"Christine Watkins has given the most thorough understanding of the Warning that I have ever read. Even though I have been familiar with many of the prophecies regarding the Warning, reading her book gave me a deeper understanding of it through the first-person accounts she shares of people who have already undergone an illumination of their consciences. She places each person in the context of their own personal journey and spiritual struggle such that when I was reading these testimonies, I felt like I was vicariously sharing in their experiences. Several of the people discussed in the book are ones I personally know. All of the stories are potentially life changing for those who read them.

Many believe we will experience this Warning, or Illumination of Conscience, in our lifetime. To prepare yourself, this informative and inspirational book will be a great help. It is hard to put down. I highly recommend it."

~Fr. John Struzzo, Ph.D., C.S.C., Congregation of Holy Cross

"If you want to live in faith, hope, and love, instead of in fear and despair, then read this prophetic book and believe the divinely inspired words of these contemporary saints and mystics. They challenge us to purify our consciences and commit our lives to Jesus, Who is the Truth and the Way to eternal life. In prayer, listen to _G_od's _P_owerful _S_pirit (GPS) gracing and guiding us to become saints by serving others as disciples of hope and healing."

~Msgr. Ralph J. Chieffo
National Spiritual Director for the Flame of Love
Pastor, St. Mary Magdalene Church, Media, Pennsylvania

"There is coming a 'prodigal son' moment for our world. It is a moment of awakening, of illumination, of warning when every person alive will see their souls in the light of divine truth—and how we are up to our knees in the pig slop of sin. It is the culmination of Divine Mercy: the 'Day of Mercy' before God purifies the world in that 'Day of Justice.' Christine Watkins has done a tremendous work in gathering the voices in the Church who have woven this thread of light and warning that may befall the world sooner than we think. _The Warning_ is an invaluable and timely manual on understanding what is coming and how to prepare."

~Mark Mallett
Catholic evangelist and author of _The Final Confrontation_

i

"I wish everyone would read this! There are so many fallen away Catholics, so many who live as if God does not exist anymore. Our era is a thousand times worse than the time of Sodom and Gomorrah. Yet our compassionate God does not give up on us, and His mercy endures forever. He is about to give humankind the strongest warning, that is, the Illumination of Conscience. This Warning might be painful, but it will save many people from the power of Satan, who is working harder than before. This has been revealed by Jesus and His dear Mother Mary. Read this book, give it to all you know. Let us all come back to the way of God before it may be too late."

~Fr. Bernardin Mugabo
Pastor of St. John the Evangelist Church, Sacramento, CA

"The Warning is a fascinating book that deals with a rarely discussed and immensely important subject in the history of Christian mysticism: the illumination of conscience. Discovering how many Christians, from mystics and visionaries to ordinary men and women, to some famous names in the world of mainstream Catholicism, have experienced this mystical grace was remarkable. It reminded me of the famous case of Alphonse Ratisbonne, who was swept up in an illumination of conscience while experiencing an apparition of the Virgin Mary in Rome, leading him from being an anti-Catholic atheist to becoming a devout Catholic priest. The case of Ratisbonne would inspire countless people, among them a young Maximilian Kolbe, to a deeper faith.

This book has the same potential. The powerful stories of this beautiful work can illuminate the minds and souls of many in their search for answers, offering them the gift of truth."

~Fr. Daniel-Maria Klimek, T.O.R.
Assistant Professor of Theology, Franciscan University of Steubenville
Author of *Medjugorje and the Supernatural: Science, Mysticism, and Extraordinary Religious Experience*

"What a blessing this book is for the Church and world. Even as one who has been studying and proclaiming the Warning for years, I received a wealth of new material that was both edifying and inspiring. That so few people—and even so few Catholics—are aware of this impending and enormous event is a tragedy, but one that Christine Watkins' new book should swiftly end. For if it were not God's will that we know of and prepare for this unprecedented, worldwide miracle of Illumination of Conscience, then heaven would not have been giving us so many revelations pertaining to it. Indeed, it is now nothing less than urgent that we all prepare to be the ones to reap the great harvest of souls that this great event will make possible. But if we bury our heads in the sand and pretend that everything is just 'business as usual,' then we shall—like the worldly who will find themselves thrust into a whole new reality through this event—be stuck spending the time after the Warning nursing our wounds instead of being the laborers in this harvest that God is asking us to be.

This book will help pull your head out of the sand. Within its pages, you will learn what the Warning will be like, as described in the revelations that speak of it. You will also learn about the personal testimonies of many saintly souls who have already received their own personal warning before the appointed time of the universal Warning, which has not been revealed but is doubtless imminent. Most importantly, you will see in this book how we are called to prepare for this once-in-a-creation event."

~Daniel O'Connor
A Professor of Philosophy at a State University of New York college
Author of *The Crown of Sanctity:*
On the Revelations of Jesus to Luisa Piccarreta and
The Crown of History: The Imminent Glorious Era of Universal Peace

Queen of Peace Media:
books, videos, blogs, prayer requests,
and more, that help you nurture your
faith and

Find your way Home.

At **www.QueenofPeaceMedia.com**
sign up for our newsletter to receive our new content.

You can browse through
**Queen of Peace Media's YouTube and Rumble channels
for help in safely navigating our tumultuous times.**
See www.youtube.com/c/queenofpeacemedia and
www.rumble.com/user/QueenofPeaceMedia.
To be notified of new videos on YouTube,
click "Subscribe" and the bell icon.

Visit Us on Social Media. Like & Follow us!
At www.YouTube.com, search for Queen of Peace Media
Rumble: www.rumble.com/user/QueenofPeaceMedia
Facebook: www.facebook.com/QueenofPeaceMedia
MeWe: www.mewe.com/i/queenofpeacemedia

ABOUT THE AUTHOR

Christine Watkins (www.ChristineWatkins.com) is an inspirational Catholic speaker and author. Her books include the highly acclaimed #1 Amazon best-sellers: *Of Men and Mary: How Six Men Won the Greatest Battle of Their Lives (Hombres Junto a María: Así Vencieron Seis Hombres la Batalla Más Ardua de Sus Vidas)*; *Transfigured: Patricia Sandoval's Escape from Drugs, Homelessness, and the Back Doors of Planned Parenthood (Transfigurada: El Escape de las Drogas, de la Calle y de la Industria del Aborto, de Patricia Sandoval)*, and this book, *The Warning (El Aviso: Testimonios y Profecías sobre la Iluminación de Conciencia)*. Watkins also authored the Catholic best-seller, *Full of Grace: Miraculous Stories of Healing and Conversion through Mary's Intercession*. Her most recent works are *Winning the Battle for Your Soul: Jesus' Teachings through Marino Restrepo, a St. Paul for Our Century; She Who Shows the Way: Heaven's Messages for Our Turbulent Times;* and *In Love with True Love: The Unforgettable Story of Sister Nicolina.*

In addition, Watkins has reintroduced an ancient and powerful Marian Consecration to the world, which is resulting in extraordinary graces for the parishes and people who go through it: *Mary's Mantle Consecration: A Spiritual Retreat for Heaven's Help,* with the accompanying *Mary's Mantle Consecration Prayer Journal (El Manto de María: Una Consagración Mariana para Obtender Ayuda Celestial y El Manto de María: Diario de Oración para la Consagración).* For details, see the end of this book.

Formerly an anti-Christian atheist living a life of sin, Watkins began a life of service to the Catholic Church after a miraculous healing from Jesus through Mary, which saved her from death. Her story can be found in the book, *Full of Grace.* Before her conversion, Watkins danced professionally with the San Francisco Ballet Company. Today, she has twenty years of experience as a keynote speaker, retreat leader, spiritual director, and counselor—with ten years working as a hospice grief counselor and another ten as a post-abortion healing director. Mrs. Watkins lives in Sacramento, California with her husband and three sons.

ACKNOWLEDGMENTS

Special thanks go to those who bravely shared their remarkable stories of undergoing an illumination of conscience, and to William Underwood, Dan Osanna, Anne Manyak, Linda Kline, and Judy Dayton for lending their keen editing eyes and golden hearts to the making of this book.

Queen of Peace Media Joyfully Announces That
The Warning
Will Be Made into a Movie by

Belladream
Films

If you'd like to know more about this effort, go to:

www.THEWARNINGMOVIE.com

THE WARNING

TESTIMONIES AND PROPHECIES
OF THE ILLUMINATION OF CONSCIENCE

CHRISTINE WATKINS

Imprimatur:
✠ Ramón C. Argüelles, STL
Archbishop-Emeritus of Lipa
Date: 5.22.2020

The Warning is also published in the Philippines, Poland, Croatia, Slovakia, Mexico, and pending publication in Spain, Colombia, and Italy. It is available in Spanish under the title, *El Aviso: Testimonios y Profecías sobre la Iluminación de Conciencia.*

Unless otherwise indicated, the Scripture texts used in this work are taken from *The New American Bible, Revised Edition (NABRE)* ©2011 by the Confraternity of Christian Doctrine, Washington, DC.

Second E-Book Edition (2020) by www.ebookpioneers.com. Books may be purchased in quantity by contacting the publisher directly at orders@queenofpeacemedia.com.

ISBN-13: 978-1-947701-09-0
ISBN-10: 1-947701-09-6

CONTENTS

A NOTE TO NON-CHRISTIANS
Before you put this book down . . .

I would primarily like to address those readers who may have grudgingly accepted to peruse this book to escape being pestered by a "religious" friend or relative who may be well-meaning, but who makes your eyes glaze over once they begin their habitual "God-talk." Having little sympathy for such piety, your heart may have sunk already if you took a sneak preview of the contents. Perhaps you noticed endorsements from priests and resolutely "Catholic" expressions that may strike you as being about as comprehensible as a particularly remote dialect of Martian. So you're at the point of giving up before you've started.

In an increasingly secular age when many in the Western industrialized nations are alienated from institutional religion, I can certainly understand such a reaction, but I would strongly urge you not to let it discourage you from reading on—at least as far as the jaw-dropping life story of Marino Restrepo, which on its own would be enough to justify publishing this volume. When considered on the level of strict logic, the central claim of this book is *not* ultimately a religious one (although it certainly has implications for questions of religion). Instead, we are talking about a universal human affirmation: that we will *all* have an experience during which we will be shown the truth of our lives from A to Z without the possibility of self-justification—a game at which, if we are honest about it, we are all specialists. Our usual options when faced with a guilty conscience—justifying ourselves, making excuses, and diverting attention to others' faults—will not be open. Our conscience will have been "illuminated" to see these strategies as the moral smokescreens that they are.

This may occur as a "life review" at the point of death, as many of those who have come "back from the brink" have testified in the form of near-death experience accounts, currently the object of intense scientific investigation (science-religion dialogue being my own area of professional research).[1] Or, as argued in the book, this may happen while we are still alive, during a dramatic worldwide event, an "Illumination of Conscience," whose purpose is that we would change our lives for the better as a result of what we discover about ourselves.

This may seem like a wildly improbable claim to make, and certainly not one that can be asserted without some hard evidence and being subjected to the most rigorous scrutiny. If it is true, then it will hold up under the microscope. If not, then it should be consigned to the category of (pious) fiction at best, religious snake oil at worst.

So what is the evidence? Essentially this: that across several centuries and quite independently of one another, many women, men and children—even a group of children—have said that they were *told* supernaturally about the reality of the Illumination of Conscience, sometimes in great detail. The very idea that some individuals may be the recipients of supernatural communications may appear totally outlandish to the mindset of *reductionist* science (not that science necessarily *has to* be reductionist), but it should be said that much of the world's religious literature is predicated on the notion that "prophets" exist. In the case of Judaism and Christianity, this is a central tenet of faith, prophetic communication being viewed as one of the ways in which God speaks in human history.[2]

Whatever way you look at them, these testimonies can be described as *doubly convergent*. Firstly, they agree with one another in an uncanny way that cannot be explained by simple copying or derivation from a "common ancestor" (to use the language of evolutionary biology). Let me just unpack this last idea a little in less scientific terms. We have a set of

---

[1] Among the leading scientific researchers into near-death experience from a medical/neuroscientific perspective are Sam Parnia, leader of the AWARE study at the University of Southampton, Steven Laureys of the Coma Research Group at Liège University, and Bruce Greyson, professor of psychiatry at the University of Virginia. One of the most comprehensive recent surveys of near-death experience accounts for a general audience, all the more interesting for not being written from an explicitly Christian perspective, is *God and the Afterlife: the Groundbreaking New Evidence of Near-Death Experience* by Jeffrey Long, M.D. and Paul Perry (New York: Harper One, 2016), an analysis of over 1000 NDE accounts submitted to the Near-Death Experience Research Foundation (nderf.org).

[2] This is affirmed by both the Hebrew and Christian Scriptures: Amos 3:7: "Surely the Lord God does nothing, without revealing his secret to his servants the prophets." Acts 2:17: "In the last days it will be, God declares, that I will pour out my Spirit upon all flesh, and your sons and your daughters shall prophesy, and your young men shall see visions, and your old men shall dream dreams."

sources here all predicting that a momentous event is going to occur to everyone in the world—and maybe sooner rather than later. Yet this prediction has no obvious literary origin. It is not found directly in Scripture and everything suggests that the sources could not have obtained this knowledge from one another. So where exactly did their information come from? The contention that it was communicated to them supernaturally may sound preposterous, but as an "explanatory hypothesis," it cannot be dismissed in the absence of a better explanation.[3]

There is, however, also a second way in which these accounts can be termed convergent. They concur strikingly with the testimonies of individuals who say that their own lives were radically changed by such an experience—an illumination of conscience—*that they have already had.* And such accounts as those gathered and composed by Christine Watkins in this book are by no means exhaustive.[4]

A testimony is nothing more than one person's story, you may object. But if you start cumulating and comparing these stories, you will quickly realize that there are *phenomena* here requiring some explanation. Why

---

[3] In the branch of philosophy known as epistemology, i.e. the study of *how* we know things, the kind of reasoning to which I am appealing here is called "inference to a best explanation" or "abduction" (which has nothing to do with aliens in this context, I hasten to add!). Scientists admittedly sometimes regard this sort of mental operation as less certain in terms of delivering *proof,* as opposed to strict mathematical "deduction," or to "induction" (making scientific observations, formulating hypotheses and carrying out tests), it is in fact the kind of thinking that governs most of our daily decision-making unless we happen to live in a laboratory! Meaning that in practical terms, it cannot be considered irrational to believe in something (provisionally) because it seems to be the best explanation available. The theory behind abduction was developed in the Scottish "Common-Sense" philosophy of Thomas Reid in the 18th century and then introduced into modern logic by the American philosopher Charles Sanders Peirce.

[4] Figures having attracted international attention and who claim that they have personally experienced something akin to the Illumination include the Polish priests and authors Fr. Adam Skwarczyski and Fr. Augustyn Pelanowski, as well as the Greek Orthodox Vassula Rydén (much contested but endorsed by several leading Catholic cardinals and archbishops). An especially extensive set of alleged prophecies on the subject that are taken seriously in Catholic circles have been attributed to "Sulema," a woman born in El Salvador but living in Quebec, who has written nearly 800 pages of supposedly inspired material in 3 volumes, published by the Swiss publishers Parvis. This material is currently only available in French; a substantial official selection of excerpts from the three volumes can be downloaded at https://illuminationdela consciencetemoins.files.wordpress.com/2015/06/pdf-comment-se-preparer-a-lillumination-des-consciences-1.pdf

are people from such diverse backgrounds, some having lived lives diametrically opposed to any kind of religious ideal, essentially having the same remarkable life-changing illumination independently of one another? And why are they having *unsolicited* experiences which they did nothing to provoke?

The best reason why the sceptic should bother to read this book can perhaps be expressed in the form of an updated version of Pascal's Wager, the argument in favor of religious belief advanced by the celebrated French mathematician and philosopher in the 17th century.[5] *If* I believe the contents of this volume to be true and decide to change my ethics/worldview accordingly, what do I stand to lose practically if ultimately the idea of an Illumination of Conscience turns out to be spurious? I lose nothing. At most, I might have renounced a hedonistic and self-centred lifestyle, like some of the protagonists in the stories that follow, which is arguably no bad thing, regardless of one's religious or philosophical outlook.

On the other hand, if I decide to discount the present testimonies and the Illumination of Conscience turns out to be a *reality* that we encounter either in this life or on the threshold of the next, what do I stand to lose? Quite possibly everything, eternally. If this call to "play the percentages" sounds like theological blackmail, then I apologize in advance, but Pascal was undoubtedly one of history's greatest minds, and although his logic has been contested by many, it has yet to be definitively refuted.

I can imagine some readers saying that, despite all the arguments above, this is still not a book for them because they do not belong to this particular religious subculture. To this I would say that neither did most of the individuals whose testimonies unfold in this book. The same event of profound importance happened to them, and they were transformed into happier people with new purpose to their lives. And that, in itself, takes some explaining.

~Peter Bannister

M.Th. in Systematic and Philosophical Theology, University of Wales
M.Phil. in Musicology, University of Cambridge

Peter Bannister is a British theologian who has worked for the Science & Religion Department of Lyon Catholic University in France and whose writings on spirituality, music, and philosophy have been published by

---

[5] See https://plato.stanford.edu/entries/pascal-wager/ (consulted September 5, 2019).

THE WARNING

Cambridge University Press, Ashgate, Routledge, the Church Music Association of America, Christian Century Magazine, and Thinking Faith, the online journal of the British Jesuits. He is also an award-winning professional musician who lives in France with his wife and plays the organ for the Taizé international, ecumenical community.

FOREWORD

by

Bishop Gavin Ashenden

Chaplain to the Queen of England
from **2008** to **2017**

Every so often a book falls into one's hands that is particularly powerful in unveiling the mystery and power of God's purpose for his Church today, and this is one such.

If you are wondering whether or not you should take the time to read it, let me strongly encourage you to do so.

We are entering a period of profound change, challenge, and spiritual conflict in which those who love Jesus will need all possible help to rise to the need to firstly deepen our own repentance; and then, using the gifts of the Spirit and the charism of the Church, to resist evil wherever we find it. We will meet that evil in ourselves, in the Church, and in the world.

We have been called into a struggle which is one of life and death, not just of the body, but more importantly of the soul. Learning the language of the soul and the reality of the spiritual struggle is a priority for the whole Church today. Not enough manage it.

In reading this wonderful book, you will find your heart opened and warmed, your mind informed and your will considerably strengthened. I, personally, devoured it, unable to put it down. It chimes wonderfully with my own experience of driving myself to death with a liter of vodka when I was 19, being taken to the courts of heaven, judged, and sent back to Earth to start again.

You will find yourself intrigued and immersed in similar stories, and in the heart and mind of God. Christine Watkins has written a book that reflects the work of the Holy Trinity among us, one that will help bring both people and the Church to life again, just when both are so badly needed.

~Bishop and Dr. Gavin Ashenden, SSC, LLB, BA, MTh, Ph.D.[6]
Christian Episcopal Church, UK.
Church Stretton, Shropshire, England
September 23, 2019

---

[6] Dr. Gavin Ashenden has since converted to Roman Catholicism and was received into the Catholic Church on Dec. 22, 2019, at Shrewsbury Cathedral, England.
See: Courtney Mares, "Former Continuing Anglican bishop to be received into the Catholic Church," Catholic News Agency, accessed July 10, 2020, https://www.catholicnewsagency.com/news/former-continuing-anglican-bishop-to-be-received-into-the-catholic-church-60055
Also see: Alyssa Murphy, "Former Anglican Bishop Gavin Ashenden: Fighting the 'Anti-Christian Program,'" with video interview on EWTN, National Catholic Register; December 20, 2019, accessed July 10, 2020, https://www.ncregister.com/daily-news/former-chaplain-to-the-queen-gavin-ashenden-fighting-the-anti-christian-pro

INTRODUCTION

There have been major "before" and "after" events in biblical history that have changed the course of human life on Earth. The first came with the fall, when the paradisiacal garden of Eden faded into a world of struggle and shame. After many generations, the deluge washed away the Earth's sin, leaving only one righteous family and pairs of animals to repopulate the land. Then the long-awaited and greatest of all events occurred, the Incarnation, markedly changing the course of mankind. God became human to save His people, and through His death and Resurrection, broke open the gates of heaven, giving to all who choose it a future even more glorious than the Eden they lost.

Today, another momentous change may be upon us in the near future, and the vast majority of people know nothing of it. This event has been given many titles by saints and holy people, including the Mother of God. They have called it the Warning, the Illumination of Conscience, the Illumination of All Souls, the Illumination of All Consciences, the Second Pentecost, the New Pentecost, the Mini-Judgment, the Merciful Pre-judgment, and the Great Day of Light.

What is this event? It is a watershed moment in time when all light from the sun will be extinguished and a thick darkness will blanket the entire world. Then a brilliant light, much like two stars colliding, will appear in the sky, leaving behind it a sign of Jesus Christ, triumphant on the cross, visible to all in His glory. From the holes of the wounds in His body, bright rays will shine forth, lighting up the Earth—and at the same time, pierce every soul, illuminating everyone's conscience. All will see their past sins and the consequences of those sins, whether or not they believe in the existence of God.

The Warning will be the greatest act of mercy for mankind since Jesus came to Earth. It will be both global and intimately personal. It will be a correction of conscience for a world gone astray.

In the Church-approved apparitions of Betania, Venezuela (1928-2004), Mary Reconciler of Peoples and Nations spoke of the coming Warning to the mystic and stigmatist, Maria Esperanza. Catholics are never required to believe in any apparitions, nevertheless, the Church assures us that this message from the Mother of God is worthy of belief[7]:

> *Little children, I am your Mother, and I come to seek you so that you may prepare yourselves to be able to bring my message of reconciliation: There is coming the great moment of a Great Day of Light. The consciences of this beloved people must be violently shaken so that they may "put their house in order" and offer to Jesus the just reparation for the daily infidelities that are committed on the part of sinners. . . it is the hour of decision for mankind.[8]*

At this point, I imagine you, the reader, responding in one of four ways. The first way: utter disbelief, even perhaps scorn. You have quickly determined that this is spiritual quackery. "Isn't this so-called 'Warning' connected to end-times nonsense?" You may have stumbled upon the obscure and specious writings of self-proclaimed visionaries who have spoken of it. Perhaps you have clicked on YouTube videos of roaming planets and Catholic art from the 50s, with the subtext, "It's the end of the world!" Or it could be that you have stumbled across websites about THE COMING WARNING or THE ILLUMINATION OF CONSCIENCE with messages from unknown "mystics" or false prophets using inflammatory language and worse yet, outdated web

---

[7] After four hundred to five hundred hours of investigation and interviews, Archbishop Pio Bello Ricardo offered his "Pastoral Instruction on the Apparitions of the Blessed Virgin in Finca, Betania": *"In consequence, after studying with determination the apparitions of our Blessed Virgin Mary in Finca Betania and after assiduously asking our Lord for spiritual discernment: I declare that to my judgement these apparitions are authentic and of a supernatural character"*. . . https://www.ewtn.com/catholicism/library/pastoral-instruction-on-the-apparitions-of-the-blessed-virgin-in-finca-betania-3647, accessed July 4, 2019.

[8] Signs and Wonders for Our Times, Volume 15-n.2, Featured Article, p. 37.
Signs and Wonders for Our Times, Special Double issue, Volume 25-n.3/4, Fall, 2015.

designs. You have understandably relegated all this to a fringe element in the Church, filled with fanatics who grab onto the latest "end time" news, like their next cigarette.

The second way: you at first judge this Warning to be too grand, unprecedented, unverified, or unknown to be true, but you're willing to turn the page to see what proof or arguments might present themselves.

The third way: you believe the Illumination of Conscience may happen, but as with all prophecies involving future events, you feel the information doesn't apply to you or your generation. People have been announcing prophecies since Christianity's inception. Even the great evangelist and apostle, St. Paul, believed Jesus would return in his lifetime.

The fourth way: you believe; you understand. You have even researched the Warning. You wonder if it will occur in your lifetime, and if it does, you hope to endure it with grace. You secretly ponder in your heart whether your loved ones might be changed, saved, or come into the Catholic Church through its unique effect.

No matter one's point of view, this book will undoubtedly be an eye-opening experience of deeper conversion for all those who desire to grow in knowledge of themselves and of God.

The first section of this book describes the Warning, based on prophecies from an impressive list of spiritual heavyweights—including Scripture: a pope declared Blessed, Pius IX; a priest and martyr, Saint Edmund Campion; a nun, mystic and Apostle of Divine Mercy, Saint Faustina Kowalska; a lay mystic and victim soul, Blessed Anna-Maria Taigi; a religious superior, mystic, and exorcist, Father Michel Rodrigue;[9] a victim soul and founder of the Flame of Love movement in the universal Church, Elizabeth Kindelmann; a priest locutionist and founder of the Marian Movement of Priests, Fr. Stefano Gobbi; a modern-day lay evangelist with a far-reaching Catholic apostolate, Matthew Kelly; a mystic and stigmatist who has received messages with the Church's Imprimatur, Luz de María de Bonilla; a modern-day stigmatist and visionary, supported by her bishop, Janie Garza; and Jesus Christ and the Mother of God through their child visionaries in the twentieth century apparition sites of Heede, Germany and Garabandal, Spain.

---

[9] To read more about Fr. Michel Rodrigue, go to www.CountdowntotheKingdom.com. Click on "Why Fr. Michel Rodrigue? A Virtual Retreat." See the Appendix for a complete bio and references.

The second section of the book provides excerpts from each of their astonishing prophecies addressing The Warning. The appendix contains the full account of these prophecies, including a biographical history of the voices behind them and what the Church has proclaimed—all carefully chosen for their credibility, if not full approval within the Catholic Church. This "behind the scenes" research is provided for two reasons. First, the lives of these extraordinary souls and the context of the two apparition sites offer a captivating and inspiring read. Second, the modern, western mind, when approaching the unknown or prophetic, often thinks, "Let me decide this for myself," giving more credence to personal discernment than sometimes even the discerning authority of the Church, which has the final say. Thus you, the reader, have more fodder for thought, should you wish to go exploring.

If such prophetic utterances seem strange or suspect to you, remember that prophecy is nothing new in the Church and even predates it by centuries in Judaism. The Bible contains approximately 2,500 prophesies, about 2,000 of which have already materialized into history with stunning accuracy. The remaining 500 or so still reach into the future. The most well-known of the fulfilled prophecies are those that foretold the coming of the Messiah. Approximately 700 years before Christ, the prophet Micah named the tiny village of Bethlehem as the birthplace of the Messiah (Micah 5:2). In the fifth century B.C., the prophet Zechariah declared that the Messiah would be betrayed for the price of a slave—thirty pieces of silver according to Jewish law, and that this money would be used to buy a burial ground for Jerusalem's poor foreigners (Zechariah 11:12-13).[i] Some 400 years before crucifixion was invented, both Israel's King David and the prophet Zechariah described how the Messiah would die, including the unique piercing of His body and sparing of broken bones, contrary to customary procedure in cases of crucifixion (Psalm 22 and 34:20; Zechariah 12:10).[ii]

If not for God, how could they have possibly known these obscure, detailed facts of something that lingered so outside of human reasoning and hope?—God becoming man. God being betrayed, humiliated? Killed?

Prophecy did not end when the Catholic councils of Hippo in 393 A.D., and Carthage in 397 A.D. and 419 A.D., determined which books would enter the canon of Sacred Scripture and gave birth to the Bible. Prophecy is a continual charism of the Holy Spirit guiding the Church and the world. Prophecy reveals the will of the Lord and at times, His plans. *"In every age the Church has received the charism of prophecy, which must be scrutinized but not scorned."*—Cardinal Ratzinger (Pope Benedict XVI)[iii]

The prophecies of the Warning fall under the category of private revelation, different from public revelation, or the deposit of faith, which ended with the death of the last apostle. The Church does not demand the assent or rejection of any private revelation (unless a particular revelation has been condemned).[10] However, the *Catechism of the Catholic Church* teaches that "even if Revelation is already complete, it has not been made completely explicit; it remains for Christian faith gradually to grasp its full significance over the course of the centuries" (n. 66). Many well-known practices in the Church have come from private revelation, such as the Rosary, the Scapular, the Miraculous Medal, the Divine Mercy Chaplet, devotion to the Sacred Heart of Jesus, the feast of Divine Mercy Sunday, and all Marian apparitions throughout history.

While the deposit of faith is now complete, and nothing more needs to be known for salvation, God continues to be as prophetically active and mercifully meddlesome as he was in Biblical times. God is still speaking. People are still receiving visions and locutions that aren't meant only for them. God is still reaching through time and space to prepare us, to give us warnings, to offer us reassurance, to help us understand what is to come so that He can carry as many of us as possible back to His bosom. As it is written in the book of the prophet *Amos: "Indeed, the Lord GOD does nothing without revealing his plan to his servants the prophets" (3:7).*

Yet thus far in salvation history, the Lord has been met, more often than not, with the hardened rejection, dismissal, or the indifference of His people. God sends His prophets. Few listen or believe. Thumb through stories of the Old Testament, and you will read a continuous saga of God calling out to His beloved Israel through His chosen prophets, and Israel's treatment of His messengers as pariahs. When Noah warned of the coming deluge and began to build the ark, how many joined his efforts? No one but his family and the animals. When Elijah, Jeremiah, Zachariah, Isaiah, and others shouted out God's unnerving words that Israel was betraying its God, they were persecuted by kings and ostracized by

---

[10] None of the private revelations in this book have been condemned by the Church. Some have been approved, and some remain in an in-between category, neither approved nor condemned. In lieu of repeating the word "alleged" before every reference in this latter category, and for the sake of preserving literary style and coherency, the Church's evaluation of each seer's messages is mentioned in the "Appendix: Biographies and Words of the Prophets of The Warning."

religious leaders. When God, Himself, came to Earth, how many embraced Him?

Scripture shares with us the ironic and somewhat frightening fact that many of the most religious people of Christ's time—those who were actively practicing their religion and eagerly awaiting the promised Messiah, were unable to recognize Him when He came. This pattern of pride and defiance will repeat itself and never change until we do. Indeed, Christ, Himself, spoke of our own future rejection of Him when He prophesied, *"But when the Son of man comes, will He find faith on earth?"* (Luke 18:8).

Why wouldn't a message as universal and earthshaking as the Warning not be preached in every church and synagogue, and shouted from rooftop to rooftop, country to country? The answer is all too clear. It lies in the unfortunate repetition of human history.

When I first asked God if He wanted me to write a book about the Warning, I told Him I could only proceed with heavenly help. The Lord would have to lead me to people who had not only experienced their own warning (small "w"), but who would allow me to write down their stories in intimate detail, and also share them with the world.

At that point in life, I had only met one such person on planet Earth and did not expect to run into copies of him. Within eight weeks of my prayer, I had met five people and learned of five others who had experienced an illumination of their conscience. Not only that, all of them gave me permission to share their stories with detail and delicacy. I took this as God's yes.

In the third section of this book, you will therefore find a collection of these people's fascinating, provocative, and acutely convicting accounts. Suddenly and against their will, they were carried through a review of their lives and shown their every sin. Two were priests, one a nun, nine were lay people, and none were ever the same.

The last story is of Marino Restrepo, which brings the reader to the climactic story of the book. It is a tale worth waiting for. Kidnapped by Colombian terrorists, this hell-bound Hollywood player underwent his illumination of conscience in brutal circumstances, and overnight became a changed man, infused with knowledge of the Kingdom of God. Today, he is a modern-day St. Paul for our century. In the unlikely case that nothing in these pages causes your jaw to drop, his story will.

The Church takes great caution with such matters, since so-called visions, apparitions, locutions, private revelations, mystical flights, or near-death experiences can be the product of a mental disturbance, an overactive imagination, a desire for attention, or a diabolical trick meant to deceive.

As a licensed clinical social worker, and for the sake of my own accountability before God and a sincere desire to help souls, I have researched and scrutinized the people and their accounts of a personal illumination of conscience, as contained in this book. I found them to be people of sound mind and solid character—men and women leading exemplary lives of faith in God and service to the Church and their fellow human beings. In addition, God's illumination of their soul produced in each of them a radical, long-lasting, and fruitful shift toward personal holiness. False mysticism never has this positive effect.

As you pore over these eye-popping testimonies, each person's account of their illumination of conscience will reveal, like the brush of a paint stroke, an insight or aspect of what it means to be a child of God. In reading people's actual experiences of seeing their sins through the Lord's eyes, you will come away with a fully painted and framed picture of the Warning, as well as a deeper knowledge of your own soul.

You may finish this book believing that God has indeed planned a Great Day of Light, when His merciful love will enlighten the dark rooms of dulled consciences. Even if you remain unconvinced, you will profit greatly from a better understanding of what you will experience when you meet God, for The Warning is little different from what meets us at the end of life.

As human beings, we prepare for the harvest, we prepare for exams, we prepare our clothing, we prepare our dinner, and we prepare our will. But who among us does the most important work of all, preparation for our death? No one escapes the particular judgment at the end of our journey, when our eternal fate is determined: heaven, purgatory leading to heaven, or hell. Our soul never dies, it simply awakens to truth. Before the judgment seat of God, all that was hidden will be revealed, and all that was falsely perceived or unjustly rationalized will be made painfully clear. Every one of us will face that moment (see Romans 14:10-12), and we will know where we are destined to go.

Whether or not the Warning occurs in your generation or occurs at all is not the most important question. The most important question that you, dear reader, can ask is: "Am I ready to meet God right now?" For one thing is certain. Live as though the Warning is real, and life from now on will hold few regrets.

ANSWERS TO COMMON QUESTIONS

What Is the Warning?

Combining completely separate sources through time and around the world, we can piece together a blueprint of this cosmic and spiritual event:

We learn from Blessed Pope Pius IX, St. Edmund Campion, and none less than Jesus and Mary, that the Illumination of Conscience will be a direct intervention from God, a "great wonder, which will fill the world with astonishment,"[11] . . . "It will be terrible, a Mini-judgment."[12] . . . God will "reveal all men's consciences and try every man of each kind of religion."[13] . . . "Miraculous and spiritual tongues of fire will purify the hearts and the souls of all, who will see themselves in the light of God

[11] Concerning the prophetic words of Bl. Pope Pius IX: Rev. R. Gerald Culleton, *The Prophets and Our Times* (Tan Books and Publishers, 1941), p. 206, http://ia800200.us.archive.org/2/items/TheProphetsAndOurTimes/TheProphetsAndOurTimes.pdf, or https://archive.org/details/TheProphetsAndOurTimes/mode/2up, accessed August 31, 2019.

[12] D. Alfonso Cenni, *I SS. Cuori di Gesu e di Maria. La Salvezza del Mondo. Le Loro Apparizioni, Promesse e Richieste. Nihil Obstat* Ex Parte Ordinis Il P. Generale D. Pier-Damiano Buffadini, February 24, 1949. *Imprimatur* Sublaci. Simon Laurentius O.S.B. Ep, tit. Abb. Ord. June 3, 1949. Accessed June 23, 2019, https://gloria.tv/like/uaZeA21Rv8dW4nTWH4kAWfMQQ

[13] Evelyn Waugh, *Two Lives: Edmund Campion and Ronald Knox* (Continuum; 2005), p. 113.

and will be pierced by the keen sword of His divine truth."[14] As a result, many will repent and be saved.

From other Catholic luminaries through to the present day, a detailed account of The Warning emerges:

At first, shadows will cease to be shadows, and instead become a most terrible darkness that will obscure the sun's light. Even the stars and the moon will fail to shine. Then the vault of the sky will be illuminated by the colliding of two celestial bodies, producing a booming noise and lighting up the entire Earth. Panic will ensue. The day will be brighter than normal, and the night will shine like the day. Then Jesus will appear in the sky on His Cross—not in His suffering, but in His glory. This sign of the Lord will be visible in every part of the world, no matter where one may be. From the holes made by the punctures in Jesus's hands, feet, and side, brilliant rays of love and mercy will fall upon the entire Earth.

These rays of light will contain the Blessed Mother's "Flame of Love" and leap out to souls due to her intercession: *"Due to lack of faith, Earth is entering into darkness, but Earth will experience a great jolt of faith,"[15]* said Our Lady through Elizabeth Kindelmann (1913-1985) of the bishop-approved Flame of Love Movement of the Immaculate Heart of Mary. *"In that dark night, heaven and Earth will be illuminated by the Flame of Love that I offer to souls."[16]* . . .*"It is so great that I cannot keep it any longer within me. It leaps out to you with explosive power. When it pours out, my love will destroy the satanic hatred that contaminates the world. The greatest number of souls will be set free. Nothing like this has existed before. This is my greatest miracle that I will do for all."[17]*

When this Flame touches Earth, everything will suddenly stop. A plane flying through the clouds will pause in mid-air. A soccer player running through the field will halt. Everyone and everything on Earth will freeze, as if time has stopped. Yet in the ensuing five to fifteen minutes, all people, whether they be Muslim or atheist, mentally incapacitated or sane, young or old, will see the sins of their lives. They will see the good they have failed to do and the bad they have done. Everyone will find themselves all alone in the world, no matter where they are at that time,

---

[14] Marian Movement of Priests, Fr. Stefano Gobbi, *To the Priests: Our Lady's Beloved Sons; 1996 Supplement* (St. Francis, Maine: Marian Movement of Priests, 1996), pp. 973-974.

[15] Elizabeth Kindelmann, *The Flame of Love* (Children of the Father Foundation; 2015-2016) *Nihil Obstat:* Monsignor Joseph G. Prior, Censor Librorum. *Imprimatur:* Archbishop Charles Chaput, Archdiocese of Philadelphia, p. 61.

[16] Ibid., p. 62.

[17] Ibid., pp. 44-45.

undergoing their own personal experience and oblivious to the world around them. The Cross will remain in the sky for seven days and seven nights.

From the start of the 20th century to the present day, heaven has provided further shape and detail to this unparalleled event. On August 2, 1934, Jesus spoke to St. Faustina Kowalska of the cosmic nature of the Illumination, which would come before the day of justice: *". . . all light in the heavens will be extinguished, and there will be great darkness over the whole earth. Then the sign of the Cross will be seen in the sky, and from the holes where the hands and the feet of the Savior were nailed will come forth a brilliant light, which will illuminate the Earth for a period of time."*[18]

The Gospel of Matthew also seems to tell of this moment, which many do not understand:

> *"Immediately after the tribulation of those days, the sun will be darkened, and the moon will not give its light, and the stars will fall from the sky, and the powers of the heavens will be shaken. And then the sign of the Son of Man will appear in heaven, and all the tribes of the earth will mourn, and they will see the Son of Man coming upon the clouds of heaven with power and great glory. And he will send out his angels with a trumpet blast, and they will gather his elect from the four winds, from one end of the heavens to the other."* (Matthew 24:29-31)

This Gospel passage tells us that *"all the tribes of the earth will mourn."* The Warning also appears to be captured in the symbolic language of the Sixth Seal in the Book of Revelation, written by the Beloved Apostle, St. John:

> *Then I watched while he broke open the sixth seal, and there was a great earthquake; the sun turned as black as dark sackcloth and the whole moon became like blood. The stars in the sky fell to the earth like unripe figs shaken loose from the tree in a strong wind. Then the sky was divided like a torn scroll curling up, and every mountain and island was moved from its place. The kings of the earth, the nobles, the military officers, the rich, the powerful, and every slave and free person hid themselves in caves and among*

---

[18] Saint Maria Faustina Kowalska, *Divine Mercy in My Soul: Diary* (Marian Press, 3rd Edition; 2003) #83.

mountain crags. They cried out to the mountains and the rocks, "Fall on us and hide us from the face of the one who sits on the throne and from the wrath of the Lamb, because the great day of their wrath has come and who can withstand it?" (Rev 6:12-17)

St. John tells us that all will be completely dark. The sun will turn black, stars will disappear, and the earth will be shaken. "Every slave and free person," meaning all people, will wish to avoid the face of God and the wrath of the Lamb. Who is the Lamb? In the previous chapter of the Book of Revelation, St. John says, *"I saw a Lamb standing, as though it had been slain."* The Lamb is Christ in His Crucified state. The earth's inhabitants will cry out, seeking protection from God's face, meaning the eyes of the Lord, Who can see their sin, for they will collectively feel as if they have entered their own particular judgment. This will happen on the "great day," and many will feel like they cannot "withstand it."

In one of the apparitions at Heede, Germany (1945), Jesus said that when the Mini-Judgment comes, *"The Earth will shake and moan."*[19] But why? Why will there be mourning? The answer comes through many voices, such as the visionary and stigmatist, Luz de María de Bonilla, currently living in Argentina, whose messages have received the Imprimatur. In a message from November 22, 2014, Jesus said:

"My beloved people, the examination of your consciences will come soon. . . Whatever moves will stop moving, for silence will reign on Earth. You will hear only the lamentations of those repenting for the wrongs they committed, and I will come with My love to once again welcome My lost sheep."[20]

God the Father revealed the Mini-Judgment in great detail to Matthew Kelly, the well-known Catholic speaker and author born in Australia, now living in Ohio, and to Fr. Michel Rodrigue, the founder and religious Superior of The Apostolic Fraternity of Saint Benedict Joseph Labre in Quebec, Canada. Through Matthew, God the Father said, *"It will be painful, very painful, but short. You will see your sins; you will see how much you offend Me, every day. . . Judgment is the best word you humans have to describe it, but it will be more like this: you will see your own*

---

[19] Ibid., Cenni, *I SS. Cuori*, Imprimatur Sublaci. Simon Laurentius O.S.B.

[20] Luz de María de Bonilla, *Venga a Nosotros Tu Reino* ("*Thy Kingdom Come*") Year 2014, with the *Imprimatur* and full support of Juan Abelardo Mata Guevara, SDB, Titular Bishop of Estelí, Nicaragua, https://www.revelacionesmarianas.com/libros/en/2014.pdf, p. 290, accessed September 1, 2019.

personal darkness contrasted against the pure light of My love."[21] Through Fr. Michel and Luz de María, the Lord shared that even those sins confessed in the Sacrament of Reconciliation will be revealed, although experienced differently. It is one thing to confess sins with words; it is another to see those sins through the light of truth and to feel viscerally how that sin pained Jesus and hurt others, extending its destructive effects, like a ripple through time.

How Did We Learn of a Coming Illumination of Conscience?

The first historical record we know of that mentions the Illumination of Conscience is from St. Edmund Campion (1540-1581), the brilliant Jesuit priest and martyr from London, who said, *"I pronounced a great day, not wherein any temporal potentate should minister, but wherein the Terrible Judge should reveal all men's consciences and try every man of each kind of religion. This is the day of change . . ."*[22]

The words of this great Catholic saint, martyred in 1581 and canonized in 1970, perfectly echo those of many prophecies to follow. A couple centuries later, God would again reveal this mysterious Illumination to a great Italian mystic, one step from sainthood, Blessed Anna Maria Taigi (1769-1837). Paupers, priests, and popes, alike, came to this humble wife, mother, and victim soul for advice because she had a most remarkable and singular mystical gift. For forty-seven years, a bright light, like a sun, accompanied her by day and by night. Blessed Anna-Maria had but to stare into it to see the most secret thoughts of persons nearby or far off; events and people of bygone days; and the details of days yet to come. Her prophecies have withstood the test of time, and hers are the first recorded words to call the event an "Illumination of Conscience": *"A great purification will come upon the world preceded by an Illumination of Conscience in which everyone will see themselves as God sees them."*[23] She also indicated that it would save many souls because many would repent as a result.

Apparently, God had only begun to alert the world of this event. A couple of decades later, He would allude to it through His longest

---

[21] Matthew Kelly, *Words from God* (Batemans Bay, Australia: Words from God, 1993), p. 70.
[22] Waugh, *Two Lives,* p. 113.
[23] Iannuzzi, *Antichrist*, p. 33. Petrisko, *The Miracle,* p. 27.

reigning pope, besides St. Peter, Pius IX (1792-1878), Vicar of Christ, whose office as has the power to catch the world's attention and belief: *"Since the whole world is against God and His Church, it is evident that He has reserved the victory over His enemies to Himself. . . all will be forced to look to the supernatural. . . There will come a great wonder, which will fill the world with astonishment."*[24] This wonder will astonish the entire world.

Might the Lord be saying to us, "Please, will you listen to my representative on Earth, now?"

Why Is God Sending the Warning?

God is sending the Warning to remedy the darkened and shadowy conscience of the world. According to His prophets, much of humanity has become blind to sin, and the Heart of the Father of all is breaking. He can no longer bear to see so many of His precious children, whom He loves beyond reason, fall into the abyss. The Father has reached out to the world with tender mercies. He has sent His Mother to Earth to help us, time and again, but too many have rejected His graces and forced His hand. It pains Him deeply to discipline us, just like a good parent reluctantly chastises his or her child out of profound love and concern, especially if that child were about to be devoured by an enemy. Would not a good parent do everything in his or her power to prevent this? God does become angry, righteously angry, not with vindictiveness, hatred, spite, or despair, but out of love. Just as a good father is angry at a person who abuses his child, so is the Father angry at those who harm themselves and others through serious sin. He wants the abuse to stop. He wants His children freed of needless pain in this life and to be with Him forever in heaven, our true home, where there is no more suffering and there are no more tears.

In Jesus's message of the Mini-Judgment at Heede, He said:

"My love has planned this action before the creation of the world. People do not listen to My calls: they close their ears; they resist grace and reject My mercy, My love, My merits. The world is worse than before the deluge. It agonizes in a quagmire of sin. Hatred and greed have infiltrated human hearts. All this is the work of Satan. The world lies in dense darkness. This generation deserves to be

---

[24] Culleton, *The Prophets*, p. 206.

wiped out, but I wish to show it My mercy. The cup of God's anger is already spilling over onto the nations. The angel of peace will not delay in coming down to Earth. I want to heal and save. Through the wounds that bleed now, mercy will win and justice triumph."[25]

On August 15, 1980, the Lord said to Elizabeth Kindelmann, *"The Church and the whole world are in danger. You cannot change this situation. Only the Holy Trinity, through the unified intercession of the Blessed Virgin, the angels, the saints, and the souls in purgatory, can help you."[26]*

"The Mini-Judgment is a reality. People no longer realize that they offend Me" (God the Father to Matthew Kelly).[27] *"Man does not look with mistrust upon the devil, instead he gladly follows and obeys him, acting contrary to the will of God"* (Jesus to Luz de María de Bonilla). *"The very fact that such judgments will come is because people refuse to convert and continue to live in darkness"* (Jesus to Janie Garza).[28] *"The Warning is not a fantasy. Humanity must be purified so that it does not fall into the flames of hell"* (Our Lady to Luz de María).[29]

"Tongues of fire will come down upon you all, my poor children, so ensnared and seduced by Satan and by all the evil spirits who, during these years, have attained their greatest triumph. And thus, you will be illuminated by this divine light . . . which will open the door of your heart to receive the great gift of divine mercy." (Our Lady to Fr. Stefano Gobbi)

God's forgiveness always knocks, but it can never enter a heart that is closed. The Illumination of Conscience will come to break open souls to the reality of God and bring willing hearts to repentance.

Recently in 2018, God the Father gave the following message to Fr. Michel Rodrigue, in which He again explains why He is sending the Warning and shares how it pains Him to do so.

[25] Ibid., Cenni, *I SS. Cuori*, Imprimatur Sublaci. Simon Laurentius O.S.B.

[26] Kindelmann, *The Flame*, p. 108.

[27] Matthew Kelly, *Words from God* (Batemans Bay, Australia: Words from God, 1993), p. 70.

[28] Janie Garza, *Heaven's Messages for the Family: How to Become the Family God Wants You to Be* (Saint Dominic Media, 1998), p. 329.

[29] Bonilla, *Venga,* with *Imprimatur* and full support of Juan Abelardo Mata Guevara, SDB, Titular Bishop of Estelí, Nicaragua, Message of March 5, 2013, p. 56, https://www.revelacionesmarianas.com/libros/en/2013.pdf, accessed September 17, 2019.

"I do not want death and damnation for any one of you. So much suffering, so much violence, so many sins now occur on the Earth that I created. I now hear the cries of all the babies and children who are murdered by the sin of my children who live under the dominion of Satan. YOU SHALL NOT KILL." ("These words were so strong," said Fr. Michel.)

"Pray and be confident. I do not want you to be like the ones who have no faith and who will tremble during the manifestation of the Son of Man. On the contrary, pray and rejoice and receive the peace given by my Son, Jesus. What sorrow when I must respect free will and come to the point of giving a Warning that is also part of My mercy. Be ready and vigilant for the hour of My mercy. I bless you, My children."[30]

What Will Happen during the Warning to Those in Serious Sin?

"For those who are not in a state of grace, it will be frightening,"[31] said Jesus at Heede. At Garbandal, Spain (1961-1965), where Our Lady first called the event, "El Aviso" ("The Warning"), the visionary Conchita said it will be *"A thousand times worse than earthquakes. It will be like fire; it will not burn our flesh, but we will feel it corporeally and interiorly. . . And unbelievers will feel the fear of God. If we die during that time, it will be of fright. . . If I could only tell you how the Virgin described it to me! . . . I am tired of announcing it and having no one pay any attention to it."*[32]

"I speak of the Warning," said Jesus to Luz de María in 2018, *"the moment in which each person will be alone before his own conscience*

---

[30] From Fr. Michel Rodrigue's live recorded talks in Barry's Bay, Ontario on July 12 and 13, 2018. Talks by Fr. Rodrigue (2 CD sets) can be purchased through Peter Frank at missionangelshq@gmail.com. All proceeds go to supporting the construction of the new monasteries, which God the Father has told Fr. Rodrigue are important for the Church's future: Fraternité Apostolique Saint Benoît-Joseph Labre (Apostolic Fraternity of St. Benedict Joseph Labre). See www.CountdowntotheKingdom.com/ why-fr-michel-rodrigue.

[31] Ibid., Cenni, *I SS. Cuori, Imprimatur* Sublaci. Simon Laurentius O.S.B.

[32] Ramon Pérez, *Garabandal: The Village Speaks*, translated from the French by Matthews, Annette I. Curot, The Workers of Our Lady of Mount Carmel, 1981, pp. 50-51.

and his sins—a moment so overpowering that some will not survive experiencing their own wickedness."[33]

The mystic and stigmatist, Janie Garza, who has the full approval of her bishop to share her messages, asked Jesus on September 9, 1995, *"Beloved Savior, will the Illumination scare people?*

Jesus answered, *"The fear that will inflame their hearts is the holy fear of the immense power of My Father, especially for those many souls that have continued to deny the existence of My Father. These will be the souls that will experience tremendous fear."*

St. Joseph said to Janie in 1994, *"For those who believe that they live in the light but continue to break every Commandment given by God, to these souls, I, St. Joseph, say that these souls will not be able to see the state of their souls and live."*

Janie responded, *"This is hard for me to know. Are you saying that people who do not live God's Commandments will die when they see their souls?"*

St. Joseph answered, *"Yes, my little one, that's how it will be for many unless they repent and decide for conversion. There is still time for repentance, but time is growing shorter with each day that goes by."[34]*

During the Illumination of Conscience, everyone will see where they would go if they were to die at that moment without the benefit of the Warning. Fr. Michel Rodrigue explained what God the Father revealed to him regarding souls destined for damnation: *"For the ones who would go to hell, they will burn. Their bodies will not be destroyed, but they will feel exactly what hell is like because they are already there. The only thing missing was the feeling. They will experience the beatings of the devil, and many will not survive because of their great sin, I assure you. But it will be for them a blessing, because they will ask for pardon. It will be their salvation."[35]*

---

[33] Bonilla, *Venga, Imprimatur*: Bishop Guevara, Revelaciones Marianas, p. 124, https://www.revelacionesmarianas.com/libros/es/2018.pdf, accessed September 2, 2019.

[34] Janie Garza, *Heaven's Messages for the Family, Volume II: Messages from St. Joseph and the Archangels* (Saint Dominic Media, 1999), p. 46.

[35] From Fr. Michel Rodrigue's live recorded talks in Barry's Bay, Ontario on July 12 and 13, 2018. See www.CountdowntotheKingdom.com/why-fr-michel-rodrigue.

What Will Happen during the Warning to Those Who Believe in and Love God?

Those who love God and their neighbor will endure the Warning with grace and be much better for it. When a friend told Conchita, The Garabandal visionary, that she was very scared of the Warning, Conchita reassured her: *"Yes, but after the Warning, you will love God much more."*[36] The visionary, Jacinta, also said, *"The Warning is for us to draw closer to Him and to increase our faith. Therefore, one should prepare for that day, but not await it with fear. God does not send things for the sake of fear, but rather with justice and love."*[37]

In a recent message on August 12, 2019 to the mystic and stigmatist, Luz de María de Bonilla, Jesus said, *"Those who behave and act in My likeness toward their neighbor, and repent with all their strength, force, and feelings, and confess their sins with a firm purpose of amendment, those children of Mine will experience the Warning like every human being will, but not with the intensity of those who stoop in the mire of sin through disobedience, ignoring My calls, those of My Mother, and My faithful Saint Michael the Archangel."*[38]

No two people will experience the Illumination of Conscience the same way, as no two people have the same sins. *"Those who would go to purgatory,"* said Fr. Michel Rodrigue, *"will see and feel the pains of their sin and purification. They will recognize their faults and know what they must correct within themselves. For those who are very close to Jesus, they will see what they must change in order to live in complete union with Him.*

The Father wants me to proclaim that you do not have to fear. For the one who believes in God, this will be a loving day, a blessed day. You will see what you must correct to accomplish more of His will, to be more submissive to the grace He wishes to give you for your mission on Earth. It will be one of the greatest signs given to the world since the Resurrection of Jesus Christ. The Father told me that the twenty-first

---

[36] "Conchita and Loli Speak on the Aviso," Garabandal Journal, January-February 2004, p. 5.

[37] Garabandal International Magazine, October-December, 2014, http://www.garabandal.org.uk/magazine.html, accessed July 4, 2019.

[38] Bonilla, *Venga,* Bishop Guevara, Revelaciones Marianas, https://www.revelacionesmarianas.com/english.htm, Accessed September 1, 2019.

century is His century. After the Warning, no one left on Earth will be able to say that God does not exist."

"I will make My light shine," said Jesus at Heede, *"a light which for some, will be a blessing, and for others, darkness. Mankind will recognize My love and My power. . . But do not fear. I am with you. You will rejoice and thank Me. Those who await Me will have My help, My grace, and My love."[39]*

Will the Illumination of Conscience Come Soon?

Only God knows the day and the hour of the Warning. The exact timing of the Lord's prophesied events throughout history has been elusive and unknown. Prophecies about a coming Messiah can be found centuries before God became man—as recorded in the Hebrew Bible, written between 1450 BC and 430 BC. (See details of these prophecies in the Endnotes).[iv] When the foretold Messiah did finally come, Jesus spoke to his disciples of the many generations of Israelites who awaited Him with great hope and expectancy: *"But blessed are your eyes, because they see, and your ears, because they hear. Amen, I say to you, many prophets and righteous people longed to see what you see but did not see it, and to hear what you hear but did not hear it."* (Matthew 13:16-17) And many of the first Christians, including St. Paul, believed that Jesus's prophecy of His Second Coming was imminent, but He didn't return in their day.

For the last five centuries, God appears to be announcing a coming Warning, through His chosen prophets in His Catholic Church, with increasing frequency and urgency. This time, again, the Lord seems to be preparing His people to receive Him, and He desires to save the entire world. But we should not, as St. Peter said, *". . .ignore this one fact, beloved, that with the Lord one day is like a thousand years and a thousand years like one day"* (2 Peter 3:8). However, it is interesting to note that the language of prophecies concerning the Warning has changed in the last few decades. Beginning in the mid-20th century, the Lord began to announce its closeness in time.

In 1945, Jesus said at Heede, *"My beloved children, the hour is near. . . The angels of justice are now scattered across the world. I will make*

---

[39] Ibid., Cenni, *I SS. Cuori, Imprimatur* Sublaci. Simon Laurentius O.S.B.

Myself known to mankind. Every soul will recognize Me as their God. I am coming! I am at the door. . ."[40]

Then again, on July 26, 1964, Our Lady said to Elizabeth Kindelmann, *"The moment is near when my Flame of Love will ignite."[41]*

Jacinta, one of the visionaries at Garabandal, said that when the Warning comes, conditions will be "at their worst." There will be persecution, and many people will no longer be practicing their religion. When asked what the world will be like when the Warning comes, she responded with one word: "Bad." Mari Loli spoke of how it will seem as though the Church has disappeared: *". . . it will be very hard to practice the religion, for priests to say Mass, or for people to open the doors of the churches.". . . "Whoever practices it will have to go into hiding."[42]*

When Mari Loli was asked on July 27, 1975, *"Can you tell us anything else about the Warning?"* she answered, *"All I can say is that it is very near, and that it is very important that we get ready for it . . ."[43]*

On September 9, 1995, Janie Garza asked Our Lord directly, *"Oh, Jesus, will this happen very soon?"*

Jesus answered: *"Our humble servant, this will happen within a short period. Do not be distracted with dates, but prepare every day with strong prayer. Many who worry about these times will not live to see these things take place. This is why Holy Scripture warns everybody not to be concerned about tomorrow, for tomorrow is promised to no one. The present day has enough trials and crosses. Know that when We speak about such things to come; this is for the people to convert and abandon their evil ways. Every day is an opportunity for souls to convert. People should not wait for such things to come to convert, but they should convert now, before it's too late!"[44]*

Our Lady's messages to Fr. Stefano Gobbi in the late 20th century also insinuate that the Warning, or Second Pentecost, is imminent.

---

[40] Ibid., Cenni, *I SS. Cuori, Imprimatur* Sublaci. Simon Laurentius O.S.B.

[41] Elizabeth Kindelmann, *The Flame of Love of the Immaculate Heart of Mary: The Spiritual Diary, Imprimatur:* Cardinal Péter Erdo, Archbishop of Budapest and Primate of Hungary (The Flame of Love Movement of the Immaculate Heart of Mary; Montreal, Canada) 2014, p. 61.

[42] Interview with Jacinta conducted by Barry Hanratty April 16,1983, St. Michael's Garabandal Center for Our Lady of Carmel, Inc., accessed July 4, 2019, http://www.garabandal.org/News/Interview_with_Jacinta.shtml

[43] Ramon Pérez, *Garabandal: The Village Speaks*, translated from the French by Matthews, Annette I. Curot, The Workers of Our Lady of Mount Carmel, 1981, pp. 52.

[44] Janie Garza, *Heaven's Messages for the Family: How to Become the Family God Wants You to Be* (Saint Dominic's Media, 1998).

To a prayer group, or "cenacle," of her Marian Movement of Priests, Mary said through Fr. Gobbi: *"And so, I invite you to spend this day in the cenacle, gathered together in prayer with me, Mother of Mercy, in the hope and trembling expectation of the second Pentecost, now close at hand"* (Feast of Pentecost, June 4, 1995).[45]

On the Feast of Pentecost, a year later, she asked those present to prepare: *"With an extraordinary cenacle of prayer and fraternity, you celebrate today the solemnity of Pentecost. You recall the prodigious event of the descent of the Holy Spirit, under the form of tongues of fire, upon the cenacle of Jerusalem, where the Apostles were gathered in prayer, with me, your heavenly Mother.*

You, too, gathered today in prayer, in the spiritual cenacle of my Immaculate Heart, prepare yourselves to receive the prodigious gift of the Second Pentecost. The Second Pentecost will come to bring this humanity, which has again become pagan and which is living under the powerful influence of the evil one, back to its full communion of life with its Lord, Who has created, redeemed, and saved it."[46]

In the 21st century, heaven seems to be announcing that the Warning will occur in this generation. Words to both Luz de María de Bonilla and to Fr. Michel Rodrigue, whose messages are currently ongoing, appear especially urgent.

On February 16, 2010, Jesus said through Luz de María: *"My Mother has announced throughout the whole world and across time what is now on the horizon."*

On March 3, 2013, Mary said: *"How close to this generation is to the Warning! And how many of you do not even know what the Warning is! In these times, my faithful instruments and my prophet [Luz de María] are mocked by those who consider themselves scholars of spirituality, by those who reach millions of souls through means of mass communication. They are misleading them and hiding the truth because I [Mary] am the One revealing the will of the Trinity, the will of the Trinity already expressed in all of my apparitions, starting from long ago."* . . . *"Those who have not believed will be put to shame."*

For some, it is hard not to wonder, "How soon is soon? Does soon mean in my lifetime?" On July 15, 2019, for the first time, Luz de María

---

[45] Marian Movement of Priests, Fr. Stefano Gobbi, *The Marian Movement of Priests; 17th English Edition* (St. Francis, Maine: Marian Movement of Priests, 1996), p. 546, http://www.heartofmaryarabic.com/wp-content/uploads/2015/04/The-Blue-Book.pdf, accessed September 2, 2019.

[46] Ibid., p. 451.

was given that answer. Saint Michael the Archangel declared, *"This is the generation that will experience the great act of Divine Mercy: THE WARNING. . ."*[47]

According to what God the Father has revealed to the Abbot of a new fraternity in the Church, Fr. Michel Rodrigue, a holy priest who has heard the Lord's voice since the age of three, "soon" means in this generation. In various talks available on CDs, he helps people understand and prepare for the Warning and the times to come, when great changes will occur in the world.[48]

"You know that you are already blessed because you are being made aware. Why do you think that God has chosen you to be here? Because you have a mission. When you go out, when you return to your home, you will feel something on your shoulder. What is it? The burden of Jesus, which is the mission of the Lord. If He is making you aware now of what will happen, it is because people will come back from their mystical experience of meeting God, searching for help, not knowing what to do. Some will be afraid; others will be in shock. You have been chosen for this time to help guide these people into the Catholic Church to receive the Good News of Jesus."[49]

Through Fr. Michel, the Lord is asking all faithful Catholics, purified by the Warning to help bring His lost, confused, and separated sheep back into His fold.

How Should We Prepare for the Warning?

The advice from heaven as to how humanity is to prepare for the Warning echoes the requests of the Blessed Mother in her apparitions of the last two centuries. She has been calling out to the world, asking us to repent, turn back to God, amend our lives, do penance to make reparation for our own sins and the sins of the world. She has called out to us,

---

[47] "The Great Warning of God to Humanity: Prophecies and Revelations Given to Luz de María de Bonilla," Imprimatur of Bishop Guevara, Revelaciones Marianas, https://www.revelacionesmarianas.com/en/warning.html, accessed July 13, 2019.

[48] To learn more about what God the Father has revealed to Fr. Michel Rodrigue, see www.CountdowntotheKingdom.com, and click on "Why Fr. Michel Rodrigue? A Virtual Retreat." Talks by Fr. Rodrigue (2 CD sets) can be purchased through Peter Frank at missionangelshq@gmail.com.

[49] From Fr. Michel Rodrigue's live recorded talks in Barry's Bay, Ontario on July 12 and 13, 2018, and at Gospa House, North Hills, California on Saturday, February 23, 2019. For more recent talks, see www.countdowntothekingdom.com/why-fr-michel-rodrigue.

pleading with us to pray, pray, pray, and to take the practices of the Catholic faith extremely seriously. The souls of her beloved children are at stake.

At Heede, in 1945, Jesus spoke with great force: *"Humanity has not listened to My Holy Mother, who appeared at Fatima to urge mankind to do penance. Now I, Myself, have come to warn the world in this last hour: the times are serious! May people finally do penance for their sins; may they turn away with all their heart from evil and pray, pray much, in order to calm the indignation of God. May they often recite the Holy Rosary, in particular: this prayer is powerful with God. Less entertainments and amusements! I am very near."*[50]

Elizabeth Kindelmann shared that Jesus said the following to her in a thundering voice, *"Before the difficult times are upon you, prepare yourselves for the vocation I have called you to by renewed tenacity and a firm decision. You must not be lazy, uninterested, and indifferent because the great storm is brewing just ahead. Its gusts will carry away indifferent souls consumed by laziness. Only those souls with a genuine vocation will survive."*[51]

Tender and fatherly advice came from St. Joseph, when Janie Garza asked him on March 19, 1966, how we should prepare:

"Pray, my little one, pray. Remain faithful to all that the Holy Spirit directs you to do. Act in everything that Most Holy Mary is calling you to. Be a strong messenger of living her messages of peace, prayer, Holy Mass, fasting, conversion, and reading Holy Scripture. Do this as a family. Do not reject God's Most Holy Name so that He will not reject you. Decide to be a holy family, to pray together, to love, and to forgive one another. This is a time of decision for all of God's children. Live as God's people, leading good, simple and just lives. Open your hearts to God's love and mercy. Every family must consecrate themselves to the Sacred Heart of Jesus, to the Immaculate Heart of Mary[52] and to my intercession and protection, that We may lead you closer to God. We will prepare you for the things to come. Live as children of the Lord, and you will

---

[50] Cenni, *I SS. Cuori, Imprimatur* Sublaci. Simon Laurentius O.S.B.

[51] Kindelmann, *The Flame,* Message of March 12, 1964, p. 205.

[52] For a powerfully effective Marian consecration, order the book, *Mary's Mantle Consecration: A Spiritual Retreat for Heaven's Help,* endorsed by Archbishop Salvatore Cordileone and Bishop Myron J. Cotta, and the accompanying *Mary's Mantle Consecration Prayer Journal.* See www.MarysMantleConsecration.com.

41

live through all these troubled times. . . Do not fear anything, but abandon yourself to the Holy Spirit who will help you to do the Holy Will of God."[53]

In 1977, when the visionaries at Garabandal were asked if they had any words of advice for people in order that they might prepare for this event, Conchita answered, *"We must always be prepared with our souls in peace and not tie ourselves down so much to this world. Instead, we must think very often that we are here to go to heaven and to be saints. Mari Loli responded that we are "to do much penance, make sacrifices, visit the Blessed Sacrament every day that we are able to, and to pray the Holy Rosary daily."*[54]

To prepare our hearts, God the Father shared this advice through Matthew Kelly on June 5, 1993:

"Poor souls, all of you, robbed of the knowledge of My love. Be ready for this judgment of Mine. . . Now do you see how important these times are? Don't wait for this Mini-Judgment. You must start to look at yourselves more closely so that you can see your faults and repent. You are fortunate to have the faith needed to read, believe, and accept this message. You must not go away indifferent to it. You must examine yourself more every day and pray in reparation.

All of you, be like the blind man. Each day you should cry, "Lord, open my eyes," and My Son will open your eyes so that you can see your wretchedness and repent.

Pray now more than ever, and remember the world's standards are a false indication of My justice. I am your God, and while I am perfectly merciful to those who repent, I am perfectly just to those who do not.

Many people think that I, your God, won't mind. "It's only little," they say. But it's not a matter of minding. I want people to love Me. Love respects little things, as well as the big things; and in most cases, these little things are not so little.

---

[53] Janie Garza, *Heaven's Messages for the Family, Volume II: Messages from St. Joseph and the Archangels* (Saint Dominic Media, 1999), pp. 201-202.
[54] Garabandal International Magazine, October-December, 2014, http://www.garabandal.org.uk/magazine.html, accessed July 4, 2019.

Do not judge your actions or others' actions. You are unable to judge. You are incapable of judging because you cannot read a man's heart.

You must love Me with your whole heart, with your whole mind, with your whole soul, and with your whole strength.

Today is the day. Do your best to renounce yourself and let Christ reign in your lives. You will never be ready for the Mini-Judgment, but some will be more prepared than others. You must aim to be one of those and bring as many others as you can to be prepared, or as prepared as possible.

Above all, do not fear. I don't tell you all this to become scared. No, simply try to become better people each day. More than this I could not ask. I am your God. I am perfectly just and perfectly merciful. You are sons and daughters of Mine. Does not a father look after his children? I send this message to spare you from any pain I can; but the pain that you experience by seeing the darkness of your soul is an act of love on My behalf. Do you not see that this will return many, many souls to a fuller love of Me? This will save many souls from the fires of hell.

This is the most important of all My messages: I am the Lord, your God. You are My sons and daughters, whom I love very much, and My greatest delight is in being with you; and I want to be with you for eternity. Anything I do is done out of love for you, My children. Trust in Me, your Heavenly Father."[55]

In summary, to prepare for the Warning is to repent, to believe in the Gospel, to love God with all our mind, heart, soul, and strength, and to love our neighbor as ourself. To prepare is to forgive and live a good, just, and simple life. The prophets of the Warning, as well as the Blessed Mother in her recent apparitions, have given us specific spiritual practices to follow: frequent Confession, Holy Mass, fasting, Bible reading, prayer from the heart—especially the Rosary, prayer as a family, visits to the Blessed Sacrament, and consecrating one's self and family to the Sacred Heart of Jesus and the Immaculate Heart of Mary. These are heaven's prescriptions for living life to its fullest in grace, and being ready to see God and ourselves as we really are.

---

[55] Kelly, *Words,* pp. 70-72.

What Will Happen after the Warning?

"I know that you think this [the Mini-Judgment] sounds like a very good thing," said God the Father to Matthew Kelly, *"but unfortunately even this won't bring the whole world into My love. Some people will turn even further away from Me; they will be proud and stubborn. Satan is working hard against Me."*[56]

"People . . . will ache for not having believed," Mary explained through Luz de María, *"but they will have already misled many of my children who will not be able to recuperate so easily, for the godless will deny the Warning and attribute it to new technologies."*[57]

"My Cross is Victory," Jesus foretold, *"and it will shine in the firmament for seven days and nights. It will radiate light constantly. It will be a preliminary sign for which My people have waited; and for those who do not believe, there will be great confusion. Science will try to give an explanation for that which has no scientific explanation."* . . . *"Even then, some of My children will deny that the Warning came from My Kingdom and will rebel against Me, uniting with evil."*[58]

"God has not given us three ways to travel, only two," said Fr. Michel Rodrigue. *"There is no grey area in between the path of evil and the path of the Lord. Those who will say, 'I don't know. I cannot make a decision,' will not be able to remain indifferent. As God says in the Book of Revelation (3:16), 'So, because you are lukewarm, neither hot nor cold, I will spit you out of my mouth.' People will have to make a decisive choice, and you will understand why because after that, they will be left with the consequences of their decision. The time of mercy will end, and the time of justice will begin. Jesus said this to St. Faustina Kowalska."*[59]

"It is the hour of decision for mankind" (The fourth message of Betania from Mary to Maria Esperanza).[60] *"Some will straighten their*

---

[56] Ibid., p. 70.

[57] Bonilla, *Venga, Imprimatur:* Bishop Guevara, Revelaciones Marianas, p. 56, https://www.revelacionesmarianas.com/libros/en/2013.pdf, Message of March 3, 2013, from the Blessed Virgin Mary, accessed September 17, 2019.

[58] Bonilla, *Venga, Imprimatur:* Bishop Guevara, Revelaciones Marianas, p. 290, https://www.revelacionesmarianas.com/libros/en/2014.pdf, Message of November 22, 2014, from Jesus Christ, accessed September 17, 2019.

[59] From Fr. Michel Rodrigue's live recorded talks in Barry's Bay, Ontario on July 12 and 13, 2018.

[60] Signs and Wonders for Our Times, Volume 15-n.2, Featured Article from www.sign.org, p. 37.

walk, others will deny My Son, thus becoming great persecutors of My elect" (Mary to Luz de María).[61]

"Those who repent will be given an unquenchable thirst for this light," God the Father said to Matthew Kelly. *"Their love for Me then will be so strong that, united with Mary's Immaculate Heart and the Sacred Heart of Jesus, the head of Satan shall be crushed. . . All those who love Me will join to help form the heel that crushes Satan. Then, as you all die naturally, your thirst for this light will be quenched. You shall see Me, your God. You shall live in My love; you will be in heaven."*[62]

During the Warning and for a short time afterward, Satan will be blinded, unable to tempt souls. Without this divine blinding, souls would not be able to see the absolute truth of their state before God, nor have the absolute freedom of will to choose God or reject Him.

"Once Satan is blinded," Our Lord said to Elizabeth Kindelmann, *"the decrees of Vatican Council II will be fulfilled in an extraordinary way. . .*[63] *Let priests and their people gather in spiritual oneness. This outpouring will reach even the souls of the non-baptized."*[64]

When the Garabandal visionary, Jacinta, was asked, *"Do you remember when the Virgin told you that the Churches would unite?"*

"The way she said it," Jacinta answered, *"was all humanity would be within one Church, the Catholic Church. She also said it was very important to pray for this intention."*[65]

Blessed Anna Maria Taigi was shown by God that entire nations would return to the unity of the Church. Many Turks [Moslems?], pagans, and Jews would be converted, and their fervor would cover with confusion the original Christians. The Lord, she said, would cleanse the world and His Church to prepare a miraculous rebirth that would be the triumph of His mercy.[66]

---

[61] Bonilla, *Venga, Imprimatur:* Bishop Guevara, Revelaciones Marianas, p. 175, Message of July 24, 2014, from the Blessed Virgin Mary, https://www.revelacionesmarianas.com/libros/en/2014.pdf, accessed September 17, 2019.

[62] Matthew Kelly, *Words from God* (Batemans Bay, Australia: Words from God, 1993). Message to Matthew Kelly from God the Father on June 5, 1993, p. 70.

[63] Kindelmann, *The Flame of Love* (Children of the Father Foundation; 2015-2018), p. 87.

[64] Ibid., p. 110.

[65] Interview with Jacinta conducted by Barry Hanratty April 16,1983, St. Michael's Garabandal Center for Our Lady of Carmel, Inc., accessed July 4, 2019, http://www.garabandal.org/News/Interview_with_Jacinta.shtml

[66] Mark Regis, "Blessed Anna-Maria Taigi," Garabandal Journal, January-February 2004, pp. 6-8.

"The Second Pentecost," explained Our Lady to Fr. Gobbi, *"will descend into hearts to transform them and make them sensitive and open to love, humble and merciful, free of all egoism and of all wickedness. And thus it will be that the Spirit of the Lord will transform the hearts of stone into hearts of flesh."*[67]

St. Joseph described a new era to come to Janie Garza: *"There will be great joy for all the faithful people of God. His children will be happy. There will be love in families everywhere. People will benefit from their labor, and they will build their homes and live to enjoy them. They will see their children's children, and all will live long lives."*[68]

"I will come with My peace," said Jesus at Heede. *"I will build My Kingdom with a small number of elect. This Kingdom will come suddenly, sooner than men think. . . My beloved children, the hour is near. Pray unceasingly, and you will not be confused. I am gathering My elect. They will come together from every part of the world, and they will glorify Me. I am coming!"*[69]

At long last, God will fulfill his promise of *"a new heaven and a new earth"* (Revelation 21:1;4) *in which righteousness dwells" (2 Peter 3:13).* The petition of the Our Father: "Thy Kingdom come, Thy will be done, on Earth as it is in heaven" will be consummated, and the awaited *"period of peace,"* promised by Our Lady of Fatima, when her *"Immaculate Heart will triumph,"* will arrive.

As Our Lady told Fr. Gobbi, *". . . sinners will be converted; the weak will find support; the sick will receive healing; those far away will return to the house of the Father; those separated and divided will attain full unity. In this way, the miracle of the Second Pentecost will take place. It will come with the triumph of my Immaculate Heart in the world. Only then will you see how the tongues of fire of the Spirit of Love will renew the whole world, which will become completely transformed by the greatest manifestation of divine mercy."*[70]

Albert Bessieres, SJ, translated from the French by Rev. Stephen Rigby, *Wife, Mother and Mystic* (Tan Books, 1970).

[67] Marian Movement of Priests, Fr. Stefano Gobbi, *To the Priests: Our Lady's Beloved Sons; 1996 Supplement* (St. Francis, Maine: Marian Movement of Priests, 1996), p. 974.

[68] Janie Garza, *Heaven's Messages for the Family: How to Become the Family God Wants You to Be* (Saint Dominic Media, 1998), p. 201.

[69] Ibid., Cenni, *I SS. Cuori*, Imprimatur Sublaci. Simon Laurentius O.S.B.

[70] Marian Movement of Priests, Fr. Stefano Gobbi, *To the Priests: Our Lady's Beloved Sons; 17th English Edition* (St. Francis, Maine: Marian Movement of Priests, 1996), p. 920.

What awaits God's faithful in this life or the next is beyond the most sublime imaginings of human dreams. As we approach the end of an era, the Warning is an extremely small passage in time, yet a monumental event in the story of mankind. Whether denied or accepted, it will proffer everyone the chance to face the reality of God and the state of their soul. The world will never be the same after the Warning, and those few who know of it in advance and prepare are fortunate indeed.

THE WARNING

PROPHETS
& PROPHECIES
OF THE WARNING

"For if this endeavor or this activity is of human origin, it will destroy itself. But if it comes from God, you will not be able to destroy them; you may even find yourselves fighting against God."

~Acts 5:38b-39

For fuller accounts of the prophecies and the prophets behind them, see the appendix.

ST. EDMUND CAMPION, SJ
ENGLAND (1540–1581)
Priest and Martyr

"I pronounced a great day, not wherein any temporal potentate should minister, but wherein the Terrible Judge should reveal all men's consciences and try every man of each kind of religion. This is the day of change . . ."[71]

BLESSED ANNA MARÍA TAIGI
ITALY (1769–1837)
Wife, Mother, Mystic

"A great purification will come upon the world preceded by an Illumination of Conscience in which everyone will see themselves as God sees them."[72]

BLESSED POPE PIUS IX
THE PAPAL STATES (1792–1878)

"Since the whole world is against God and His Church, it is evident that He has reserved the victory over His enemies to Himself. This will be more obvious when it is considered that the root of all our present evils is to be found in the fact that those with talents and vigor crave earthly pleasures, and not only desert God but repudiate Him altogether. Thus it appears they cannot be brought back in any other way except through an act that cannot be ascribed to any secondary agency, and thus all will be forced to look to the supernatural. . . There will come a great wonder, which will

---

[71] Evelyn Waugh, *Two Lives: Edmund Campion and Ronald Knox* (Continuum; 2005), p. 113.
[72] Thomas W. Petrisko, *The Miracle of the Illumination of All Consciences* (St. Andrew's Productions, 2000; second printing 2002), p. 27.

fill the world with astonishment. This wonder will be preceded by the triumph of revolution. The church will suffer exceedingly. Her servants and her chieftain will be mocked, scourged, and martyred."[73]

ST. FAUSTINA KOWALSKA
POLAND (1905–1938)
Nun, Mystic, Apostle of Divine Mercy

Jesus to St. Faustina: *"Write this: before I come as the Just Judge, I come as the King of Mercy. Before the day of justice arrives, this sign in the sky will be given to mankind. All light in the heavens will be extinguished, and there will be great darkness over the whole earth. Then the sign of the Cross will be seen in the sky, and from the holes where the hands and the feet of the Savior were nailed will come forth a brilliant light, which will illuminate the Earth for a period of time. This will take place shortly before the last day."*[74]

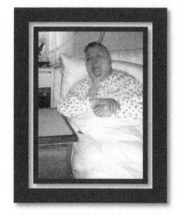

APPARITIONS OF OUR LORD AND OUR LADY AT HEEDE, GERMANY
(1937–1940, 1945)
GRETE GANSEFORTH
Mystic and Stigmatist
(1924?–1996)

Jesus to Grete Ganseforth: *"I am very near. The Earth will tremble and will suffer. It will be terrible, a Mini-Judgment. But do not fear. I am with you. You will rejoice and thank Me. Those who await Me will have My help, My grace, and My love. For those*

---

[73] Rev. R. Gerald Culleton, *The Prophets and Our Times* (Tan Books and Publishers, 1941), p. 206, accessed July 29, 2019, http://ia800200.us.archive.org/2/ite ms/TheProphetsAndOurTimes/TheProphetsAndOurTimes.pdf

[74] St. Faustina Kowalska, *Diary of Saint Maria Faustina Kowalska: Divine Mercy in My Soul, 3rd Edition* (Marian Press, 2005), #83.

who are not in a state of grace, it will be frightening. The angels of justice are now scattered across the world. I will make Myself known to mankind. Every soul will recognize Me as their God. I am coming! I am at the door."[75]

ELIZABETH KINDELMANN
HUNGARY (1913–1985)
Wife, Mother, Mystic, Founder of The Flame of Love Movement

Our Lady to Elizabeth Kindelman: *"My Flame of Love is burning. It is so great that I cannot keep it any longer within me. It leaps out to you with explosive power. When it pours out, my love will destroy the satanic hatred that contaminates the world. The greatest number of souls will be set free. Nothing like this has existed before. This is my greatest miracle that I will do for all. . . No need for this miracle to be authenticated. I will authenticate the miracle in each soul. All will recognize the outpouring of the Flame of Love."*[76]

APPARITIONS OF OUR LADY AT GARABANDAL, SPAIN
(1961–1965) Visionaries: CONCHITA GONZALEZ, MARI LOLI MAZON, MARI CRUZ GONZALEZ, AND JACINTA GONZALEZ

Conchita to Dr. J. Dominguez in May, 1973:

A: The most important thing about that day is that everyone in the whole world will see a sign, a grace, or a punishment within themselves. They will find themselves all alone in the world, no matter where they are

---

[75] Ibid., Cenni, *I SS. Cuori*, Imprimatur Sublaci. Simon Laurentius O.S.B.
[76] Kindelmann, *The Flame of Love* (Children of the Father Foundation; 2015-2018), pp. 44-45.

at that time, alone with their consciences right before God. . . Sometimes there are people who cannot see their own evil, for as it is said, they close the eyes of the soul not wanting to see inside. . . It is to open our soul to God and to bring repentance to us.

We will all feel the Warning differently because it will depend on our conscience. It will be very personal. Therefore, we will all react differently to it because your sins are different from mine.

Q: Will the Warning cause physical harm?

A: No, unless it is something that results from the shock, as, for example, a heart attack.

Mari Loli on July 27, 1975:

Q: It is said that you have mentioned that at the time of the Warning, everything will stop—even planes in the air. Is this true?

A: Yes.

Q: Can you tell us anything else about the Warning?

A: All I can say is that it is very near, and that it is very important that we get ready for it, as it will be a terrible event. It will make us realize all the sins we have committed.[77]

Jacinta in February, 1977:

"The Warning is something that is just seen in the air, everywhere in the world, and immediately is transmitted into the interior of our souls. It will last for a very little time, but it will seem a very long time because of its effects within us. It will be good for our souls, in order to see in ourselves our conscience—the good that we have failed to do, and the bad we have done. Then we will feel a great love toward our heavenly parents and ask forgiveness for all our offenses. The Warning is for us to draw closer to Him and to increase our faith. Therefore, one should prepare for that day, but not await it with fear. God does not send things for the sake of fear, but rather with justice and love. He does it for the good of all His children so they might enjoy eternal happiness and not be lost."[78]

Note: In keeping with the honor of the Church's Imprimatur, St. Pope Paul VI's words on The Warning have been omitted in this book's second printing, for no

---

[77] Ramon Pérez, *Garabandal: The Village Speaks*, translated from the French by Matthews, Annette I. Curot, The Workers of Our Lady of Mount Carmel, 1981, pp. 51-52.

[78] Garabandal International Magazine, October-December, 2014, accessed July 4, 2019, http://www.garabandal.org.uk/magazine.html

other reason than the reference was taken from a recorded reading of the written source, rather than the source itself. Pope Paul VI was no stranger to Garabandal. In 1966, the visionary Conchita Gonzalez was called to Rome and met privately with Paul VI, who addressed her with the words, "I bless you, Conchita, and with me, the whole Church blesses you." Conchita wrote, in an autographed letter to Fr. Gustavo Morelos that same year, regarding her visit with the Pope: "Reverend Father: My trip to the Vatican was very happy, everything went very well. They told me to keep it a secret and so I cannot be more explicit."

Later, Pope Paul VI also spoke publicly on the subject, saying, "Garabandal is the most wonderful work of humanity after the birth of Jesus. It is the second life of the Blessed Virgin on this earth" . . . "It is very important to make these messages known to the world."[v]

FR. STEFANO GOBBI
ITALY (1930–2011)
Priest, Mystic, Founder of
The Marian Movement of
Priests

Our Lady to Fr. Gobbi: *"What will come to pass is something so very great that it will exceed anything that has taken place since the beginning of the world. It will be like a judgment in miniature, and each one will see his own life and all he has done, in the very light of God."*[79]

MATTHEW KELLY
AUSTRALIA, UNITED STATES (1973–)
Husband, Father, Speaker, Writer,
Founder of the Dynamic Catholic
Institute

God the Father to Matthew Kelly: *"The Mini-Judgment is a reality. People no longer realize that they offend Me. Out of My infinite mercy,*

---

[79] Marian Movement of Priests, Fr. Stefano Gobbi, *To the Priests: Our Lady's Beloved Sons; 17th English Edition* (St. Francis, Maine: Marian Movement of Priests, 1996), pp. 784-785.

I will provide a Mini-Judgment. It will be painful, very painful, but short. You will see your sins; you will see how much you offend Me, every day.

I know that you think this sounds like a very good thing, but unfortunately even this won't bring the whole world into My love. Some people will turn even further away from Me; they will be proud and stubborn. Satan is working hard against Me.

Poor souls, all of you, robbed of the knowledge of My love. Be ready for this judgment of Mine. Judgment is the best word you humans have to describe it, but it will be more like this: you will see your own personal darkness contrasted against the pure light of My love."[80]

JANIE GARZA

UNITED STATES (1955–)

Wife, Mother, Mystic, Stigmatist

Jesus: Our humble servant, the illumination that will take place will be for a short period. During this time My Father will allow all of humanity to see the state of their souls as My Father sees their souls. This will be a time of great grace when many souls will repent and return to My Father. Those souls that die will die from great shock to see the state of the darkness which exists in their souls.

Janie: Beloved Savior, will the illumination scare people?

Jesus: The fear that will inflame their hearts is the holy fear of the immense power of My Father, especially for those many souls that have continued to deny the existence of My Father. These will be the souls that will experience tremendous fear.

Janie: Will all people convert?

Jesus: Many will convert, but many will not.

Janie: Oh, Jesus, will this happen very soon?

Jesus: Our humble servant, this will happen within a short period. Do not be distracted with dates, but prepare every day with strong prayer.[81]

---

[80] Matthew Kelly, *Words from God* (Batemans Bay, Australia: Words from God, 1993), p. 70-72.
[81] Janie Garza, *Heaven's Messages for the Family: How to Become the Family God Wants You to Be* (Saint Dominic Media, 1998), p. 329.

SERVANT OF GOD, MARIA ESPERANZA
VENEZUELA (1928–2004)
Wife, Mother, Mystic, Stigmatist, Visionary of the Apparitions at Betania, Venezuela (1976–1990)

Our Lady to Maria Esperanza: *"The love of my Jesus will be the door that will open hearts to give access to a beautiful era that must revive people to a glorious teaching of unity. Take advantage of time because the hour is arriving when my Son will appear before everyone as Judge and Savior. You must be in the necessary conditions to live with Him on that Great Day. Do not think that it is distant."*[82]

The Fourth Message of Betania—Our Lady to Maria Esperanza: *"Little children, I am your Mother, and I come to seek you so that you may prepare yourselves to be able to bring my message of reconciliation: There is coming the great moment of a Great Day of Light. The consciences of this beloved people must be violently shaken so that they may "put their house in order" and offer to Jesus the just reparation for the daily infidelities that are committed on the part of sinners. . . it is the hour of decision for mankind."*[83]

LUZ DE MARÍA DE BONILLA
COSTA RICA, ARGENTINA (1962?–)
Wife, Mother, Mystic, and Stigmatist

Our Lady to Luz de María: *"How close this generation is to the Warning! And*

---

[82] *The Appeals of Our Lady: Apparitions and Marian Shrines in the World.* "Apparition of the Virgin Mary at Betania."
[83] Signs and Wonders for Our Times, Volume 15-n.2, Featured Article from www.sign.org, p. 37.

how many of you do not even know what the Warning is! In these times, my faithful instruments and my prophet [Luz de María] are mocked by those who consider themselves scholars of spirituality, by those who reach millions of souls through means of mass communication. . . The Warning is not a fantasy. Humanity must be purified so that it does not fall into the flames of hell. People will see themselves, and in that moment, they will ache for not having believed, but they will have already misled many of My children who will not be able to recuperate so easily, for the godless will deny the Warning and attribute it to new technologies.[84]

FR. MICHEL RODRIGUE

Priest, Mystic, Exorcist, Abbot and Founder of The Apostolic Fraternity of Saint Benedict Joseph Labre

CANADA, FOUNDED (**2012**)

God the Father to Fr. Michel Rodrigue: *"Pray and be confident. I do not want you to be like the ones who have no faith and who will tremble during the manifestation of the Son of Man. On the contrary, pray and rejoice and receive the peace given by my Son, Jesus. What sorrow when I must respect free will and come to the point of giving a Warning that is also part of My mercy. Be ready and vigilant for the hour of My mercy. I bless you, My children."*[85]

---

[84] Luz de María de Bonilla, *Venga a Nosotros Tu Reino* (*"Thy Kingdom Come"*) Year 2014, with the Imprimatur and full support of Juan Abelardo Mata Guevara, SDB, Titular Bishop of Estelí, Nicaragua. Message of March 3, 2013, from the Blessed Virgin Mary, p. 56, Revelaciones Marianas, https://www.revelacionesmarianas.com/libros/en/2013.pdf, accessed September 17, 2019.

[85] From Fr. Michel Rodrigue's live recorded talks in Barry's Bay, Ontario on July 12 and 13, 2018. See www.CountdowntotheKingdom.com. Click on "Why Fr. Michel? A Virtual Retreat."

THE WARNING

TESTIMONIES OF THE ILLUMINATION OF CONSCIENCE

It is not only through the sacraments and the ministrations of the Church that the Holy Spirit makes holy the People, leads them and enriches them with His virtues. Allotting His gifts according as He wills (cf. 1 Cor. 12:11), He also distributes special graces among the faithful of every rank. By these gifts He makes them fit and ready to undertake various tasks and offices for the renewal and building up of the Church, as it is written, "the manifestation of the Spirit is given to everyone for profit" (1 Cor. 12:7). Whether these charisms be very remarkable or more simple and widely diffused, they are to be received with thanksgiving and consolation since they are fitting and useful for the needs of the Church.

~Second Vatican Council, *Lumen Gentium,* 12

C. ALAN AMES

A Visit to a Violent Alcoholic

C. Alan Ames is a Catholic mystic who began his healing, speaking, and writing ministry in 1993, after undergoing an unduly dramatic conversion involving heavenly visitors and a personal illumination of his conscience. Since then, the Lord has sent him around the world to heal and convert thousands, through his holy zeal and extraordinary charisms with which the Lord has gifted him. Alan lives painfully the Passion with the hidden stigmata, which is sometimes made visible. Today he has published over twenty books and continues to receive messages from the Holy Trinity and the saints. Alan's ministry enjoys the full and explicit support of the archbishop of Perth, Australia, where he resides. See www.alanames.org.

In 1993, when I was forty, I traveled frequently for my job as a sales manager for a pharmaceutical company in Perth, Australia. On one of my work trips, I flew to a city called Adelaide and went through my monotonous routine of checking into to a hotel and sitting on the bed to watch television. Though normally a heavy drinker, I hadn't downed any booze because I didn't generally consume alcohol on a work day. While I was watching the evening news, all of a sudden, directly in front of me appeared a horrific-looking man who reached his arms forward and began to choke me. He had dark skin and bulging eyes, with lips drawn back in a snarl that exposed his ghastly teeth; but I was less concerned with his appearance than the fact that he was strangling me! I tried to use my martial arts moves against him, having been captain of the Australian team in the Aikido World Championships, but my hands passed right through his body. Nothing I could do would stop his stranglehold. After a few minutes of useless fighting, the veins in my neck were about to burst, and I believed I was taking my very last breath.

Then an audible voice in my head said, "Pray the Our Father!" That was the last idea I would have come up with, but in desperation, I started to pray it, and the strangling stopped. Then I stopped and the strangling resumed. Every time I ceased to pray, the strangling started, and every time I resumed, the strangling stopped. To add to this nightmare, I was trapped and couldn't move. I tried repeatedly to get out of the hotel room, but the terrifying man kept me pinned in a stranglehold—and this went on all night.

The experience was so strange and frightening that I thought I'd gone mad: "That's it. I'm absolutely crazy." I'd heard of people who drank in excess and would see pink elephants traveling up the wall, so I figured I was one of them. Then I saw my neck in the large hotel mirror. To my amazement, it was bruised; therefore, I couldn't deny the attack was real. Yet I couldn't accept it either.

The next day, I heard the same voice in my head that had told me to pray the Our Father. He told me he was an angel whom God had sent to help me. I didn't believe in the existence of angels. To me, they were nothing more than make-believe fairies. He said God had sent him because God loved me and wanted my love. "If God exists," I answered back to this "fairy" in my head, "surely He wouldn't love someone like me!"

I had good reason to think I was a poor candidate for love. God had always been the furthest thought from my mind, and troublemaking the first. I was born on November 9, 1953, in Bedford, England, north of London, to an English dad and an Irish-Catholic mum from the county Kerry. She was often praying the Rosary, attending church, and trying to bring me up in the faith, but I had no interest in religion whatsoever. Ignoring her efforts completely, I preferred to leave the house in order to play and steal money, causing my mum multiple heartaches. Coming from a poor family, I was hateful toward those who had toys, who had holidays, who had things I couldn't have. Even from a very early age, I didn't believe God was real. Perhaps a group of wise men had gotten together and jotted down guidelines on how we should live without hurting each other, and wrapped it up in this story called Jesus.

At age twelve, I started drinking alcohol and was brought before a court judge for taking money out of the candle box in St. Edmund's Church in Edmonton, London. At age fourteen, I had the worst record of all the students at a Jesuit school in Stamford Hill, and was finally expelled for stealing. I thought the only way I was going to get treated with any dignity was to follow in the footsteps of my father: an aggressive, alcoholic gambler. People were frightened of him and gave him a grudging respect, which he gained through violence. I copied his habits, including his constant drinking, because alcohol gave me good feelings and numbed me to all the bad things in my life. But the next day would always come, when everything felt worse, so I would drink again to drown the consequences.

I lived in a dangerous part of London with my parents and my four brothers. In my teen years, I joined a motorcycle gang and became extremely violent. Most of my friends were like myself: thugs and thieves. My best friend killed someone, another friend was murdered at the age of seventeen, another was blinded in a fight, and another tried to murder an older woman. I learned Aikido because at 5 feet, 7 inches tall, I realized there were a lot of men out there much bigger than I. When a man who had been protecting me was put in prison for twelve years for murder, I worked hard to better protect myself and eventually achieved a fourth-degree black belt, later becoming captain of the Australian team in the 1992 World Championships in Tokyo. I had a very bad temper, and the martial arts taught me how to use it to harm people: break their bones, punch them, kick them, and even kill them. I hurt others out of jealousy because they seemed to have what I didn't—money and the love of a happy family.

At age eighteen, I met my Australian wife-to-be and covered up my real self so she would like me. She noticed me drinking a lot but didn't realize I was addicted to the stuff. She must have loved me. She married me. We lived in London, and life was hard for me there as an uneducated, struggling warehouse worker, so my wife said, "Let's go to Australia. Life is better there." I agreed, and we moved to Perth in 1976.

Several years later, I managed to obtain my job with the pharmaceutical company by lying to get the position. To keep the job, I had to actually study the topic of medicine, and my learning paid off because I stayed there for ten years, rising to sales manager. It was a great job, an easy job, which paid lots of money and provided plenty of opportunities for raising Cain.

Drinking is very popular in Australia, and I fit in quite well. Outside of work, much of my life revolved around carousing, fighting, stealing, swindling, and lying. I believe the only thing I didn't do was murder, but I came frighteningly close to it a few times. I lived for power, money, and a good time at all times. But suffering always dragged down my dreams because my pleasure came from sin and addictions, with their lingering imprint of pain, hurt, loneliness, and emptiness.

My life was a dark one when the angel started to visit me. Even when I heard his voice, I still didn't believe that he existed, so I said to him, "Prove you are real." And he did. He started to tell me of different things that would happen in my life, which I shared with my wife—and to our amazement, they all came true.

The angel was gentle, but I didn't listen to him; therefore, in his stead, God sent in the big guns. One night, when I was again in the city of Adelaide, but staying in a different hotel, St. Teresa of Avila appeared in my room, wearing a brown Carmelite habit. Her face looked hawkish and stern, like that of a strict school teacher. She proceeded to give me a kick up the back side, saying I needed to change my life completely to avoid going to hell, which she then described in frightening detail. That woke me up. Before then, hell was only a made-up myth to trick people into living better, but now, if that place existed, I certainly didn't want to go there.

St. Teresa explained to me that I had to start loving God and my fellow men. Each person, she said, is created in the image of God, and to love Him would naturally mean to love other people, regardless of their differences or behavior toward me. Then she revealed what could also be mine: she told me all about heaven. "That is where I want to go!"

"You can reach paradise," she said to me, "anyone can. If you live your Catholic faith, you are guaranteed heaven." Then she insisted, "Pray, pray the Rosary!" and asked me to go get one.

I didn't want to pray. Prayer was boring, so I looked for excuses: "Where can I get rosary beads at this time of night?"

"There is a shop around the corner that is open and sells rosary beads."

"At 9:30 at night? That's impossible!"

"You go there!"

"This is totally nuts," I thought to myself, as I walked outside. Turning the corner, I saw a religious shop. It was open, and they were stocking inventory. St. Teresa directed me downstairs where many rosaries were on display. I couldn't believe it. She showed me a brown rosary, which I later discovered was the color of the Carmelite order to which she belonged. "Get that one!" she urged.

Rosary in hand, I went back to the hotel room. Standing in front of St. Teresa, I resumed my litany of excuses: "I can't pray this. . . so many prayers, too many Hail Marys and Our Fathers . . . I can't do this!" Each night, as an insurance policy, I was accustomed to saying ten seconds of prayer. I figured if I died in my sleep, God would take me to heaven— that is, if it existed.

"Pray the Rosary," she insisted, "and pray fifteen decades!" which equals three entire Rosaries. "Ugh." I didn't like prayer, so I started a big argument with St. Teresa. "You must pray," she said, "and you must pray the Rosary because you risk losing your soul! *You are going to hell unless you change!*" Needless to say, she won the argument.

I didn't really know the Rosary, so she explained to me how to pray it. She said that I should see it as a window into the life of God on Earth, that I should place myself beside Jesus and walk with Him through His life. By doing so, His grace would reach inside of me and touch me in a powerful way. "Every prayer of the Rosary," she told me, "is a step away from evil and a step toward God. See the Rosary as a chain you are hanging around the neck of Satan, which will weigh him down and break his grasp on you."

From my first Rosary prayer, I felt a peace, a happiness, an excitement within. I couldn't stop laughing, and I couldn't stop crying. No drugs or alcohol could have given me what I was feeling at that moment. The more I prayed, the stronger this feeling became, until suddenly, I had finished fifteen decades. I wanted to continue. . .

"Why is this happening?" I asked St. Teresa. "When I see other people praying, they often have long faces and look miserable, as if they were forced to pray. Yet this is really joyful, wonderful stuff. Don't other people experience what I'm experiencing in prayer?"

"Well, often they don't," she answered, "because so often when they pray, they're thinking about themselves. They're focusing on their lives, their problems, their concerns. When you focus on self, God gets pushed aside. When God comes second, and self is first, your heart actually starts to close to God and stops His grace from filling you. However, when you focus on God in your prayers and look past yourself, past the world, that is when your soul opens, and God pours His grace in abundance deep inside of you."

She said I should tell people that when they begin to pray, the first thing they should do is turn to the Holy Spirit and say: "Lord, I can't pray properly. I'm weak; I'm human; I'm fragile. I'm easily distracted, taken into thoughts of myself and the world. But you, Lord, lead me past that. Help me to pray properly. Help me to focus on the Father, the Son, and You, Holy Spirit, so that my soul can be opened, and I can receive the grace that is there for everyone in prayer."

She continued, "Once you do that, once you seek God's help in prayer and in all you do, then you can start to experience what prayer is meant to be: a joyful gift of God's love. If prayer is a burden, a chore, a duty, this is often because prayer is self-centered and not God-centered. Remember, in all things God must come first. Look to God in everything, and then you will receive His joy in all you do."

From the moment I started to pray the Rosary, Satan's grasp on me weakened. My addictions fell away, and I had many of them—alcohol being the primary one. This is nothing I did, but a grace from God. Anyone who has been addicted to alcohol knows how hard it is to quit, and I stopped immediately. In moments of temptation, when I felt weak and so alone, hurt, rejected, and unloved, I was freed and strengthened by remembering St. Teresa's words to me: "Every time you feel a desire to do wrong, think of Jesus. Just think of His Name, think of Him suffering on the Cross, or see the Host before you. Keep concentrating on that and you will see your desires fall away."

Soon after St. Teresa of Avila paid me a visit, other saints came to speak to me as well. The first three were St. Stephen, St. Andrew, and St. Matthew, who encouraged me to read Holy Scripture, which I did. When I went back to England for a holiday, they directed me to walk into St. Edmund's Church, the same church where I had been caught stealing as a child.

I ended up staying for Mass, which was unusual for me at the time. Afterward, as I knelt and prayed in front of a Sacred Heart of Jesus statue, it suddenly began emanating a white light and came physically alive before my startled eyes. Then the statue transformed into the Blessed Mother dressed in white, with light shining forth from within her. So much love was in her smile, and her beauty defied words. How can I adequately describe her? Her eyes were blue and her hair black. She may have been my wife's height, about five feet, six inches. But this says little. . . I could see her heart circled in white roses and superimposed on Jesus's Sacred Heart. Never had I heard about the Immaculate Heart of Mary, and only the next day, from a glance at a prayer card, did I realize what I had seen: their two Hearts as One.

I was further stunned when Blessed Mother Mary began speaking to me from the living statue. Her first words were, "Pray, pray, pray." In my flustered and flawed logic, that meant increasing my Rosary prayers by three times, so I began to say many decades of the Rosary, every day. Mary also told me she was my mother and that God has given her a wonderful grace to bring people deeper into the Heart of Jesus. From that point on, she would visit me and do just that.

In 1994, Blessed Mother Mary said to me one day, "My Son is coming to you," and before me was Jesus on the Cross, telling me He loved me and He wanted to forgive me. It was the greatest day in my life, but also the most difficult because I was shown how all my sins, from childhood to the present, had contributed to His suffering and dying. There were so many of them! It seemed as though I was sinning every second of my life.

I saw how every time I had hurt someone, I was hurting Jesus. Any time I told a lie, I was lying about Jesus as He suffered and died. Every time I gossiped about people, I was below the Cross with those gossiping about Jesus as He hung in agony. Any time I made fun of others, I was making fun of Jesus as He died for me. Even the smallest sin, even the thoughts I had toward others—of dislike, anger, hate, or frustration—seemed so big. And to see my grievous sins was absolutely terrible.

Jesus showed me the state of my soul, which was putrid. He revealed how my sins not only hurt other people but often led them into sin, such as when they tried to imitate me or responded with anger or violence. I felt so ashamed, so unworthy and offensive. I wanted to run away but couldn't, and Jesus wouldn't leave me. Worse yet, He kept me telling me He loved me and longed to forgive me.

Then the view changed, and I saw Jesus in the Garden of Gethsemane, taking into his Heart the pain, the hurt, the suffering from my sins and everyone else's from the beginning through the end of time. It is no wonder He sweated blood. I saw the strokes of the whip and the crown of thorns as my sins. I saw Jesus carrying the Cross and myself sitting on top of it with my pride, making it heavier and heavier. I saw each of the nails, the thrust of the spear. . . I saw Jesus hanging on the Cross just loving me, and calling out that He wanted to forgive me no matter how much I hurt Him. "Through all those times," He said, "I was still there by your side loving you."

I fell to the ground crying, seeing how much throughout my life I had hurt my sweet, gentle, and wonderful Lord. I didn't want to live. I begged

Jesus to let me die and to send me to hell because I didn't feel that I should exist anymore. But Jesus kept calling out to me. For five hours, I cried and cried, curled up on the floor, sobbing like a baby, begging Jesus, "Let me die, let me die!" To see His Blood running down His face as He called out to me through His suffering, "I love you, and I want to forgive you," was the deepest pain I've ever felt in my life.

Eventually with His grace, I built up the courage to ask for His forgiveness. Reaching out across a chasm of shame, I said, "Forgive me, dear Jesus."

"I do forgive you," He answered. At that moment, I felt a tremendous weight of sin being lifted from me. His love touched my soul in such a wonderful way that I never wanted to lose His presence again. Possessing Him, I knew, was the most important thing in life. I felt refreshed, renewed—a different person! I couldn't stop telling Jesus that I loved Him and wanted to love Him forever. I knew I could never hurt Him again purposefully, and I never wanted to be away from Him. I fell in love with Jesus that day, and I totally committed my life to God.

After I asked for the Lord's forgiveness, He said to me, "Go to Confession."

"Wait a minute!" I responded. "I've been through five hours of crying my eyes out, begging You to let me die and send me to hell, while You took me through all these sins I committed, and then You said you forgave me. Now, why do I need to go to Confession?" I thought Confession was a power trip for the priest. After you tell him what you've done wrong, he tells you off, gives you some prayers as a punishment; then you go outside, say them as quick as you can, and rush out of the church. The next time you see the priest, you avoid him.

Knowing my thoughts, Jesus said to me, "It's not that at all. You need to have the grace through the sacrament to help you through your weaknesses." So I learned directly from the Lord that He gave us Confession to help us, strengthen us, purify us, cleanse us—to bring us closer and closer to God and to heal our souls.

"It is important that you go," Jesus told me. "You must confess all your sins."

So off I went into the confessional box and said, in essence, "Please, Father, forgive me, for I have sinned. I stole this little thing and told this little lie, and forgive me for anything else I have done." I figured that covered it. I didn't want the priest to know how bad I really was.

When I came out of the confessional, Jesus said, "Understand that when you don't confess all your sins, you hold onto the pain and hurt and suffering that comes with them. If you do not confess all of your sins, it is easy for Satan to lead you into more sin because you are not only left feeling bad about yourself, but you also have that sin residing on your heart, on your very soul. It remains a weakness there, a doorway where evil can enter and lead you further away from God. It is also important that you continue to recognize your mistakes, and once you do, come to Confession and ask for forgiveness. Do not push them aside and say they are not important. Understand that it is important to get rid of every sin."

I went back to Reconciliation the next day and confessed all the big sins I could remember. I was in the confessional box such a long time, crying and blubbering, that I started to feel very sorry for the priest.

Many times, I have said to St. Stephen, St. Matthew, and St. Andrew, "Why me? There are so many good people who come to church because they love God, so many religious people, yet you are talking to me who has been so bad, who *is* so bad. I just don't understand."

They explained, "It is because God loves you, and He loves you the same as anyone else. The only difference is how much you love God. Also, God appearing to you, someone who was so far away from Him, shows that His love is there for everyone, even the worst sinner, not just for a select few."

When Jesus forgave me from the Cross, and I accepted, I told Him that whatever He asked of me, I would do, regardless. And He keeps me to that. Every time I don't want to do a request of His, He reminds me of that promise. When God came into my life, the first thing I wanted to do was quit the job I thought I would never leave in order to do His work, and that is exactly what Jesus asked of me. He said: "It's going to be difficult. It's never going to be easy until the day you die. But don't give up!"

From the beginning of my ministry in 1994, I have sought the sanction and guidance of the Church. The Archbishop of Perth, Most Reverend Barry Hickey, first supported me for seventeen years. I saw him frequently, and he appointed a spiritual director who checked all of my writings and supervised my work. After him, Archbishop Timothy Costelloe and his Auxiliary Bishop Don Sproxton have given me their support, which is documented in writing.

The mission Jesus gave me is to go out into the world and tell people that God loves them, and that He doesn't want to condemn or punish them. Since 1994, the Lord has sent me around the globe to be His instrument of healing, and to bring people closer to Him and His Church.

The Lord has said so often that there is a day of judgment coming. No one knows when it is, and I do not profess to. What Jesus says to me is to tell people to pray, receive the sacraments, turn back to God, love God, and love each other. Then when that day of judgment comes, they will be rewarded by God, not punished.

I believe that the Warning or the Mini Judgment, which many people are concerned about and some are looking forward to, is akin to what the Lord took me through. I hope I will never have to experience it again, but I am sure that I will. By suddenly taking away those rose-colored glasses through which we see only the goodness in ourselves and think of how wonderful we are, by showing us how we have really been living and how offensive to God our sins are, He hopes we will not want to sin anymore.

"Change, pray, receive the sacraments, love each other; do not hurt each other. Live in God's love and avoid hell because if you do not, that is probably the place where you will go." This is the message, the message He gave to me, the message He is giving to anyone who will listen. God is real, and He is offering everyone His love, His love forever in heaven.

Jesus:

[Let] the greatest sinners place their trust in My mercy. They have the right before others to trust in the abyss of My mercy. My daughter, write about My mercy towards tormented souls. Souls that make an appeal to My mercy delight Me. To such souls I grant even more graces than they ask. I cannot punish even the greatest sinner if he makes an appeal to My compassion, but on the contrary, I justify him in My unfathomable and inscrutable mercy.

~Diary of Saint Maria Faustina Kowalska, #1146

FATHER STEVEN SCHEIER

A Priest Condemned to Hell

I was ordained in the diocese of Wichita, Kansas, in 1973. For the first twelve years of my priesthood, my ministry didn't center around service to God's people. Rather, it focused on how God's people, especially my brother clerics, thought Fr. Scheier was doing. I could not stand peer rejection and wanted to be one of the guys. Deep within me was the stifled thought that I wasn't the priest I should be; but I hid my betrayal of a few commandments with a sugar coat of friendliness, to the point that people thought I was a good priest, and I remained convinced that I handled my day-to-day existence very well.

It was fashionable for the priests around me to act like regular guys, who happened to wear Roman collars, and this fact shone most brightly from the pulpit. We didn't proclaim morality, dogma, and what the Church is all about—saving souls. We proclaimed what people wanted to hear—peace, love, and joy—instead of what they needed to hear. "God help" the priest who wasn't popular because that meant the money didn't roll in, and I was in charge of a parish, Sacred Heart, nestled in the small Kansas town of Fredonia.

One day, I decided to get advice from a brother priest about a parish problem I was having, which meant a trip to Wichita, about eighty-six miles away. The fastest way there was via Highway 96—a dangerous, hilly road without shoulders and heavily trafficked by semis and large trucks. Around four o'clock that afternoon, I was driving east, headed home. And that is the last thing I remember.

I collided head-on with a pickup truck carrying three people from Hutchinson, Kansas. Not wearing a seatbelt, I was thrown out of my vehicle, landed violently on the ground, and lay unconscious at the scene. I suffered a major head concussion, and the scalp on the right side of my head was ripped from my skull. Part of the right side of my brain was sheared off, and many of my brain cells were crushed.

Traveling just behind me was a Mennonite nurse from Frontenac, Kansas, who pulled over and stayed with me until an ambulance arrived. She later told me that as I lay in her lap, I tried to say the "Hail Mary" over and over. She wanted to help me but didn't know the prayer. I thank God for her because she told the ambulance drivers that I probably had a broken neck and to treat me accordingly. She was right.

My second vertebra was crushed, a traumatic injury "affectionately" called "the hangman's break" because when a person is hanged, the C2 vertebrae breaks and the person asphyxiates. Had my head been turned either way at the scene of the accident, I would have died.

Apparently, I was taken by ambulance to a small hospital in Eureka, a town nearby. The doctor in charge sewed my scalp back on my skull. He told his sister, who was also a nurse, "There's not much I can do for him," and called a LifeWatch helicopter from Wesley Hospital in Wichita to come and pick me up. I was still unconscious. As the doctor and his sister watched the helicopter lift off the hospital grounds, he said to her, "He won't make it to Wichita."

The helicopter landed on top of Wesley Hospital, and I was rushed to the trauma center, where I was treated and then admitted to the intensive care unit, only five blocks from where I grew up. My mother, a widow, could see the helicopter land from her home. Already a worrier, she rushed to the hospital when notified it was me. One of my parishioners called the hospital that evening to see how I was doing, and was told I had a fifteen-percent chance to live. I hope to God my mom never knew.

I would later learn that the three people in the oncoming pickup truck, into which I collided, survived. I also learned that on the evening of the accident, the doors of Sacred Heart Parish were opened for people to come in and pray for me at any time. In the days that followed, parishioners gathered to pray a Rosary on my behalf once in the morning and again in the evening. That first night, the Evangelical, Baptist, and Methodist churches all opened their doors. The Assembly of God minister in Fredonia spent the entire night in prayer for me, and the Mennonites added me to their prayer line. My gratitude to all of them is immeasurable.

A few months into my recovery, one of the physicians said to me, "Father, we doctors thought that had you lived, you would be in an iron lung for the rest of your life, looking up at the ceiling, paralyzed from the neck down. For obvious reasons, I can't do this, but I'd like to write 'miracle' on your chart because, indeed, you are a miracle. Anyone reading your report would have to come to that conclusion."

I did not need to have any surgery, and the hospital staff told me I recovered in record time. I was fitted with an orthotic device called a cervical thoracic orthosis, otherwise known as the "halo." The device circled my head, held in place with four screws driven directly into my skull—two in the front and two in the back, so that I could not bend or move my neck. The symbolism of God's seemingly forced holiness through His Divine Mercy was not lost on me. The required "halo" fit onto an irremovable steel "jacket," which I also had to wear. For eight months, I was not able to move my head in any direction, and my temples, like detonated minefields, still bear the indentations from the screws.

A month and a half after the accident, I was released from the hospital, wearing my halo and jacket, and returned to my childhood home to recuperate with the help of my mom, my younger brother, who lived in Wichita, and another brother who was on leave from the navy and in the house night and day, to my benefit.

My bishop had kept my parish open, calling for a substitute priest who said Mass on weekends. After seven months of this arrangement, when I had recovered well enough, I was assigned back to Sacred Heart Church. I had to go out and buy another car and face my trauma, which was very difficult. Even harder was driving the same highway back to my parish. But I'm glad I did it.

My parishioners were quick to tell me of their concern and their prayers for my recovery and return. The people of Fredonia, and especially of Sacred Heart Parish, are a God-fearing people who take their religion very seriously. When I returned, I noticed and appreciated how they did not demand much from me because of my near-fatal accident which greatly helped my performance.

Not long after my return, I began reading the Gospel of Luke, Chapter 13, verses 6 to 9, while saying Mass on an ordinary weekday—or so I thought.

And he told them this parable: "There once was a person who had a fig tree planted in his orchard, and when he came in search of fruit on it but found none, he said to the gardener, 'For three years now I have come in search of fruit on this fig tree but have found none. (So) cut it down. Why should it exhaust the soil?' He said to him in reply, 'Sir, leave it for this year also, and I shall cultivate the ground around it and fertilize it; it may bear fruit in the future. If not, you can cut it down.'"

As I was reading from the lectionary, something extraordinarily supernatural occurred. I'm German, and as far as I knew, things like this didn't happen. The page itself, from which I was reading, became illumined and enlarged, and rose off the lectionary toward me, while at the same time, I began to vaguely remember a conversation taking place.

Attempting to remain calm, I finished Mass as normally as I could, then retreated to the rectory, plopped down in my lounge chair, and nervously drank about four cups of coffee. "Why," I wondered, "did this particular Gospel bring back so many memories, and memories concerning what?"

Then suddenly everything came back to me. A conversation had indeed taken place, and it had happened very shortly after the accident, as my body lay unconscious. I had been taken before the Throne of God, before the judgment seat of Jesus Christ! I didn't see Him, but I heard His voice. What happened next took place instantaneously, as far as "time" is concerned. Jesus Christ spoke to me, reviewing my entire life on earth, and He accused me of sins of commission and omission that were unrepented, unconfessed, and unforgiven.

I had planned at my particular judgment to spout a lot of excuses: "Well, Lord, you know she was a pretty feisty woman, so it was easy to lose patience with her"; "But, Lord, he made me do it." "Lord, I had a bad day"; "I didn't feel too good, You know, and that was the reason why I didn't do this or that."

But when talking to Truth personified, alone before the judgment seat, excuses don't exist. No rebuttal is possible. To each offense, I easily agreed. The only thing I could do when Jesus spoke about particular instances in my life was to say internally, "Yes . . . Yes, that's true."

When the Lord finished, He said, "The sentence that you will have for all eternity is hell." I knew before He even said it what my fate would be. Jesus was doing nothing but honoring my decision. "I know this is what I deserve," I thought. "That is the only logical thing He could have said."

Then another voice that filled me with horror said, "Come on down. You belong to me."

At that moment, a female voice, the softest and sweetest voice I had ever heard, said, "Son, would You please spare his life and his immortal soul?"

The Lord then said, "Mother, he has been a priest for twelve years for himself and not for Me. Let him reap the punishment he deserves."

At that, I heard her say again in response, "But Son, if we give to him special graces and strengths and come to him in ways that he is not familiar with, we can see if he bears fruit. If he does not, then Your will be done."

There was a short pause, which seemed like an eternity. Then His voice came back and said, "Mother, he's yours."

I have been hers, and she has been everything, ever since. The Blessed Mother has indeed lived up to her promise. Routinely, supernaturally, there are things she has told me and done for me that I have not deserved. I can now speak from direct experience that the Blessed Mother is our advocate, our "lawyer," before God. We can't imagine the power God has given her. Neither can we fathom how much she loves us.

At the foot of the Cross, Jesus looked down upon her and the apostle He loved and said, "Woman, behold your son," which meant, "Mother, I give mankind to you as your sons and daughters." She takes that very literally and seriously. We have a mother. She will come to anyone's aid, as she did for me. I was not special. She loves me as much as she does anybody else, and who would not want, as their lawyer, the Mother of God? I learned that with regard to the Trinity, not One of Them, not One can say no to her. It's impossible.

One might think that I'd already had a special devotion to the Blessed Mother, therefore it was no wonder she interceded for me. To this, I have to say, "No!" which indicts me as a priest. The angels and saints were to me like imaginary playmates, make-believe friends. They were not real!

When I regained consciousness after the accident, one of the things I somehow understood very well was that God and his angels and saints are the only reality that exists. We are the ones in the shadow world. We have only one home, and it's not here on Earth. Our priorities are often mixed up, as mine were. I should have been living to help God save my soul and bring others to heaven, which is what a priest is called to do anyway. That's where I should have invested, not in the future I was pursuing—happiness on earth as a retired priest.

My parishioners would never have guessed I was headed for hell. That is how much I had fooled them. One of the things that amazed and surprised me during my judgment was that Jesus didn't take a popularity poll. I couldn't say, "Why don't you get his or her opinion of me, and then make up your mind?" He knows everything. *He knows.* I realized right then that He's the only One Who matters, and He is what I almost lost for all eternity. I had only Him to please, and my concern with pleasing (or trying to please) countless others was a total waste of time and energy.

I wasn't prepared to be a Catholic priest. This life is one of sacrifice, and I didn't love the priesthood, as many men do. To make matters worse, I was forever running from the cross. I have since learned that if we run from the cross, there is always a bigger one awaiting us. Our crosses are not long-lasting, they are not eternal, and God and His Mother carry them with us, making them as sweet as They possibly can. What brought me to the sentence I received was a string of broken commandments. For twelve years, I pantomimed being a priest. My homilies, my life in the parish, people's comments about me—everything had to give me self-assurance. If I didn't feel uplifted, I wasn't the only one who suffered, for I had my sinful ways to escape pain. My priesthood, the Lord told me, was only the bitter icing on top of a rotten cake.

The Lord had previously alerted me to stop offending Him through two small traffic accidents, which preceded the major, nearly fatal one. I once said to my former pastor, "I feel that another accident is coming, and the next one will be the big one." It was. The Lord had His ways of warning me, but I purposefully didn't listen because of the pleasure I was experiencing—and He wasn't about to take it away from me. He wasn't about to take *that* away from me.

I did believe I was in mortal sin, but it didn't make any difference because I used the Sacrament of Confession regularly, but only as "fire insurance." I felt sorry to be threatened with eternal damnation by Almighty God, but I didn't feel religious sorrow from the realization of hurting the One I should love. I was afraid of consequences in the way that a man feels sorry he committed adultery because his wife would kill him, if she were to find out.

Sorrow for sin out of fear of God's punishment is okay, if a desire to amend one's life is present; and repentance from a heart in love with God is ideal. Appropriate use of Confession means to have a desire, a firm purpose of amendment, but I wasn't about to change my life. I was in the unfortunate situation of not caring, taking things for granted, and assuming I had all the time in the world: time to convert, to become a good priest, to change. All the while, God was warning me, "Steven, there is no time."

Perhaps worst of all, I was not very spiritual—my prayer life was practically nil. I never said the Divine Office, the daily prayers required of a priest. A priest without prayer is dead; a priest without the Blessed Mother is dead; a priest without the Blessed Sacrament is dead. I didn't mind saying Mass, but I didn't mind missing Mass, either. My collar does not save me, for I am under the same commandments as anyone else. The only difference between myself and the laity is that I am held more accountable. If the devil traps the pastor, he can get the whole parish. I was allowed to come back to tell others, particularly priests, that hell exists, and we are liable to end up there. My mission is also to tell people Divine Mercy exists, and God's love outweighs His justice.

I learned my lesson, but it took Him breaking my neck and the threat of eternal damnation just to get my attention. But I would go through the whole experience again, if need be. I would never want to go back to the way I was—ever.

I am often asked how I have changed since the accident. While I will never be able to adequately answer that question, I can say that I am more accepting of the behavior of others and less judgmental. I have to discern and judge good from evil, but I can't condemn. And my sense of time and its sacredness has altered drastically. I see clearly now how we waste an incredible amount of precious time on frivolous, stupid things. I cannot turn the radio on in the car anymore. I have to be praying, saying the Rosary—doing something productive. I'm unable to take a vacation, so to speak, or just lie on the beach. That, to me, is a waste of time. I'd rather make a retreat with God.

I have been told I am a walking icon of God's mercy because of what He's done for me, and that is true. Mother Mary has heard me say to her many times, "I hope you haven't bet on a dark horse." How does one thank someone who helped save their eternal soul? How? What can a person do? How much can one pray? Thank you is not enough.

It has been twenty-five years since the day of my salvation, and I'm still trying to be a better priest. All I can say is that I am trying. I always feel I could do more. I am much more concerned about my salvation and whether or not I'm doing the right thing. It seems I have to work harder than others, if that is even possible. Each day I get up, I say, "Dear God, sustain me. Help me to do Your will." One might automatically assume that those who have seen or heard Jesus or the Blessed Mother have got it made. They don't. They're accountable. God gives gifts, but not without obligation, for He desires something in return. I believe God expects me to come through.

Right now is the time to tell the Truth. God has asked that of me and of all His faithful. To tell the Truth is to pay a consequence, such as being disliked, talked about, ridiculed, or avoided—the peer rejection that I formerly dodged at all costs. Only through suffering can  we come to deeply know and embody religious values. This is martyrdom, in a way—an unbloody martyrdom, and we are all called to be martyrs. We can be, and we will be.

Today I am not blind to heaven's pleas, as I was in the past. What is of paramount concern to me nowadays is the fact that the majority are not paying any attention to the Blessed Mother, who is warning us of where we are heading. At her apparitions in Akita, Japan, she said that she could not hold back her Son's strong arm anymore. The Twin Towers were a wake-up call. We didn't heed it. More will come. God is having us fall on our knees before Him, and He hopes that we'll stay there.

The mercy of Our Lord, Jesus, far outweighs His justice. But He, Who is so patient, merciful, and loving, has told us, through St. Faustina Kowalska, that we should take advantage of His mercy while we still can. Time runs out for all of us. When He comes as Judge, it will be too late for His mercy. The Blessed Virgin Mary is not only warning us, but marking out for us a detailed plan of how to get to heaven: prayer from the heart, especially the Rosary. That is how concerned she is, which is no surprise, because we are her children, and she loves us more than we could possibly understand. I found that out.[vi]

Jesus:

In the Old Covenant, I sent prophets wielding thunderbolts to My people. Today, I am sending you with My mercy to the people of the whole world. I do not want to punish aching mankind, but I desire to heal it, pressing it to My Merciful Heart. I use punishment when they themselves force Me to do so; My hand is reluctant to take hold of the sword of justice. Before the Day of Justice, I am sending the Day of Mercy.

~Diary of Saint Maria Faustina Kowalska, #1588

VINCE SIGALA

God Chooses Who He Will

I was a joyful kid. My earliest memories of childhood were beautiful. I'm not sure when all that changed for me. I only remember that my home was happy, and then it wasn't. I remember sitting with Mom and Dad on the couch and laughing and being tickled. I can recall running to my dad and yelling with glee, "Daddy!" when he came home from work, and how proud my dad looked when I caught my first fish. My father meant more to me than anything or anyone. He was my hero.

My memories jump from that wellspring of goodness to seeing my father brought home by the police, to seeing him cursing, screaming, and beating my mom with a belt, to feeling him grip me to his chest with a butcher knife to my throat, threating to kill me if mom didn't give him money for another heroin fix, to seeing my hero in prison for burglary. I remember the concrete floor and the brick walls, as I ran down that long hall to hug my daddy. But now he was dressed in an orange jump suit. I don't remember seeing my father very much after that. Mom divorced him while he was in prison because she feared if she did so when he was out, he would kill her.

My mother, brother, and I were then on our own. Mom was often gone from our home in Salinas California, working two jobs to pay the bills, and I only heard from Dad around Christmastime and birthdays. I remember one Christmas Eve, in particular, when Dad called to say he was coming over with a big surprise for my younger brother and me. Throughout Christmas eve night, I was overwhelmed with anticipation and sheer joy, and every second of Christmas day, I asked, "Mom, when is Dad going to be here?" But Christmas day came and went. I vividly recall lying at the foot of the front door, crying uncontrollably, while my mom tried to comfort me. All I could say was, "I want my dad. I just want to see my dad." He never came. Didn't even call.

That Christmas night of 1974, when I was only five years old, a seed of anger burrowed into my heart. It had no direction, but was planted deep. By the time I started fourth grade, babysitters, whom my mom knew and trusted, had molested me three times. I felt dirty and different, depressed and filled with disgust, but tried to hide my feelings, even from myself.

Exactly one year later, on Christmas morning, when I was in second grade, I had my first mystical experience, but wouldn't have known to call it such. My mother took my brother and me to Christmas Mass, and afterward, we walked out the front doors of St. Mary of the Nativity Church in Salinas, California, to where Fr. Richard O'Halloran was greeting parishioners. Standing near the pastor, I looked up and saw the glory of God shining behind him. It was a light much different from the sun's. It was pure, like crystal, but imbued with color and moving, shining, regenerating from within itself—alive, glorious, and exceedingly beautiful.

In the fourth grade, Mom moved me from a public school to a Catholic one in our town of Salinas. I was as wild as the day was long, a real source of penance to the nuns who taught me the faith, and a reason for all the teachers to look forward to the weekend. Initially, I hated the transfer, but it turned out to be one of the best decisions my mom ever made.

From the moment I entered Catholic school, I knew, by no will of my own, that I would marry a girl who went to the same school, had the same number of letters in her first name as in mine, and that my first born would be a son. I spent a lot time in class wondering and looking around the room trying to figure out who it might be. This was a big deal to me. None of the girls had the right number of letters, and if they did, I didn't find them attractive. Oddly, I somehow understood that this was simply going to happen, and the incongruence of reality ate at me. I just couldn't figure it out.

In the sixth grade, I began attending a youth group called "Son Beams," whose director, Cheryl Ward, took us teens under her wing, like we were her own, as did the woman who assisted her, named Faye. At first, I went to this group at Cheryl's house for the snacks and the girls, but as I continued showing up, something started to tug on my heart. In one of our meetings, we wrote a letter to Jesus, and that "something" revealed itself to me as "Someone." For the first time in seven years, I met Someone with whom I could share freely about my dad, Someone who I sensed would not only listen and understand, but who really cared.

In one of our last meetings, when I was in the 8th grade, the lower grades were invited to Cheryl's for an open house of sorts so that us older, graduating kids could invite them to the youth group. I noticed a young girl in the fourth grade, sitting on the arm of a light-brown chair. I introduced myself: "Hi, my name is Vince."

"Hi, I'm Heather." I stood there staring at her big green eyes and blurted out, "Wow, you're really pretty. If you were older, I would ask you out." I had unwittingly just introduced myself to my future wife: same school, same number of letters as V-i-n-c-e-n-t, and our first born would be a nine-pound, ten-ounce baby boy named Christian. It never occurred to me that the girl I'd spent so much time trying to find would be four grades below me—God's sense of humor.

Time went on, and I attended a different youth group for older kids, although I never got as much out of it as the one at Cheryl's house. I didn't receive holy corrections anymore, my personal relationship with God was no longer a priority, and I got the feeling that I was more of a nuisance to the leaders than anything else. One night, I found myself in a most insignificant dilemma, which to my teen brain, seemed gargantuan. I liked two girls who both liked me, and I wasn't sure which one to go out with, and not going out with either of them was not an option. I called Cheryl to ask her for advice, and she answered in her typical form: "Well, Vince, God could answer that question a lot better than I could. Why don't you just pray about it, ask the Lord for an answer, and then open your Bible and start reading?"

I said, "OK," hung up and did what she said. No answer. So, I called her back. "Nothing happened, and I did exactly what you said."

Cheryl told me to do it again. "This time, pray with your heart. Really talk to Him, Vince. Ask for an answer and believe that you will receive one." So again, I prayed—this time hard, opened the Bible, and began to read. From the first words my eyes fell upon, God spoke to me clearly and directly. His Word sliced through me and had nothing to do with my question.

The Scripture passage I opened to was Isaiah 48: *"Hear this, O house of Jacob called by the name Israel, sprung from the stock of Judah, you who swear by the name of the LORD and invoke the God of Israel without sincerity, without justice. . ."* I sensed God speaking directly to me about my insincerity towards Him, and He convicted my heart to its core. By holding up a mirror, God opened my eyes. Then came another message in verse 6, which struck my heart, but I didn't understand its meaning:

"From now on I announce new things to you, hidden events you never knew. Now, not from of old, they are created, before time you did not hear of them, so that you cannot claim, 'I have known them.' You never heard, you never knew, they never reached your ears beforehand."

Years later, this is exactly what God did. He would reveal to me visions of future events concerning the world and the Church. But that verse would have to wait. Meanwhile, in verse 20, came the calling: "With shouts of joy declare this, announce it; make it known to the ends of the earth, say: *'The Lord has redeemed his servant Jacob.'"* I believed that the Lord was commanding my spirit to proclaim redemption, specifically my own, and to preach the Gospel in all Truth and without compromise, but I felt a little fearful because it sounded like God was angry with me. I called Cheryl back. She quickly calmed my spirit, but also said: "Well Vincent, it sounds to me like Someone's talkin' to ya. You want my advice? I'd listen to what He's sayin'." I imagine Cheryl hung up the phone that day, started laughing, and called a couple of friends who knew me, saying, "You'll never guess what just happened."

The next day, I went to school, Bible in hand, telling all my friends to stop sinning and to turn to God. "God is real!" I exclaimed. "And He loves you." They didn't know what to make of it—I'd gone from being one of the "cool guys" to preaching repentance—and neither did I know what to make of it. All my "best friends" no longer wanted to be around me. I could be overly aggressive, and they were paying Christianity lip-service, like I had done. I began to give talks at the youth group retreats and felt a holy desire to share God's love with others, especially with one of the girls. We prayed together, talked on the phone for hours about Jesus, and ended up a "couple" at the tender age of thirteen. I loved her, but she also became an idol.

At the end of the eighth grade, she broke up with me. She learned that being a true Christian came with persecution and began to distance herself and then broke away, not only from me, but from God. I watched in despair as she returned to the comfort zone of being accepted by those who knew nothing of God and sought the things of the world to make them happy.

I felt alone again and without spiritual direction. The youth leaders tried to be there for me but couldn't understand what I was going through. Neither could I. For me, this was so much more than a young couple splitting up. The pain that crashed down upon me was tenfold what I had experienced with my father. I desperately wanted her salvation and was in absolute anguish. The only words that made any sense to me were the Lord's, when he said, "My soul is sorrowful, even unto death."

Still seeking spiritual direction, I went to a priest in our diocese of Monterey, to a church in my hometown, but in one of our "private meetings," he put his hand on my leg. Before this, he had bought me gifts. Preceding his transfer to another parish, he had called my mother, asking for her permission to take me to a cabin in the mountains, and my mother forcefully hung up on him. When he touched my leg the way he did, I knew exactly what was happening. I had already been there, and I ran. I ran from the youth group, from the pain, from everything and everyone.

I entered an all-boys' Catholic school and spent the majority of my free time sitting alone, reading my Bible, trying hard to understand why a God Who supposedly loved me so much would allow me to experience such pain. The little contact I did have with others usually happened in a negative way, since I quickly became a target of older bullies. But I was unwilling to be pushed around, so their taunts often led to physical confrontations. It didn't take long for them to learn not to mess with me.

Playing football in my freshman year provided my only bright spot, since it allowed me to channel my anger and not only stay out of trouble for it, but receive praise. Had my coaches known the rage from which my aggression came they would have never encouraged it. But raw violence was part of the game. I never intended to simply make a tackle, but to punish and hurt the opponent, which didn't bother me in the least. Concern caused pain, which I'd had enough of.

By the end of the year, my mother received a letter from the school, saying that I would not be allowed to return due to numerous fights. As a result, I went back into the public school system and into a rapid descent toward a living hell.

I entered my sophomore year with the mentality that I could count on no one but myself. My dad didn't care about me. Those I trusted had violated me. A priest had failed me. Did God, Who had showed me His love, only do so to allow me to experience even more pain? Hurt became anger; anger matured into hate; and hate devolved into blind rage.

On the second day of my sophomore year of high school, I got in a fight during lunch hour, the beginning of a long string of violent altercations. My target: a boy who had taunted me the previous summer, calling my mother names and talking "big behind my back," but never confronting me head on. I spotted him in the field with nowhere to run. With my friends egging me on, and his friends doing the same to him, I approached him. He told me he didn't want to fight. I didn't care. I unleashed years of fury on this poor kid. I hit him so many times in the face that I broke my hand, as he was begging me to stop. The next thing I remember was holding him by the back of the hair and smashing his

face into the gravel track, then standing over him and repeatedly kicking him as hard as I could in the head and the face, with heavy Colorado boots. Had my friends not pulled me off of him, I don't know that I would have stopped. I will never forget the boy I saw when his friends helped him to his feet. His face no longer resembled a face. All I could see was blood and torn flesh. That image, like an ugly scar, is burned into my memory.

The next eight years of my life blurred into an unholy mix of heavy metal music, violence, drunkenness, drug use, and unbridled sex. I swallowed the great lie that Vince was no longer a "victim" of the world but in control of it. The reality was, the moment I decided to take control was the moment I completely lost it. I couldn't get through the day without getting high on marijuana, which numbed me from everything I wanted to forget, and which led to hard drugs, like cocaine. Through my frequent fornication, I began to judge

women based on their appearance and how good they were in bed. I woke up next to women whose names I didn't even know.

But there was one girl who, for me, was different. She had lived around the corner from me for a number of years in Salinas, but I only got to know her better through a mutual friend when I was twenty-one. We

started to do most everything together and soon were best friends. After three years, I mustered enough nerve to kiss her. My feelings for her were genuine. We started dating, and when her parents decided to relocate to Lodi, they gave her the choice to leave behind everything she knew and have college paid for, or remain and be mostly on her own. She decided to stay, and she moved in with me. When I was twenty-four and playing lead guitar in a band with a promising future, my nineteen-year-old girlfriend announced that she was pregnant. Her name was H-e-a-t-h-e-r. In an instant, a distant memory came rushing back—the same number of letters, the same school! And we soon learned that the child in her womb was boy. I told myself that my son would never know ugliness in his father, like I had known in mine. So I quit the band, got a higher paying job, and married her.

We bought our first home, and things seemed to be going well. Though we fought quite often, we made our relationship work for the sake of our son, Christian. Because we were making a lot of money together, our relationship seemed to find its strength in materialism. I had gotten my contractor's license and was doing custom flooring in the Monterey Bay area for fancy homes and high-end clientele: Clint Eastwood's properties, Del monte Shopping center, The Monterey Bay Aquarium, to name a few. My work ethic and job integrity stemmed from my mother's example of how hard I saw her work when I was young. So our family's little world revolved around three things: work, money, and baby. Neither my wife or I were living our Catholic faith, not even close.

About five years into our marriage, it began to sink. The spark was gone, and we had grown apart. Nothing was making us happy. I fell into a deep depression, and one night, I pondered taking my own life. I remember sitting on our bed with a loaded gun in my hand, as my wife cooked dinner and my nine-year-old son played in the living room. I reviewed my life: I had taken numerous drugs and downed gallons of alcohol; I had hurt a lot of people in fights; I had slept with countless women. And here I was, a husband and dad, trying to do things right, and more miserable than when I was doing everything wrong. True joy, I thought, must be a myth. The only thing stopping me from putting the gun into my mouth and pulling the trigger was the faint sound of my son's voice in the other room.

That night, in a last-ditch effort to save our marriage and save me from myself, my wife gave me a book she had just bought. Hardly religious, she handed me *The Purpose Driven Life* by Rick Warren, and from the first page, I knew Who was speaking to me. I knew what was missing.

The only real joy I had ever felt had never come from the world. The next day, I called Cheryl, whom I hadn't spoken to in years and asked her what I should do. She told me the place to begin was Confession and recommended I see a particular priest: "Fr. Jim Nisbet is a world-renowned Scripture scholar with great wisdom. Listen to him." Then she confided, "I've been praying and waiting for this phone call for a long time."

Determined to follow her advice, I went to see the priest. Sporting jeans with holes in the knees, dirty sneakers, and a tank top, I walked into his office. "What can I do for you?" he asked.

"I need to do a confession. I have a calling."

In the most intellectual voice I've ever heard, he asked with a smirk, "Really. What kind of calling?"

"A calling to preach the Word of God."

Fr. Nisbet smiled, looked at me like I was a nut, and appearing to hold in his laughter, said, "Okay," and proceeded to hear my confession. At Cheryl's suggestion, I asked if it would be okay to meet with him on a regular basis. He almost never took on spiritual direction in this manner, but by the grace of God, said, "Yes."

That year, I met with Fr. Nisbet regularly and began to immerse myself in prayer, particularly the Rosary, the Scriptures, and daily reception of the Eucharist. With great anticipation and an all-consuming need to receive the Body and Blood of Christ, I practically ran into church for Mass each day.

Fr. Nisbet encouraged me to forgive all those in my past who had hurt me. Even to the point of trying to contact the babysitters who had molested me, to tell them in person or over the phone that I forgave them. I did try to reach them, but to no avail. I was, however, able to reach my father. When I called him, I got right to the point. "Dad, I want to let you know that I forgive you for everything you did to me and to our family." My father immediately broke down crying and said, "Thank you." A great weight was lifted from both of us that night, not to say that it was easy. It was the hardest phone call I've ever made.

At the beginning of 2003, I began to experience unusual phenomena, not unknown in the Church, but definitely unknown to me. I began to receive private revelations through visions and locutions, without having a name for them. As far as I knew, the only people who experienced stuff like that were those recorded in the Bible. And why on earth would such things happen, especially to someone like me, who had offended the Lord in so many ways? I was just trying to come back to the Church.

THE WARNING

The first vision happened when I was sitting on our living-room couch one evening.

Suddenly, I found myself in the midst of a large crowd of people. They were all yelling loudly amidst a lot of angry pushing and shoving, but for a few who were weeping, mostly women. I could not understand the language they were speaking and felt both surprised and disconcerted, for no other reason than I found myself there in the blink of an eye by no will of my own. The people were dressed in what appeared to be Middle-Eastern attire, and the road on which we stood was paved by hand in cobble stone. No sooner was I able to orient myself when I caught glimpses of a certain man through the crowd. All attention was on him, as he slowly made his way toward me from my right. The pushing, shoving, and yelling was increasing to a violent intensity. I could feel my body being pushed back and forth, and I struggled to maintain my balance.

The man came so close as to pass in front of me, just three people away. I could make out his hair, which was somewhat long and completely soaked in what looked to be his own blood. The one-piece white garment he wore was filthy and also stained with blood in places. I could see clearly his crown of thorns, and the front and left side of his head where the thorns were deeply embedded into his scalp; but it was the swelling of these wounds that drew most of my attention. They were large and purple, filled with blood underneath the skin, disfiguring his brow. A large, heavy beam of wood lay across the back of his shoulders and neck, with his arms tied to it at the elbows, and his forearms hanging toward the ground. He was stumbling, barely able to take his next step.

As a spectator, I didn't know that this man was the Lord, until just after the vision ended. Yet I distinctly remember thinking that I must help him— that I had to do something to help him. No sooner did I take one step forward to reach him through the few people in front of me, when another man on my right pushed me out of the way with great force. I stumbled to my left, and as I regained my balance, the man walked up to the Lord at arm's length and threw a large rock, about the size of a brick, as hard as he could. It crashed into the side of Jesus's head with a brutal force. The sound of the impact was gruesome and mixed with a gush of air that released from his mouth, and a low, gasping moan. As he fell away from me to the ground under force of the blow, he tried to brace himself from the fall, but couldn't because his arms were tied to the wood. When he landed, his arms crumpled under the weight of his body and the wood, with the front his face taking the brunt of the fall onto the stone path. He lay there, rocking from side to side in obvious and unbelievable pain. People then began to kick him in the stomach, head, and legs.

Oh, how real this vision was. I was there, no differently than I am here on Earth now. The vision ended as quickly as it began. What an enormous price the Lord paid for my sins! Until then, I had never truly understood the sheer brutality of the Passion of our Lord, and I shuddered with the realization of how He had felt every strike, every kick, every punch I had ever inflicted on a fellow human being.

Heather entered the living room, and I walked up to her in tears. She asked me what was wrong, and I collapsed to my knees in front of her, wrapping my arms around her hips. Crying profusely, all I could say was, "He loves us so much. Heather, He loves us so much."

My second vision came about a week later and was just as real as the first. This time, whether I wanted it or not, understood it or not, the Lord began to do exactly what He said He would when He first spoke to me through Isaiah 48:

"From now on I announce new things to you, hidden events you never knew. Now, not from of old, they are created, before time you did not hear of them, so that you cannot claim, 'I have known them.' You never heard, you never knew, they never reached your ears beforehand."

In the late morning, I left the house to run a few errands, and suddenly . . . *I saw the sky opening and Jesus coming on the clouds of heaven. It was as if the air, itself, opened to reveal the unseen. The Lord was enormous, and I was made to know that everyone, no matter where they were on Earth, would see this. His hands, which still bore the wounds from the nails, were down by his waist and turned outward, as though presenting himself, and He was surrounded in great power and glory. White clouds moved with great speed and power, and were inflamed with a reddish orange fire; and white lights, small and bright, which I understood to be angels, darted to and fro around Him.*

This experience would seem to bring with it at least some trepidation. But I had no fear. On the contrary, I was filled with a joyous sense of victory, something I have never felt before or since. My triumphant exuberance was so strong that I wanted to leave everything and run to the Lord as fast as my legs could take me. This feeling remained long after the vision ended.

I didn't tell anyone about the vision and still knew nothing of mysticism. I had no idea that such things still happened, while I knew they were happening to me. To be honest, part of me grew concerned. Although not to the point of panic, thoughts entered my mind that I might be losing it. Everything was moving so fast: I would receive one vision and barely had enough time to realize what had happened before another would take place.

During this period, I would stay up very late reading the Scriptures and talk to Jesus throughout the day. Even though my sleep habits had changed, I never woke up tired, and my prayer life didn't interfere with my work in any way. My morning routine was to get up, make some coffee, pray the Rosary or read Scripture, get ready, drop off my son at school, and head to morning Mass before work.

Within several days of the vision of Jesus in the heavens, my small fear of being crazy would be replaced with a holy fear of God. It happened on April 9, 2003, a day that I awoke very early, at about 4 a.m., compelled to get out of bed and pray. I walked down the hallway of my house, and as I approached the kitchen, I was immediately taken away. All I know is that the "I," whom I know to be "me," with all of his hopes, fears, feelings, sights, smells, and touch, was no longer in my hallway.

A great flash of blinding white light temporarily impaired my vision, and as my eyes adjusted, I could see before me, a round lake of water, bearing little resemblance to any on Earth. It looked more like a thin slice of crystal, smooth as glass, with light emanating from beneath its surface. In the center of the lake, stood a tree-like fountain, which poured forth multi-colored lights, like streams of water.

Both the ground around the lake and the sky above it were pure light. Across the lake, I could see human figures dressed in white robes, too bright to make out in much detail, due to the immense brilliance of a great white light to the right of me in my peripheral vision. This glorious light, like crystal, yet alive, was God himself. As I tried to focus on the human figures conversing amongst themselves, suddenly appearing in front of them was the Lord, Jesus Christ. I could clearly see his face, his beard, his hair, and the outline of his ankle-length robe, which glowed with brilliance. Tall and strong with sharp features and white hair, like pristine snow, he looked like a king.

Facing toward my right, he began levitating, slowly and purposefully, toward the great light that was the Father. Then with his right hand extended forward, and the back of his right shoulder facing me, he reached into the light, whose brightness obscured my view of his extended arm. When he brought his hand out, he was holding the scroll with seven seals from the Book of Revelation (Chapter 10). The scroll appeared off-white with a hint of bronze, and was about three feet long. Its seals were thick, round, and the color of dark-red blood. The Lord then faced me and looked directly at me. Immediately, my entire being seized with a tremendous fear of God. Unable to move or breathe, I felt petrified, as though I were about to die. His pupils were flames of fire that pierced through the center of my soul. Nothing was hidden from His gaze. All that I had ever done in my life lay absolutely bare before him.

In a flash, Jesus began to show me, interiorly, my past sins and their consequences. I had no control over what was happening to me. I saw every transgression that I had knowingly and unknowingly committed. What I had thought were little things, like yelling at my brother or my mom, weren't little at all; and my sins of omission, actions I should have taken but didn't—which I didn't know were sins at all, struck my heart with tremendous regret and sorrow.

Nine years of my life had passed in a blur, and I didn't realize how far I had fallen into darkness until I was shown its true ugliness. The more that I saw, the more it got worse. Everything had been about me and my pleasure. The world had been my playground. Whatever I wanted I went and got; and whatever I couldn't easily get, I went somewhere else to find. Christ, the King and Lord of All, was exposing my deceit and anger—my physical and emotional violence— my lust and abuse—my arrogance and slander—my materialism and greed—my idol worship and vanity—my alcohol and drug use—my partying and rock music . . . all the things I held in higher esteem than God. Most of my life had been wasted, spent pleasing myself and impressing others, but not Him.

Particularly devastating was seeing the destructiveness that my actions had on other people, for I had led many of God's children into sin. One event stood out like a glaring nightmare. After having sex with a girl, I introduced her to cocaine, and then we lost contact. Three years later, I saw her. She was hardly recognizable. Addicted to crack, she looked old, crinkled, gaunt, and wearied. The Lord showed me how she had let herself be used sexually and physically, over and over again. My inordinate desires had destroyed her life.

The Lord revealed how Satan had used my twisted view of sexuality, caused by the three molestations in my life, to turn me into an instrument of death. The abuse predisposed me to lust, rather than love, and from my lust came fornication, and my fornication led to two young women getting abortions, which then made me partially guilty of murder.

I was shown how when I was a little kid, around five years old, someone gave my older sister a playboy magazine, and I felt so upset and hurt that I ran into another room and started crying. Then later in life, when I looked at pornography, I saw nothing wrong with it at all.

What horrified me and left me shaking the most was seeing the nature of sin itself. It does nothing but destroy and is infinitely worse than poison. Poison can kill the body, which is temporal, but sin can kill the soul, which is eternal. Jesus revealed to me that every sin, large or small, is significant. A little lie was more serious than I thought because Jesus looks at our hearts. The lie may seem small, but the deceit within us can be huge. Or with slander—casting another in a negative light, thinking it and speaking it can look the same in God's eyes because God sees the seed of judgment in our hearts. The slander is simply an expression of it. When Jesus said in Matthew 5: 27-28, "You have heard that it was said, 'You shall not commit adultery.' But I say to you, everyone who looks at a woman with lust has already committed adultery with her in his heart," He meant exactly what He said.

God revealed to me how sin spreads like a malignant cancer. Just the simple act of treating one person negatively initiates a spider-web effect. If I yell at someone in the morning and put them in a bad mood, they take that with them into their day and spread it easily to others, who in turn, bring the anger home with them, and take it out on their loved ones, who bother their neighbors, and so on . . . and so on . . . and so on . . .. Like the many branches of an infinite and insidious tree, it expands from one small sprout. Every single sin multiplies this way, even those we think are hidden, affecting both the physical and the spiritual realms, travelling across generations, sometimes continents. Sin unveiled is a gruesome thing.

What happened next shocked me to my core. I was standing before Jesus, with no memory of how I had come back to the Church two years earlier and repented. The Lord of heaven and earth was hiding this from my awareness because He was about to let me fully experience what would have happened to me had I died in my sins.

Jesus gave me my personal judgment. Immediately, I saw my sentence within His eyes. The verdict was hell for all eternity. I was frozen, speechless, in overwhelming, silent terror. I knew I deserved it, and there was absolutely nothing I could do to stop it. The experience felt frightful beyond sheer horror. I couldn't argue back. I couldn't talk my way out of anything. I fell silent before the divine truth that justice demands. I was undergoing my personal judgment in miniature, and by the life I had lived, I had freely chosen my sentence: an eternal "fiery furnace, where there will be wailing and grinding of teeth (Matthew 13: 42b)." Human language cannot convey the regret that seized me.

As Jesus took the scroll from the Father, I was also made to understand that this judgment, unique to each individual, is coming upon the world. Every person on the face of the Earth will experience their personal judgment, either while alive or at death, and every single sin will have to be accounted for.

What made the experience so scary for me, and what makes me so concerned for the world is that at death, there is no way to alter one's sentence. There is no way to go back and change things, to correct the wrongs. It is absolute. For me, the door to heaven had locked with an iron deadbolt, and my fate was to be sealed *forever*.

My experience in the heavenly realm stopped as quickly as it began, and I found myself back at the end of my hallway. There was a distant echo of holy chanting in the air, and my body was trembling uncontrollably from head to toe.

As the day went on, I prayed harder than I ever have in my life, begging God for mercy, begging Him to give the world more time, as we are not ready for this. For the sake of poor sinners, for humanity, for the sake of His Holy Name, I begged Him to have mercy!

It took close to seven months for me to come to the full realization of what had happened that morning in the hallway. I was not only shown my sin for what it truly was, but what everyone will experience, in essence, during what I later learned is called "The Warning." To recollect it even now brings tears to my eyes and an overwhelming sadness for the world, simply because I know what awaits each person if he or she does not repent and turn back to God. There will be many who will not survive this. Their bodies will physically not be able to withstand an encounter with their sin, as seen within the Holiness of the Living God.

Simply put, they will die of sheer fright at the sight of their own sin. That is how I understood this. Some will drop dead, some will convert, and others will completely reject God and become possessed by Satan.

A day or so after this experience, I was approached by two women I did not recognize. They stopped me in the parking lot after morning Mass, as I was walking to my truck, and offered me a pamphlet. "We feel like we're supposed to give this to you." I inquired a little, and they said it was information about a pilgrimage. I'd heard of pilgrimages before—Fr. Nesbit had led many to the Holy Land—but they were talking about a place I'd never heard of and couldn't even pronounce: Medjugorje in Bosnia-Herzegovina. I took the pamphlet to be polite. The last thing on my mind was a Marian pilgrimage to anywhere. My marriage was a mess, I was going through radical changes, and while I did pray the Rosary, I would have never considered myself a Marian devotee. A relationship with the Mother of God was foreign to me.

About a week later, on April 14, 2003, I decided to take a break while on the job. Walking out of the house I was working on, I noticed a bench on the front porch, sat down, said a little prayer, and reflected on the graces I'd been receiving. One of my work habits was to turn on my truck radio and listen to either Christian preachers or Christian music. My ears tuned into the voice of a man preaching on the airwaves. Naive to the fact that Catholics and the Catholic Church are looked down upon by so many different denominations, I was of the belief that we were all Christians, we all got along, and there was no rift between us at all.

The man was teaching about "the rapture," the end times, and reading from the Book of Revelation. I had never been catechized on what the Church taught on such things, and have since learned that there is no such thing as pre-tribulation rapture—a moment when all the good people will be taken away, or raptured, and all the wicked will be left behind to undergo the final tribulation. Nor is this pre-tribulation rapture anywhere in the Bible. Toward the end of his sermon, the preacher paused and said sarcastically, "Boy, the Catholics will be surprised when it happens," followed by laughter and applause. Something was very wrong. I'd known a lot of wonderful Catholics—Cheryl, Faye, Fr. Nesbit, the nuns who taught me, to name a few—and if anyone was going to be raptured, it should be them. The guy was a good preacher, and I enjoyed listening to him, so I couldn't understand this and immediately bowed my head, closed my eyes, and said to Jesus, "Lord, please give me understanding of your Word."

When I looked up, my eyes fixed on a tree across the street, and the volume of the preacher's voice began to lower in my hearing until it was gone. Simultaneously, I began to feel a current, similar to a growing wind, but spiritual in nature. It grew in strength, swirling around to envelope me, and I found it harder and harder to breath. Then it stopped. Air was no longer there, as if I no longer needed it to live. I found myself frozen and unable to move, staring at God's Glory appearing before me. This was different than a vision. His manifestation of Glory was physically in front of me. I could still make out the tree and the scene across the street through it . . .

The Glory of God was like crystal, yet living, with every color of the rainbow slowly emanating long, luminous, translucent shards outward from within it. It exuded a powerful heat, which could consume all things in any moment, but stayed controlled and purposefully didn't overwhelm me; and it possessed a quality of purity not of this world.

Within the vision of Glory, scenes of moving images, sharp and in full color, began passing before my eyes in slow motion: The Lord was showing me future events concerning a great tribulation in the world, which shook the depths of my soul. Transfixed, I saw a coming world war, a nuclear exchange between world powers, great social unrest, worldwide chaos, people possessed by Satan, future chastisements— mankind, by its own actions, bringing itself to the very point of extinction. I saw the infiltration of the Church by those in league with Lucifer, a massive persecution of the Church, from within and without, with priests being murdered, churches sacked and burned, and the Eucharist trampled and profaned by soldiers with faces of death. The Earth was made desolate, and destruction reigned everywhere. It appeared as if every demon in hell had been unleashed on the Earth, while man unleashed the most terrible weapons upon himself.

When the vision stopped, I ran to my truck, turned off the radio, grabbed my Bible, and opened to the Book of Daniel. I somehow knew what I had been shown was written there. I had only read a few scattered verses in Chapters 7 through 12,[vii] when strands of luminous golden wheat woven together in three ropes came up through the left-hand side of my Bible and buried themselves into the right. The golden light of the ropes shone brighter and brighter, accompanied by a sound like the strong hum of an electric current. As the three ropes bore down into the pages with tremendous force, the sound and the light came to a crescendo, and two words came into my mind: "totally binding." That is to say, I knew that the vision must happen. That there is no way around it, and no amount of prayer can stop it. It is written. It is part of God's plan of purification, decreed by Him through His holy prophets, and according to His will.

The Lord gave me another vision in which I believe I was shown a divine act of God through which the truly faithful were protected from a certain and devastating chastisement of divine justice.

I was suddenly standing in the back of a church. Behind me were two, solidly heavy, large wooden doors. There was no way through this entrance from the outside and no way out from the inside. I was made to know that the doors had been locked by God Himself. Outside of the doors, there was great confusion, chaos, horror, fear, and death. As I looked toward the altar, a priest was elevating the Sacred Host, and people were kneeling in the pews and in the isles, some with their heads touching the ground. Not a sound came from any of them, only great reverence and silence. When the Host had reached its highest elevation, crystal clear water, somewhat thick and with light emanating from within it, flowed out from the Sacred Host and into the air. This water was alive, and it slowly washed over everyone there.

I was then transported at lightning speed to another church somewhere else in the world, where all the above happened again, only faster. I sensed that this Mass was being held around the world at the same time. The same scene was shown to me repeatedly, only faster each time it happened. I understood the water from the Host to be some type of divine protection from what was happening outside of the sanctuaries.

Later, God would show me the victory of God's Holy Church and His people in the world, preserved and renewed by the Spirit of Almighty God through the intercession of the Blessed Mother, after all that was unholy had been removed.

As I stood outside on a dirt path, I saw a group of about fifty to a hundred people walking in the same direction away from me, as if going somewhere. I sensed their great reverence for the Church and the Sacraments. God was their first love, far and above all else, and their love for one another was without barriers. They were smiling and laughing as they talked and interacted with one another. The adults appeared to be in their late twenties to early thirties, and were accompanied by a few children running around, just being kids. The sky was extremely clear with no pollution, the clearest I'd ever seen it. Various plants were scattered to my far left and right, and the path disappeared into distant rolling hills covered in grass. All of creation, the sky and the land, was renewed with divine life. The peace of God, which lies beyond all human understanding and fulfills human longing, had been poured out upon the Earth.

I was seeing a future world where there is no sickness or pain, where life is much simpler and people live much longer than they do now. I noticed that people's skin radiated in a way foreign to what we know now. Everyone looked beautiful, healthier, and more luminous because of God's presence within them. There was no sign of makeup, hair spray, or revealing clothes. People walked around comfortably in loosely fitting pants and tunics, which were light in color, different from any styles of today. Nothing looked modern, and yet everything looked new.

I distinctly remember one man at the tail end of the group. He turned to look back at me and smiled warmly, as though inviting me to hurry up and join them. He had a beard and semi-long hair. He resembled Jesus, but in the vision, I was not made to know who he was. Only when the vision ended did I realize that the man was Jesus guiding and shepherding His people into a new age of peace.

Overwhelmed by these revelations, which were bringing me to my knees, I called Cheryl and Faye, and they both encouraged me to continue to see Fr. Nisbet. "Tell him everything," they said, pushing me through my hesitation to speak, for fear of the priest's response. "He's your spiritual director, after all." Father was a little intimidating to me, for no other reason than his great gift of wisdom. He was a living encyclopedia who seemed to know everything about everything. I finally did tell Father about the visions, although I did not go into a lot of detail, at first, perhaps because I was still in a semi state of shock. I remember sobbing, "It's going to be a slaughter," unable to understand why all this had to be.

In his familiarity with uncommon spiritual gifts, Fr. Nisbet recognized the words and visions I reiterated to him as prophetic revelations from God. At that time, I still had no idea that I was prophesying. I just felt confused, overwhelmed and deeply saddened, and wept every time I relayed to Father what I'd been shown. Father's reaction was the complete opposite, nothing less than uncharacteristic outbursts of sheer joy. "Make sure you land on the foot of faith," he said. "Realizing the glory to which you've been called will help to deal with the burden that comes with it."

"But, Father. Couldn't God find someone else?"

At one point, out of curiosity, I asked him what he was learning from all this. Fr. Nesbit looked at me, smiled, and said, "I'm learning that God chooses who He will."

Soon I would receive a difficult test of faith and trust. I had been honest with Fr. Nesbit, and now I had to be honest with my family, so I shared with them what was happening to me. My wife, my friends, my brother and his family quickly abandoned me. Even my in-laws thought I had taken a crazy pill. Only my mom, Cheryl, Faye, and Fr. Nesbit believed me. At one point, my wife walked up to me as I was studying the Scriptures and said, "Vince, you're changing, and I don't know if I can live like this."

Holding back tears, I responded, "Heather, no matter what happens, I will always love you." She turned and silently walked away.

A few years passed, and in 2005, our family, still intact by the grace of God, moved to another town in Northern California. Many of our friends had moved there, and Heather wanted to be closer to her mother and best friend, as well as pursue better career opportunities in the San Francisco Bay Area. Now I was far away from my spiritual director and missed our meetings tremendously. In this new place, I went to see my new pastor to share with him what was happening to me, by the suggestion of Fr. Nisbet, with the caveat, "Don't be surprised if he thinks you're cuckoo."

"He won't think I'm crazy," I thought to myself. "He's a priest. He'll understand." I should have heeded the warning. Within minutes of our meeting, I could sense the he was having a hard time believing me. Since passiveness is not one of my stronger traits, and once I get going, I find it hard to stop my tongue, I persisted. Finally, I think out of sheer frustration with me, he brought up some of the sins I had confessed three days earlier, told me that the saints didn't do this kind of stuff, and referring to Proverbs 26:11, threw out: "But, then again, every dog will return to its own vomit." Then he basically excused himself from the meeting so as not to waste anymore of his time. He is actually a humble and obedient priest. It was not his intention to hurt me.

I prayed about this, saying, "Jesus, he won't listen. He doesn't understand. I thought it was Your will that I share this, and he just won't listen!" The Lord responded in a locution by asking me a question, "Why are you so impatient with my brother? Oh, my child, how often, how many times in your life have I spoken to you, and you haven't listened? Have I ever been impatient with you?" Humbled by the Lord's words and by my selfishness and pride, I began to pray every day for this priest.

Shortly after the visit with my new pastor, I was walking to my car after attending a weekday Mass and Rosary, and was approached by a woman I didn't know, again in the parking lot of a church. "Sir!" she yelled. When I turned, she was hurrying over to me. "I'm sorry to bother you, but I really felt I should give this to you. It's information about a pilgrimage to Medjugorje." This time, I paid close attention. She explained what was happening in this place I still couldn't pronounce, and how she believed that Our Lady was appearing there. I took her pamphlet home and mentioned it to Heather, but the thought of flying halfway around the world seemed like a far-fetched dream.

Around that time, the Blessed Mother was becoming more real to me: a true and tangible mother, not just a distant and powerful figure attached to my Rosary beads. Feeling terribly alone in the world, my marriage all but over, my flooring business and reputation as an installer nonexistent, since I had to all but start from scratch, and finding nowhere else to turn for help, I pleaded for guidance from Mary. Walking into the church, I knelt in her alcove before a large statue of Our Lady of Fatima, and just cried. I asked her to please help me to understand all this stuff that was happening to me, to know what I was supposed to do with all of it—and to save my marriage. When I eventually looked up at her statue, a soft white light with smaller but brighter lights within it was raining down upon her. Through a locution, I heard the Blessed Mother say, "Come to my place." I knew she meant Medjugorje.

I decided to go. When the day of departure came, Heather helped to get me through the airport and sent me off in the general direction of my departing gate. I was like a kid who was completely lost. I had no idea what I was doing, and to say that I was nervous would be an understatement. I didn't know my way around airports at all, and I was terrified of flying. As I sat in a window seat, waiting for the plane to take off, I wanted to jump out. "This is a mistake," I thought to myself. "I shouldn't have done this." When the engines kicked in and asphalt began to speed by, all I could think to myself was, "What in the world are you doing? This is crazy. You're doing this for no other reason than because you heard a voice? Oh, boy this is really bad."

During the flights to Bosnia-Herzegovina, I didn't sleep a wink. When I arrived with my pilgrimage group, I was just happy to be on the ground. Our tour guide, Matilda, one of the visionary Mirjana's aunts, gave us a brief summary of Medjugorje and how the apparitions there began. This interested me somewhat, but I had read a book on Medjugorje before we had left and knew most of the story already. I noticed that now that I was finally in "Mary's place," a spirit of peace came over me that I'd never felt in the United States, and my doubts that our Blessed Mother had personally invited me vanished.

It was in "her place" that my mystical experiences began to tie together. I went there searching for Mary, for answers, for peace, and I found all three. In Medjugorje, the Holy Spirit began to teach me the

magnitude of all of Our Lady's messages to the Church and the world. Within them, heaven's plan is being revealed. What I had been shown regarding imminent future events corresponded to past messages from apparitions of Our Lady, which I knew nothing about. The Spirit planted a seed of curiosity in me, which led me to learn of her apparitions in La Salette, France; Fatima, Portugal; Garabandal, Spain; Akita, Japan; and Kibeho, Rwanda, among others. In late 2002, when God's revelations to me began, I had no idea of the illumination of conscience, or "The Warning," as prophesied at Garabandal. The Holy Spirit also showed me how Our Lady's authentic apparitions were connected, not only to each other, but also to Jesus's revelations to St. Faustina Kowalska, the saint of Divine Mercy. The most profound realization of my pilgrimage was that Our Lady's messages are continuing to unfold, and Medjugorje is the culmination of them all.

The pilgrims around me didn't know what God had revealed to me. To sit with them and hear them occasionally inquire with each other about the Medjugorje secrets, the last of which involved chastisements, was difficult. Many times, I would retreat to my room or climb Cross Mountain in Medjugorje and cry to God because if they truly understood what they wanted to know so badly, they would have never wasted time inquiring. Instead, they would have just prayed. Whenever I needed motherly comfort, I called on Mary, and her love touched me so gently that it, too, brought me to tears. I would need this same comfort in the years to come because, in time, I would receive forty-five to forty-eight visions, locutions, and revelatory dreams combined.

I tried to call Heather a couple of times but could never get a hold of her. She would not hear from me for about seven days and wondered if I was dead or alive. But I was very much alive. With each day that passed, the graces intensified. I befriended an acquaintance named Loretta, who ran a Catholic bookstore back home, and she and I decided that we wanted to spend one whole day in prayer. The next day, we separated from the group and went to Confession, Mass, prayed the Rosary on the Hill of Apparitions, and chatted with Jesus and each other all day long. We were like Catholic kids in a candy store of miracles, while the Lord presented Himself to us in different ways, all day long, like a Dad spoiling His kids on a field trip. No matter what we asked of Jesus, it happened almost immediately. I wanted to ask a priest a question, and suddenly, a priest approached us, just to talk. Loretta said she was thirsty, and someone offered us a drink. We both wanted to see the miracle of the sun and suddenly, a lady cried out, "Look at the sun!" And I was staring directly into the sun without difficulty and watching it spin like a disk. A cross appeared in its center, like on a Host, and then it began to spew out beautiful colors. On one side of this spinning disk, the light formed a red heart, which looked almost like a soft cloud, but with sharp edges, and on the other side, an exact replica in blue: symbols of the Sacred Heart of Jesus and the Immaculate heart of Mary.

But the greatest of all these graces was the time we spent that day in Adoration of the Blessed Sacrament. Bowing my head, I poured out my silent concerns to God. I prayed for my marriage and my wife's conversion, and I prayed to understand what the Lord was calling me to. When I looked up, I saw the Host turn the color of blood and begin to beat like a human heart. When we left the adoration chapel, I took my rosary from my pocket and noticed that all the links of its silver chain had turned gold.

When the time came to leave, our group stayed one night in Dubrovnik before we took our final flight back home to the states. I finally got ahold of Heather, and the first thing she said to me was that I sounded different. We talked a little, and I let her know when and where to pick me up from the airport. I felt very sad that I had to leave because in Medjugorje, I felt at home. A big part of me wanted to stay there for the rest of my life. As

I sat on the plane, again in a window seat, I looked down at the ground as it sped by. This time, I had no fear of flying.

When I returned home, a second test came. In its eleventh year, my marriage still teetered on shaky ground. Heather and I just couldn't seem to connect, and divorce had entered both our minds, more than once. I began to pray fervently to Jesus about our relationship, asking Him what was wrong, what I could do to fix it, and Jesus showed me how through the years, I had taken my wife for granted so many times. He showed me the gift that she truly was, and how I often didn't really listen to her or see her concerns as genuine.

The next year, I dragged my wife and my eleven-year-old son, Christian, to Medjugorje because I knew that getting them there was the only hope of saving my marriage. Almost refusing to go, they complained the entire journey there and throughout the first two days of our pilgrimage. But Mother Mary prevailed. She touched my wife in a profound way, showing her that it was okay to hurt, to be vulnerable, to be a little girl in her Mother's heart. Mary began to bring about my wife's conversion back to Jesus, back to the Church.

When she was at the outdoor Croatian Mass, sitting on a large piece of wood on the ground, still pondering why she was there, during the "Sign of Peace," a woman behind her said, "Peace be with you" in Croatian. Heather turned and shook the woman's hand and turned back around. Something about the woman's sincere kindness made Heather quickly turn back to tell her thank you, but the woman was nowhere to be seen, as if she had never been there. To this day, Heather believes this woman might have been an angel in human form.

As the pilgrimage continued, so did the graces. I could see the Lord working on my family, and the atmosphere of daily Mass and prayer was starting to rub off on my wife and my son. One night as we were walking through a field, after getting some ice-cream, my son yelled out, "Look at the light!" Heather and I looked up in the direction where he was pointing, and sure enough, there was a light, soft and warm looking and light orange in color. It was very high on a mountain, not Cross Mountain and not Apparition Hill, but a high place in between them. This is significant because there is no way to climb up to that area, which is rugged with rocks and overgrown brush. The light then began to float straight down the mountain, without swerving as a person would do. Two women just behind us fell to their knees and began to pray. My family stood in awe, watching the light descend to the bottom and slowly disappear.

Three days before we were to leave, Heather had already signed us up, with no prodding from me, to return to Medjugorje the same time the next year. My wife went from telling me she wanted a divorce, to complaining about going to Medjugorje and wondering why she was even there, to looking forward to returning as soon as possible. All of this change happened to her within one week. It is Our Lady, the Queen of Peace in Medjugorje, whom my wife and I credit with saving our marriage.

Heather eventually made her Confirmation, became a Mass coordinator and a member of the liturgy committee, as well as a member of our church's pastoral council. She has volunteered to coordinate buses to the Walk for Life in San Francisco and has given her testimony to local parishes.

Today, any visions or messages I receive along with those from the past, I have and will submit to a certain holy priest, who is also my current pastor and an official exorcist. I do not share any of them easily or without his approval. I pray that what I have been allowed to share helps the Lord save and heal His beloved people. Can you imagine watching your children continually run into a busy street, telling you it's not a problem, despite all your warnings? Can you imagine knowing full well that it is only a matter of time before you will literally have to watch, as they get hit by car and die? So it is with the Father when He looks at this world. God is tender and gentle, and He loves us far beyond what we could ever imagine. That is why He is preparing to give us a merciful warning, so

He can gather His children in His loving arms and keep us safe and happy forever.

One of the last visions I have received is the one I consider to be the most pivotal of all because an instruction given within the vision itself, and the instruction was not just for me, but for anyone who will listen. This indelible experience happened in early 2015, in the middle of the night:

I was asleep in bed with my wife. Suddenly, I was awakened. I sat up very quickly and looked to my left. At the entrance to our bathroom, adjoined to our bedroom, was an enormous man. He was praying on both knees with his head lowered and his hands pressed together under his chin. Our vaulted ceilings are about thirteen feet tall. Even so, the back of his head grazed the ceiling, so the size of this creature when standing would have been at least twenty-five feet tall. His white, ankle-length garment also glimmered with gold, and a solid-gold-colored sash wrapped around his waist. His hair was a color in between blonde and light brown, and his feet, also very large but in proportion with the rest of his body, were strapped in brownish bronze woven sandals. I could plainly see a cut or bruise on his upper left cheek, and while his garment was beautiful, it was discolored and soiled from what appeared to be wounds underneath the fabric. He looked extremely sad and very tired.

I was startled to say the least, not only by his presence in my room, but by the sheer size of him. I jumped out of bed and quickly reached in my night-stand drawer to grab a fire arm I keep in my room for protection. No sooner did I point the weapon in the creature's direction, when he turned his head and looked me, saying," Please don't do that." At these words, a great calm came over me. I lowered the weapon to my side and just stared at him. His face was gentle, as were his eyes, but he still appeared heavyhearted. He then said, "Tell the people to pray the Chaplet of Divine Mercy, every day, and to offer it in reparation for the sins committed by the United States."

Then he was gone. My wife had slept through the whole thing. In the days that followed, through contemplation and prayer, I was shown that this man is the guardian angel of the United States, and he is losing the battle for our country to Satan and his demons. Our prayers, specifically the one he requested, strengthen not only him, but all the angels who fight with him. He is petitioning us for help. I came to understand that we empower the angels through our prayers, just as we empower the demons with our sin. While our sins and indifference open the doors to the devils and their curses, our prayers and petitions open the doors to God's strength and blessings.

We are in desperate need of prayer and penance, of sacrifices for love of God that give way to waterfalls of grace. May we surrender all that we are and all that we have to Jesus before the Day of Justice arrives. Woe to those who would take this period of mercy for granted and put off their conversion, thinking that they can wait until the last hour. To grow in holiness can only come by way of God's grace and mercy. To grow in holiness takes time. And that time for grace and mercy is now.

Jesus:

Let all mankind recognize My unfathomable mercy. It is a sign for the end times; after it will come the day of justice. While there is still time, let them have recourse to the fount of My mercy; let them profit from the Blood and Water which gushed forth for them.

~Diary of Saint Maria Faustina Kowalska, #848

SISTER NICOLINA KOHLER

Caught in His Eyes

I grew up a nice Catholic girl in the small, quaint town of Oberschwappach, Germany. Playful and flirtatious, without much religious depth, I made fun of nuns in their habits, calling them traffic obstacles and walking chapels. But God's sense of humor is better than mine. At age nineteen, I entered the novitiate of the Dominican sisters of Oakford, an order of active contemplatives and missionaries, to become a nun in full habit.

The nuns attended the same Catholic boarding school as I, and they naturally attracted the young, with their superior the age of thirty-two and the others in their twenties. Although I wasn't known for my piety, they liked me, and I liked them, too. But what spoke to me most was their spirit. While open and fun, full of laughter and very human, they also showed a serious and contemplative side as they sat in church for hours of prayer, communing with God in peaceful silence or singing the divine office in angelic tones.

At age twenty-six, vested in my very own blue and white habit with a white veil and knee-length skirt, I took my final vows to live out the commands of the Gospels as a Dominican sister, taking a strict vow of poverty, begging for food two times a year.

Three years later, my order assigned me to live in Northern California, my home ever since. In the span of time, I was placed in charge of postulants, then candidates, then finally novices—sisters in their first year of religious formation. In my own estimation and that of my community, I was a good nun who loved God and prayer and people.

In 1984, I celebrated my twenty-fifth jubilee year of religious life and was granted a sabbatical. Desiring to spend it gaining more insight into the connection between the Old and New Testaments, I traveled to the Holy Land, specifically to the Ecce Homo University, situated on the Via Dolorosa in Jerusalem, overlooking the road that Jesus walked to His Crucifixion. I was on holy ground.

Our study of Scripture and scenes in the life of Jesus included excursions to the very places where the events happened—all within walking distance: the Church of Mount Zion on Mount Zion itself; the Church of All Nations at the Garden of Gesthemane; and the Church of the Last Supper, which I cherished because I have a great devotion to the Eucharist. There I could pray best.

But there was one place where I didn't want to go. At the end of the Via Dolorosa, only a twenty-minute walk away, stood the Church of the Holy Sepulchre, also known as the Church of Golgotha. It is said to be the place of the Lord's burial and Resurrection, above the actual ground where He was crucified.

But I wasn't interested in Calvary. Each year when Holy Week came, I couldn't wait to celebrate Easter, my favorite time of year. Holy Thursday was fine, but then Good Friday had to come. Why couldn't we just skip over the torture? It seemed so hard and horrible. Dying, death, and suffering didn't make much sense to me, and I often wondered why Jesus had to be crucified.

My generation of Germans, the youth of World War II

Germany, didn't understand why the disaster of the Holocaust had occurred. Why didn't the generation before us stand up for the Jews and all those being persecuted when such horror was happening? We had lost faith in grownups to make right decisions and believed in obliterating war. Never again should suffering and death happen.

And yet it happens anyway. No one can escape misery and sickness and death. But after twenty-five years of being a nun, I was blind to that. I wanted to make the world a better place, make it beautiful and whole, without understanding that the world also had to suffer, get old, and die.

At the Ecce Homo, I began the school semester alongside forty-two people from thirty-two different countries, already accomplished in their various fields of ministry. One of these students named Ruth had been teaching at a Lutheran seminary in South Africa. Since my order, the sisters of Oakford, is based in South Africa, she had met some of the sisters there. This connection immediately drew us together, and we became friends. Having a curious mind and an open heart, she liked to hear me speak of Catholic beliefs. Ruth had focused her study on the Passion and death of Our Lord Jesus, and her fascination with Calvary had carried her many times along the Via Dolorosa to the Church of the Holy Sepulchre.

One semester into our school year, Ruth came to me and asked, "Would you like to come with me to the Church of the Holy Sepulchre? I don't think you've been yet. We can go early in the morning at 4:30 a.m., when they open up the church." She wasn't pushy but enthusiastic and more than accommodating. She thought it would be wonderful for me to escape the throngs, to walk alone with her when the streets are dark and silent, when the rest of the town is asleep and only a priest or a monk might hush by—to enter into perhaps the most sacred place in the world.

I was slow to answer as I searched for an excuse. I really didn't want to go and hadn't examined why not. I'd told myself that I wanted to study Calvary thoroughly, that I'd go there with the teachers and the class when I felt prepared. But the other students, all forty-two of them, had already gone to the Church of the Holy Sepulchre several times each by that point.

Not hearing a response, Ruth asked, "Do you have an alarm? We would have to leave here around 3:30 in the morning. I can do all the arranging since we'll need to get permission to leave that early."

I felt conflicted, but I didn't want to lose face. I was a Catholic nun after all, the only one at the school, and one in full habit, at that. Reluctantly I said to her, "Make sure when you get up that you see a light under my door." Secretly I hoped I would just sleep through it all.

At 3:30 a.m., there was the knock at the door. Darn. "Sister Nicolina, are you up?"

I opened the door ajar and said tersely, "Yes, I am up."

"We are leaving in exactly ten minutes."

Darn.

Into the dark morning, we stepped outside and moved along the paved, upward slope of the Via Dolorosa, the way Our Lord walked toward Calvary. The original road lies far beneath the ground, below the centuries. One city on top of another has buried Jesus's steep path, back in time.

After only a short walk, we reached a corner and Ruth stopped. I wondered why. Looking up, I saw the first Station of the Cross: a shrine bordered by an iron gate, depicting a relief image of Our Lord condemned to death. She dropped to her knees in the center of the small street. I cringed. Bewildered and upset, I stood there looking at the stark picture of Jesus being condemned to death, and watching this mystery envelope Ruth.

I didn't sign up for this. She didn't tell me this was part of the deal. "So, if this is the first station," my mind raced, "I hope we're not stopping at thirteen more of them! How long are we going to be here? Let's just get this church visit over with. Well, I sure hope we're done in time for our class at nine." I had already felt reluctant to go, and now I was fully resistant. There wasn't a prayer in my heart—not a one.

Then we went to the second station: Jesus Carries His Cross—the third station: Jesus Falls the First Time—the fourth station: Jesus Meets His Afflicted Mother. At every stop, I just stood there; never knelt, never prayed. Ruth dropped to her knees each time and went deep into herself, with her head on the ground or resting gently on the station's image. This wrinkled my brow. "What a spectacle. Why did she have to do that?" Dawn was coming and people were filling the street. No one else was acting this way; everyone was going about their business. This wasn't being done in my way or my time. "Why couldn't we just walk normally up to Calvary?"

We came to the sixth station at the base of a distinct incline. This time, the station depicted Veronica wiping the Lord's face and receiving His imprint on her cloth. The relief looked newer than the others since it was built onto the side of the Chapel of the Little Sisters of the Poor at a later time. Jesus's face shone clearly in the likeness of the image on the famous Shroud of Turin.

When Ruth again fell on the ground with her face down, I didn't look at her this time, but at Jesus's face. Suddenly, His image on the cloth spoke to me through a memory.

Twenty-five years earlier, on the night before my final vows, I was staying overnight at a retreat center. The only sister prepared to make vows with me in a ceremony the next day was seized by great doubts and darkness. I remembered how ready I felt to give my life completely to the Lord, how I longed to give my lifetime vow of being a nun for Him. I couldn't understand her upset and worried that the next morning would find her on the run. "Would the vow ceremony happen without her?" I wondered. I felt like a woman on the night before her wedding day, unsure if she was going to have a ceremony.

Throughout the night, I tossed and turned, the other sister's turmoil causing me to barely sleep in the retreat center. As dawn cast the first ray of light across my bed, I opened my eyes, sat up, and saw that over me hung an image of Jesus's face on the Shroud of Turin. I hadn't noticed it before. Jesus's eyes were closed, just as they are on the actual shroud. But as I continued looking at His face, He literally opened His eyes half way. Then He focused directly on me with a long and deep look of such love! I actually saw His pupils focus, and His penetrating eyes didn't just look into mine, they stared through my soul. His gaze touched me with such an infusion of ecstatic peace and total love that I knew no matter what my sister was going through, all would be well that day, and I would give my life to the Lord.

While I stood next to Ruth on the pavement of the Via Dolorosa, transfixed by the memory of Jesus's face on the shroud, the Lord's love came into my soul again, so strong and real that I found myself on my knees with my head bowed low, unaware of how it happened. The remaining stops along the Stations of the Cross then became a real journey up to Calvary. From that moment on, I was no longer walking with Ruth. I was walking with Jesus.

No longer did it bother me whatsoever how long we stayed on our knees. I couldn't have cared less how dramatic this might look. Many more people passed by, some even pushed into us. I didn't see them. I had become part of the real Story.

Ruth continued to guide us forward. In ancient times, the hills once rose abruptly, with Jerusalem built on top of one, and Calvary jutting upward from it. Steep inclines in the natural rock of the area were now covered by time and civilizations, but parts of the rock, on top of which Jesus was crucified, remained exposed within the Church of the Holy Sepulchre.

When we arrived at the church, Ruth motioned toward a basement door. As we stepped inside, she told me that one can still see the rock of the hill of Calvary rise sharply inside the church structure. This was the rock in which the Cross of Jesus had been mounted. People had built around it over the centuries, for no one dared to remove it. In an area next to a staircase, we would be able to touch that same rock with our hands.

Now vulnerable, I started seeing so much more in Ruth, and I am sure she noticed the change in me. As she climbed up the stairs, letting her hand rest on the rock of Calvary, I saw great devotion in her touch. With a beautiful tone of reverence, she whispered, "This is the rock," as if to say, "This, my friend, is holy ground."

Ruth continued walking ahead of me, sharing her knowledge, as I absorbed every word. Within the Church of the Holy Sepulchre, different Christian factions with their separate chapels have each staked their claim through their unique forms of ornate art. Styles clash and modern decor stands next to ancient, since the chapel has been destroyed many times. I could feel the divisions of centuries. Protestant Christians usually do not worship or pray in the Roman Catholic or Orthodox churches in the Holy Land. But here she was, honored to be there, full of love, reference, humility, and awe.

At the top of the stairs, we entered into an area where Russian Orthodox monks were chanting their morning hymns of praise. In somber silence, we stood and waited by the place where Jesus's Cross was laid on the ground and He was nailed to it.

When the monks finished their morning praise, now was our moment to enter their Russian Orthodox chapel situated directly on top of the place of crucifixion. Most pilgrims were not yet awake, and Ruth knew that once the chanting ended, a certain monk guarding the site would fall back to sleep around 7 a.m. This would provide us a window of time when nobody would bother us or rush us along. We would have this hallowed place to ourselves.

"That altar in front of us," Ruth whispered, "stands directly over a hole in the rock where the True Cross was inserted. It was specially erected over the Cross because an altar is for sacrifice, and this is where *The Sacrifice* for us and for our sins took place. But you cannot get to the rock of The Cross unless you kneel down."

She paused for a moment in reverence, and then spoke again. "You can go underneath the altar and touch the rock, but everyone has to go on their knees. When you get to the place where Jesus died for you, you have to become very small."

Then I watched as Ruth went first. She knelt down and crawled underneath the altar, where I could no longer see what she was doing. Only one person at a time was allowed to enter, and normally for only five minutes. After praying in silence under the altar for ten minutes, Ruth came up and gestured for me to kneel down.

Not knowing what to expect, I dropped to my knees and lowered my head under the altar. All at once, complete darkness surrounded me. I reached my hand down into a pitch-black hole in the rock. At that moment, time was suspended. Whether I stayed in my body or traveled out of it, I do not know.

I saw the Cross in front of me, even though my eyes were closed. And on the Cross was Jesus, nailed alive, looking directly at me. His eyes were soft and kind. They held no condemnation, no desire to complain or punish. They were so filled with love that in the illumination of His gaze, I saw my unworthiness as I never had before. Held by His look of pure mercy and understanding, I couldn't help but cry and cry over my sins, which were many and repellent. I would have dissolved in a flood of tears, if He hadn't wrapped me up in grace and sustained me with His eyes.

The experience felt so big, so overwhelming. I had been living a lie in so many ways, yet I felt no need to hide or lower my head out of embarrassment or shame, like I would before another human being. Jesus took off my mask, my outer shell, my painted-on face, so I could see my real self. Stripped naked before Him, I didn't feel demeaned or have to cover up anything. His gaze felt different than anything I'd known before.

I saw my pride. I saw my life of betrayal, how much I hurt Jesus and others with each little sin. It all added up to an attitude, a stand, a lifestyle. I didn't see specific moments, rather a larger picture, which made it more horrible. He remained on the Cross in terrible pain, as His penetrating, all-knowing, all-loving stare infused me with interior knowledge. I knew everything about myself at once, and all was painfully clear. He showed me my soul as He saw it, bringing into focus the ugliness of my sins with all my excuses erased, so He could pull me straight to His bosom without any lies or barriers, and I could rest my head on His heart without any fear or pride.

Jesus didn't show me my noble qualities and talents. They still remained in His gaze, precious and good, but He didn't bring them forward. My gifts, He revealed, were not for selfishness or show, but for service.

I saw how I tried not to make a show of myself, yet wanted to be seen. My self-assertion suddenly appeared devious. I had given it all the right names while denying my real motivation. I'd always thought I wasn't a proud person, and yet I was simply proud in a deceptive way. Being a colorful personality, I could wiggle my way into the middle of almost any group. If I didn't make it into the center of people's lives, I walked away and became the center somewhere else. When leaving a group behind, I'd think to myself, "I don't like them"—a judgment born of the big "I," selfishness, because my vanity hadn't been satisfied. If you would have asked me, "Are you proud and vain?" I would have said with confidence, "No."

In relationships, I saw how I got my own way, not in a pushy manner, but by being cute. People served me very easily, especially when I was young. I was entertaining. I was fun. I had a big smile. But all of it was fake and not true virtue. This stood out very clearly, and it wasn't pretty.

Growing up in Germany, my siblings had to suffer from my selfishness. My eldest sister always had to pick up after me because I never followed through with anything having to do with work. I said to God what I said to everyone, "I am not made for work. I am made for fun." My brothers would even say to me, "You're not beautiful like a cover girl, but you have personality. You wind men all around your little finger, then exit like a butterfly."

"Oh, no. That's not true. I would never want anyone around my little finger," I would reply, while loving the swarms of attention. One sin I didn't see within myself was jealousy. That sin I never understood. If somebody else was getting all the attention, I didn't bother getting jealous. "Well," I'd think, "he's not the only person in the world," and I'd go find someone else to adore me.

The Lord showed me my temper. When I got very angry, I would shoot people to the moon in my mind. "Wow," I'd sometimes think. "There are so many people up there on the moon now. The sky is full! I'd better cut this out. Perhaps one day someone might shoot *me* to the moon, and I'll have to spend my eternity with *them*!"

Cutting through my ego, Jesus revealed my devious shortcomings in religious life as well. As a young nun, I believed I could become holy quickly if I followed all the order's rules and regulations. I made an idol of my religious practice. Thinking I was somehow holy by following all the rules also reduced my idea of holiness to "no big deal." At the root of my perception was pride, which creeps stealthily in to destroy all good deeds.

I fooled myself into thinking I was doing all the right things, while the truth was, I was breaking the rules all the time. The sisters had to be back in the convent by 10 p.m. with lights out, for instance, and I sometimes feigned going downstairs into the chapel in order to watch a night movie in the recreation room. After compline prayers at 7:30 p.m., "profound silence" was expected in the convent until the next morning, and at times, a few of us would sit in the car chatting, instead. I made excuses like, "I wasn't in the house, so the rule didn't apply to me." My inward deception helped me think of myself as following the rule perfectly and with the heart. I was never guilty. I was a good nun.

We sisters didn't have strict rules after the Catholic Council of Vatican II (1962-1965). Yet Jesus showed me that my breaking the ones still in place was a sin. I'd taken a vow of obedience before God. Period.

As for gluttony, I didn't indulge too much, but Jesus reminded me that I'd snacked all my life, which is not a convent virtue. In the poverty of our order, there is never much extra food around. The convent rules say you shouldn't eat outside of mealtimes unless you're sick. "This is not a hidden sin," I half-jokingly tell the sisters now in the convent house in California. Like some of the other nuns, I love to open the fridge at night to search for anything left to snack on, and I have my excuses that go with it.

In addition to food, the Lord showed me my many other attachments: to position, planning, people, and attention; and to my own ways, opinions, and desires. When it came to people crossing my plans, my mood always grew sour because my most excellent agendas had to be redone, and they were perfectly tight without wiggle room. My gift of intertwining my heart with my mind became a problem when I took things personally. In a meeting, I could hold a strong opinion. If somebody with a louder voice said, "No way, Nicolina," I would feel personally offended because my idea felt like part of my own heart.

Respecting and honoring my elders and superiors who were older than I came easier than obeying my superiors who became younger and younger over time. I sometimes treated them as though they were still my novices and entered into power struggles.

By God's grace and no merit of my own, I easily outshined the other sisters in my good works, never thinking anything amiss with it. But the Lord showed me what was wrong: I made my abilities the measure for other people, believing, "What I can do, you can also do." My standard of judgment was "Me."

Jesus also revealed my personal pique over hearing people say untrue things about me. I had always thought I had to defend myself and tell everyone the way things really were. Highly offended, I would speak quickly to correct any misquote or misinterpretation, without love or a forethought. Jesus didn't like that, and He showed me clearly why not. I was to say, "Lord, You know what I said, did, or meant, so I do not have to justify myself because You are the more important One. You know everything." Why would I need to correct myself before people? That's not to say that the Lord doesn't want us to defend ourselves against abuse or a misjudgment that would cause serious harm. But He knows the truth, He is the judge—no one else; and usually that is good enough.

As the insights continued, one after the other, Jesus brought to light my indignation over people saying true things about me. The sisters often said to me, "Nicolina, you're flirting."

I would say, "Why is this guy always hanging around me?"

"Because you don't see the way you look at him and flirt with him." I called it being friendly. I was perfect, so why were they making me out to be imperfect?

I was also shown how I had to free myself from my attachment to friends. Friends could be part of my life, but once again, one of my strengths, my love for and intimate connections with people, was also my weakness. People walked easily into my heart, and I allowed them to push Jesus further out. I could easily wrap my thoughts and time around someone and then acknowledge Jesus only once in a while. But the Lord wanted my primary focus to always be on Him. In Him was everything I needed.

Having a cardiac condition, I had learned to control my emotions so as not to aggravate my heart. But under the altar of sacrifice at Calvary, I had no emotional control. My conscience seized my heart with inexpressible torment, and only by crying uncontrollably could I release it. My tears flowed not from embarrassment, but from seeing the signs of suffering on the Lord's body and on His face, due to *my* sins. "This is all for you," His eyes said to me. "I did this all for you." That message thrust a fiery sword through my heart, causing a searing, stabbing pain. I wanted to die, and yet didn't, because I longed to be worthy of the love in His eyes.

Never before had I experienced the agony of my own sins because I had always explained them away. Jesus had loved me to the point of death, and I hadn't tried hard at all to love Him in return. Instead, I snuck around in side-stepping, slippery ways, which meant that the way I said and believed I lived my life, I didn't. Looking like a saint and not being one hurt the most.

So much transpired in that mystical encounter with the crucified Jesus that I lost track of time. At least two hours had passed when I finally crawled out from underneath the altar. I emerged with an indelible mark of unworthiness on my soul, along with the unshakeable knowledge of being sublimely loved and adored. How one can receive both at the same time, only God knows.

I missed my 9 o'clock class but didn't care. Ruth had already gone back to the school. She had waited a half hour and then left, realizing that I wasn't just under the altar of sacrifice. I had gone somewhere else. Clusters of pilgrims now bustled about, coming and going, but no matter how chaotic the crowd, people were falling to their knees and faces. Grace was striking unexpectedly, and I could see signs of great miracles happening in people's hearts. What Ruth had shared with me about touching the rock of the True Cross was not known by most pilgrims, so they never saw me down there underneath in the darkness—gone.

Jesus had chosen to give me the greatest graces in Calvary and not in a site I felt drawn to, like Bethlehem or Nazareth. Nowhere was I so profoundly touched as in the place where I was most reluctant to go.

People have often said to me, "Oh, you are a good nun." Well, don't believe it. We cannot go by what people say, good or bad. We have to look at Jesus Christ, and then we know who we really are.

The Lord touched the deepest places of my personality and changed me. But the revelation is not finished. That moment was a grace, a onetime, extraordinary event. But eye-openers continue along the journey, whenever He chooses, to shape me into His own image and likeness, and I see myself again in another light. These are moments we cannot get on our own. They can only come through the Lord's gaze.

Now when my wishes and desires are not met, when life is hard and painful, I can lock glances with Jesus and bring meaning and purpose to it all and not run away. I can unite my own little crosses with His and

suffer them with Him, in Him, and for Him. When wrapped in Jesus's beautiful and penetrating stare, even when we are facing the harshest truths, or suffering the greatest pains or injustices, we can endure, we can hold on. We get the strength.

Many times, I have reflected on this journey with Ruth, for it was our walk up to Calvary that turned my heart around. No longer was Good Friday a day to jump over. Now I wanted to lengthen it. I wanted to enter more profoundly into Jesus's suffering and ponder at length His great love—all because of what I saw in His eyes. Those eyes.

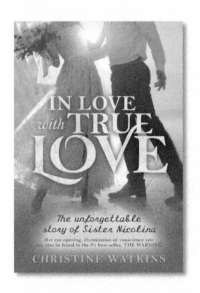

Also read the enthralling short story of Sr. Nicolina, once a feisty, flirtatious girl who fell in love with the most romantic man in all of post-war Germany. Little did they imagine the places where love would take them...

In Love with True Love: The Unforgettable Story of Sister Nicolina offers a glimpse into the grand secrets of true love—secrets that remain a conundrum to most, but become life itself for a grateful few.

Jesus:

So I turn to you, you-chosen souls, will you also fail to understand the love of My heart? Here, too, My heart finds disappointment; I do not find complete surrender to My love. So many reservations, so much distrust, so much caution. To comfort you, let Me tell you that there are souls living in the world who love Me dearly. I dwell in their hearts with delight. But they are few. In convents, too, there are souls that fill My heart with joy. They bear My features; therefore, the Heavenly Father looks upon them with special pleasure. They will be a marvel to angels and men. Their number is very small. They are a defense for the world before the justice of the Heavenly Father and a means of obtaining mercy for the world. The love and sacrifice of these souls sustain the world in existence. The infidelity of a soul specially chosen by Me wounds My heart most painfully. Such infidelities are swords which pierce My heart.

~Diary of Saint Maria Faustina Kowalska, #367

FATHER RICK WENDELL

The Man Who Died before He Lived

It's a miracle I'm alive. I grew up a thrill-seeker. When life got too mundane, I'd test its limits. My friends and I had our own versions of extreme sports. We started out with rope swings over the river, and then over cliffs. We fought each other with BB guns and played toss with fireworks, which blew off my friend's hand. We went camping in weather twenty-degrees below and drove at speeds over a hundred. Four of my high school friends died in high-speed car wrecks, but that didn't slow me down.

The result: three operations on each of my wrists, five surgeries on my left knee, one on my right, two broken ankles, a separated left shoulder from jumping off moving freight trains, and a snapped collarbone from performing flying bicycle stunts—not with a decked-out mountain bike, but a Schwinn with a banana seat. My mother said she was just trying to keep me alive. When I was sixteen, wearing my Boy Scout uniform with a merit-badge sash and driving my '69 Ford Mustang, a police officer chased me down, jumped out of his car, pointed his gun at me, and yelled, "Put your hands on the roof, kid!" I "didn't know" how to drive a car unless it was going full blast. My parents absolutely forbade me to have a motorcycle, so when I turned eighteen, I made sure to get one. It only took me a few months to spin out in a death-dealing crash followed by eight hours of surgery. After that, people began saying, "God is saving you for something special." "Nah," I thought. "I'm just lucky."

Achievements came easy. Mom found me poring over her medical books when I was five. I sculpted, appreciated fine art, played leads in musicals, and was captain of our high-school hockey team, with the temper to go with it. I was truly a Renaissance kid in a good sense, but my personal morals flew all over the map. At the end of my senior year at Hill-Murray High School in Maplewood, Minnesota, I went to five

121

proms with four girls. After having gone with one of my girlfriends to each other's proms, we unexpectedly saw each other again with different dates at a third prom. When I graduated, five hundred people paid to come to my party, replete with a live band, porta-potties, and four sixteen-gallon kegs of beer—to start.

Coming from a practicing Catholic family, it was assumed that my two brothers and I would say grace before meals, prayers before bedtime, and attend parochial schools. Being late for Mass was not an option because mother would make us sit in the front row. Not my idea of a thrill. Since businesses weren't open on Sundays in the 1960s due to the blue laws, our family would have a formal meal at grandma's house after Mass every Sunday. Catholicism was a family given, but my 1970s Catholic high school faith formation was dangerously thin and punctured with holes. "God loves you," we were told. "You'll figure it out."

I spent my first year of college homebound, doing independent study connected with the nearby University of Wisconsin because I had forty-five pounds of plaster on three broken limbs. When I recovered, I couldn't get away from home fast enough, so I escaped to St. John's University, a Catholic college in Collegeville, Minnesota. I didn't witness any examples of faith among the monks on campus, and we students weren't required to go to Mass on Sundays, so we didn't. My immorality mushroomed because of the lack of moral guidance, and I became increasingly disillusioned with the idea of faith. Intellectually, I couldn't prove that God didn't exist; but He wasn't relevant in my life, and he or she, or whatever, certainly wasn't important enough for me to modify my behavior.

Although I'd been told God was all love, I never felt him and certainly didn't understand him as a loving father, perhaps because I never experienced my own father's love. The only time Dad told me he loved me was on Christmas Day after downing a couple bottles of champagne. Even though I was always an honor student, was voted outstanding artist in high school for my sculpting and pottery, and excelled in sports, especially contact sports, Dad never came out to watch a single one of my games and couldn't find his way to offer a hug or a compliment. Rather, he criticized me. When I was fourteen, my father hit me for the last time, perhaps because I was getting bigger and stronger, or perhaps because my smile of sheer rage immobilized him. I swore in my heart that day that I would kill him if he touched me again (a curse I placed on myself that had to later be broken by Jesus Christ).

After earning a Bachelor of Science pre-med degree from the University of Wisconsin in River Falls, I worked for a short time in a hospital emergency room to build my résumé in order to attend medical school (like my mom had). Late one Saturday night after I'd survived another terrible motorcycle crash, the contract doctor in the emergency room, whom I deemed very cool, sat me down and said, "Rick, you can do this job. You have the ability. But being a physician is not what I do, it's who I am. And I'm not sure that you would be happy." I listened and instead sought out the deepest snow available, which I found in Little Cottonwood Canyon, Utah. Between hitting the slopes in wintertime as a professional skier, and lifeguarding and riding Harley Davidsons in the summer, my days became a living cliché of sex, drugs, and rock 'n' roll.

In my opinion, there was only one way to go—full on, top speed—ready to risk my very life for the next thrill. It was the 80s, when cocaine use was fashionable, not criminal, in certain crowds. I showed up in places within the drug trade where no one should go, and I met with people no one should see, for the spirit of evil within them was palpable. I attempted feats so perilous that if I didn't complete them, I would die. Perched on one ski, atop a three-hundred-foot cliff, I stopped twenty-five feet away from plunging to my death. My face was a historical map of cuts and scrapes, and every inch of my back had been bruised or lacerated—the markings of a young man trying to prove himself to a father who didn't care. But the biggest scars were on my heart.

When I found out that I could make better money in construction than lifeguarding, I left the slopes of Utah to form a little construction company back home in Minnesota. By age twenty-seven, I had fifteen men working for me, building high-end, custom, golf-course homes. Enjoying the income, I purchased my family home, a waterfront property, and decorated it with a big boat and a string of cars and motorcycles. I was young, in shape, arrogant, and everything I tried to do I could do well. The world shouted success at me with my possessions, money, power, and popularity, not to mention girlfriends. In time, I was engaged to be married to my trophy girl—the prettiest and wealthiest one of them all. To add to her good qualities, she could pound booze almost as hard as I could and liked the same stuff on pizza.

So that was my life before God changed everything.

One day, when I was age thirty and in perfect health, I needed stiches because of a large nail that gouged my face, due to a construction accident. My body went into anaphylactic shock from a reaction to the anesthesia that was used—and I died. For two and a half hours, I was gone, cold to the touch. My body was going to be shipped to a harvest center in St. Paul, Minnesota, where they would eventually pronounce me brain dead and harvest my organs. I have AB positive blood, a type found in less than 2 percent of the population, so I am very valuable in parts.

Suddenly, my arm shot up off the hospital bed and wrapped around my startled mom and fiancé. Soon I was sitting up and talking completely healthy. In the two and a half hours that my body was dead, my soul was in the very presence of God, and soon after that, I was shown that had I not been brought back to life, I would have entered hell for an eternity. This entire story can be found in the book, *Of Men and Mary: How Six Men Won the Greatest Battle of Their Lives.*

Needless to say, I came back a changed man. The Lord let me know, without compromise or uncertainty, that I was not the lord of my life. He was. The Blessed Mother also reached out to me through an invitation to go to one of her pilgrimage sites: "Medjahoochee," or "Medgegookie." (None of us from North America knows how to say Medjugorje, pronounced me-ju-gó-rya.) I read a book by Fr. Joseph Pelletier on the first five days of the apparitions in this small town in Bosnia-Herzegovina, the former Yugoslavia and wasn't at all skeptical: "If something this incredible is going on in the world today," I thought, "I want to be like the apostle Thomas and go put my fingers in the Lord's wounds." I wanted to "touch" Mary's presence. I'd heard about Fatima and Lourdes and other sights of Marian apparitions, but they were far away and long ago. The Medjugorje apparitions had begun in 1981. "Are they still happening?" I wondered. Within a short time after that, I found myself traveling with my mother to this unpronounceable place across the world. It was there that God revealed my sins to me.

The first evening we arrived, I was sitting on an outdoor bench of the sunny side of the parish church, St. James, to listen to the lilting sounds of the Rosary, coming through the loudspeaker in Croatian, followed by dozens of different languages harmonized into one voice: "Holy Mary, Mother of God, pray for us sinners now and at the hour of our death. Amen." In the middle of the Rosary, at 6:40 p.m., small church bells played "Ave Maria," announcing the arrival of the Mother of God, whom the locals affectionately call "Gospa." "So, Mary is appearing now on earth to one of the visionaries," I thought to myself. Then all went quiet, extremely quiet, and the atmosphere grew still.

People from around the globe, from Asia, Africa, Europe, and America—wearing cameras, robes, loafers, and tennis shoes, respectively—started to look up and point toward the sky. Joining them, I stood transfixed as I watched the sun shimmer and throb and shoot off beams of light. At intervals, its center turned opaque, with the outside spinning in one direction, then the other, displaying changing and swirling colors. After a few minutes, I diverted my eyes, realizing I wasn't supposed to be able to stare at the sun without going blind. I even looked for a bright spot in my vision, which naturally comes from optic fatigue. It wasn't there. Turning to the woman next to me, I asked, "Do you see that?"

"Yes, the sun is spinning!" she exclaimed, and then I learned that women describe colors differently than men. Purple, as far as I knew, could be "light purple" or "dark purple." "It's lavender!" she began. "No wait, it's turning violet, now mauve . . . actually, more like mulberry or magenta. . ." As she continued to name all the colors on a paint wheel, I thought of how I wanted to share the experience with my mom but didn't know where she was, so I began walking toward the back of the church along a pea-gravel path in search of her. At the point when I stood directly outside of where the Tabernacle resided inside the church, I was suddenly taken away . . . and shown my life.

I saw all the sinful events of my life up through the present moment. It was an illumination of conscience, an experience more intimate and vivid than a movie, more realistic than a 3-D image; and I had the sense that God was there, somewhere behind me, watching everything. I was aghast to learn the implications of my sin, how my actions or inactions were so much bigger than one single event and had a ripple effect on others across time and eternity. I didn't know that human beings were related in this way. Bawling uncontrollably, all I could say over and over again was, "I'm sorry. I'm so sorry. I didn't know." But what was clear was that in every situation, I had a choice, and I chose poorly.

The first scene God showed me was of myself as a five-year-old boy, reaching up to steal a Matchbox car, which hung from a store rack, and I felt how it broke God's heart. He loved me beyond all telling and would have given me anything. Simultaneously, God communicated the intricacies of deliberation that went into my choice. At that tender young age, I knew that taking the car was wrong. I knew my parents or my grandmother would have happily paid for it. I had no reason to steal it. God revealed to me all those things we never think of. ("It's just a toy car. What could it hurt anybody?") But my small action hurt relationships of trust. Insurance had to pay. The owner of the store had to pay. His and others' trust in their fellow human beings was further eroded, which changed their behavior—and so on, and so on. There were losses within me, as well. There was the loss of innocence. Once I performed that deed, I could never take it back. It could be confessed and forgiven, restitution might be made, but a reality would still hold that would remain part of my experience. And that could never be changed. Yet after I stole it, I didn't repent; therefore, every subsequent theft became that much easier.

Then I saw, in mind-boggling detail, scenes of my moral descent into all that the world and the devil had to offer me. At first, my conscience knew that there was an undeniable selfishness attached to my transgressions because I was created and taught to know better. But as my sins grew progressively worse, my conscience became ever more muted, until in time, the voice of truth in my life was either actively ignored or shut out completely. Materialism, power, and pleasures became my gods. I saw my attachment to the forty-foot motor yacht, the big house on the river, the cool cars, the clothes, the sex, the drugs. Not once did I think of consequences because consequences didn't come to me. Without experiencing the negativity of my actions and rationalizing away any that came, I made my pursuits acceptable in my own mind. Embracing the mentality of the world today, I believed, "If they don't catch me, if they don't charge me, if they don't bring me before the magistrate, then what I'm doing is okay." God was giving me immediate and intimate knowledge of this human folly. He was exposing my cherished lies and those I embraced from society. If abortion was legal, if contraception was prescribed, didn't that make them okay? No. If state legislators legalized marijuana for everyone and called it medicinal, wasn't it always so? No, they were liars. What mattered was what God thought, what God said. But I had preferred to be ignorant of God.

I believed the damning lie that simply because two people "consent" to a sexual act, it is therefore justified. With each encounter I had with a woman, I was fully responsible for my part and partially responsible for hers. The degrees of culpability and the far-ranging, rippling repercussions were different for each act and each person. Sometimes a woman wanted to please me because she had every intention of having a deep relationship that involved marriage, and I had no intention of that whatsoever. Sometimes I had better intentions, but my sin was still sin. I could never give back what I had taken from so many women, sometimes her virginity, which was crushingly serious—worse than beating her. Even if I had run after her and told her I was sorry a thousand times, her relationships with men throughout her life would still be affected, not to mention her eternal soul. Every one of my sexual sins, like all sin, involved pain and suffering, but I hadn't allowed myself to see.

My mother wanted me to behave differently toward women, but I appeared to be cavalier and uncaring about her feelings, which wasn't the truth. In the illumination, I felt her pain within myself. She was so disappointed. Long before she moved into my home, she would visit and try her best to help me, but I continued to insist that she embrace my behavior in order to have a relationship with me. It was against her sensibilities, so she couldn't accept it, but she loved me anyway. My response was to turn my back on her physically and emotionally. "I'm not coming over to your house. I'm not seeing you!" I bellowed. This was the woman who bore me into the world, who loved me, whom God had chosen as my mother. When reliving this moment, I felt the slicing pain of rejection that had stabbed my mother's heart to its core.

Even choices that didn't seem serious to me were, and my good intentions were never enough to cover them up. When someone passed me a joint at a rock concert, for instance, even if I didn't intend to do drugs when I was there, I still bore the responsibility for my choice to take a hit, however disinterestedly. One particular scene that bore my fingerprints was profoundly disturbing. I had sold drugs to a certain guy on more than one occasion, then moved away and never saw him again. When I returned to that area, I was sitting in a local tavern where a man told me that the guy had committed suicide. In the illumination of conscience, I was shown the event of his death. It is still so hard for me to accept and to know that in certain and real ways, I was part of his decision-making process to end his life on Earth. In seeing the ripple effects of my sin, I learned that he was holding his family together. When he died in such a way, he crushed each one of his family members. Their suffering, in turn, afflicted every relationship they had with others, and so on, in a spiral of pain.

All of the sinful events of my life passed before my eyes and through my emotions, in the eternal presence of God, where there could be no deception, no rewriting of history, no mitigation of circumstances. It was what it was. All my back stories were being erased and my guilt exposed. Like most human beings, I had rewritten the unconfessed sins of my past, creating skewed interpretations in my mind to downplay any personal culpability and disperse blame. I had decimated every one of the Ten Commandments. Intense remorse flooded my soul. I felt devastated by the heavy weight of truths about myself that I didn't want to see, didn't want to feel, didn't want to own. People had died because of my actions. I witnessed moments in my life that made me incredulous it was even me. Mortified, I just wanted to go away, to curl up and die, but I couldn't escape. I believe that had I seen the condition of my soul without the merciful support of God, I would have experienced a despair so great that I couldn't have gone on living.

When I came out of the illumination, I found myself kneeling and looking up at the miracle of the sun, still spinning and pulsating with color. Then I glanced downward to see the front of my shirt and the flagstones beneath me wet with tears. A few feet away, sitting on a bench, was my mother. I could see from her posture that she, too, could see this miracle of the sun, so I got up, walked behind her, wrapped my arms around her and rested my chin on her shoulder, cheek to cheek. Together we looked up at the most powerful energy source known to man, which God was manipulating at his discretion because he created it, and he isn't bound by the laws he made. In the presence of such a miracle, we were like little kids cuddled up in innocent awe, observing the power of God.

"How could it be," I wondered, "that scarcely any time has passed?" It then occurred to me that I had just experienced the whole of my life in the same few short minutes that Mary, the Mother of God, had appeared on Earth.

So that was my first day in Medjugorje. The next day, I woke up with an all-consuming desire to go to Confession. Donning a light jacket, I walked through the mist and rain drops, underneath scattered clouds toward St. James church. Sitting down on a wet bench, I thought to myself, "I would have liked to have gone to confession to Fr. Mike Canary"—a priest from Ireland I had met the night before, who was a late vocation. I had sensed from his demeanor that he would understand the gravity of the sins I had committed and give me a harder penance than simply five "Hail Mary's."

I didn't think of my ponderings as prayer, but no more had I finished my thought than Fr. Mike walked into my peripheral vision. For the next three hours, we sat together on that bench, huddled under his umbrella, while I told him my sins. Like St. Padre Pio, he could read into my soul; he knew the details of my sins before I said them. When I had trouble voicing my most shameful and embarrassing moments, he would help me by reminding me of particulars: ". . . and this is what you were doing . . . but this is what you were thinking . . ." When I finally finished, he gave me my penance: "You go to the mountain, the Mountain of the Cross. You take your shoes off, not as a penance, but an equalizer for all the infirm and elderly, the sick and the less able who come here. You are young and strong, and you climb that mountain in your bare feet, and you pray for every person you've ever hurt." Then he laid his hands on my head for absolution, and heat came out of them and into me. I didn't know what it was. I just knew that it was.

As I climbed the mountain, I could remember the name of every person I'd hurt. I could remember the lies, the seductions, the cheating, the thefts. . . I sobbed all the way to the top, and since I left my shoes at the bottom, I sobbed even more all the way down. At the base of the mountain, where a crucifix stood, I prostrated myself and begged Jesus for my life. I knew that I could walk this life perfectly from that moment on, and I would never be able to make up for all the harm I had done.

When I finally stood back up, I felt truly forgiven. I had never felt that way before in my life. I put my tennis shoes on and thanked God for his extravagant mercy. Then I walked back to the church, where I ran into Fr. Mike again. He said, "Come with me," and I followed him into a room with rows of metal folding chairs and people singing hymns. He called it a healing service. I didn't know what that meant and didn't think I necessarily needed one. I was happy because I felt forgiven. But, "What could it hurt?" Fr. Mike pulled out a purple stole, creased from being folded in his pocket, placed it around his neck, and walked to the front of the room. People stood up one at a time and walked over to him. When it came my turn, and I was standing about three feet in front of Fr. Mike, my mouth opened involuntarily, and I heard my voice say, "I have many scars on my heart, and what I want is the Holy Spirit." Putting my hand over my mouth incredulously, I thought, "Okay, that was weird. I wasn't gonna say anything."

Fr. Mike didn't utter a word. He picked up a small vial of holy oil, made the sign of the cross on my forehead, put his right hand on my head and then on my heart. All of a sudden, the Holy Spirit descended with great force, and I was afraid, not from fear, but awe. The Spirit stopped right above my heart. The experience wasn't merely psychological, physical, spiritual, or emotional, and it dwarfed any human drug or sexual sensation. What I underwent was the most explosively powerful event of my life. For those who know the original Star Trek series, I liken it to putting one's head into the "anti-matter." Fr. Mike said, "Let there be no more doubt. Let there be no more fear," and in that moment, my spirit expanded, as though taking in the biggest breath of air possible. The more I opened myself, the more he filled me, until there was no distinction between God and me. When I finally came back to consciousness of my surroundings, I found myself lying on the floor. Fr. Mike had his hand on my heart and was praying over me along with an eighteen-year-old young man named Bill Curry, who only six months earlier, had been a face-down drunk; but God delivered him from his addiction in Medjugorje.

My feet were sticking straight out and my body lay stiff, as though it had been jolted with a million volts. I could have easily served as a plank between any two of those folding chairs. Gradually, as my body began to relax, a delightful warmth I'd never known entered my soul. I had felt happiness before when winning the big game, falling in love, achieving success, and celebrating Christmas, but I'd never known what true joy really was. When I got up, I immediately embraced Fr. Mike, who said I almost broke his back I hugged him so hard. But I couldn't help it. I loved him! I loved everybody! It was sappy, and I didn't care. The experience so filled me with the Spirit of God that I could feel my heart beating with love for all of his creatures; it so cleansed my soul that I could almost feel people's bad thoughts. I walked outside into the cold outdoor air wearing a T-shirt and a smile, with no need of my sweater because I was emanating intense heat.

So that was only my second day in Medjugorje. The following day was the Feast of Corpus Christi, the Body of Christ. At dawn, as I lay in bed, I experienced another mystical event. This time, I found myself standing in a field of tall grass, about six to eight-inches high, with a wooden fence on my left, which travelled down a slope before me. A soft wind blew waves through the grass, making the underside of the blades appear silver in the sunlight. Then Jesus came. He walked up the slope in my direction and stopped a few feet in front of me, off to the left. He looked exactly like I would have expected him to. The only image I've seen that resembles his face was captured by a young artist named Akiane Kramarik,[viii] a girl who could miraculously paint like a master, as a child, without any training whatsoever. She was allegedly transported to heaven and recorded on canvas what she witnessed. The face of Jesus she painted was the face that I saw. He appeared to me wearing a soft, cream-colored, inner garment flecked with brown, and over it, a dark brown outer robe with banded strands of four or five threads woven in a checkered pattern. I could clearly make out his bearded face and his intense, but inviting eyes.

Then without speaking, Jesus communicated to me, "I want you to be a priest."

I was completely taken aback. "You've got to be kidding. I am the worst sinner, ever, and we've just been through this!"

"Yes," he responded.

"But I'm engaged to be married. I love my fiancée. I've named my kids. The dress is bought. The country club is rented. Critical mass has been achieved. And sorry to say it, but I've been treating her like my wife already." I had never, ever, ever, ever thought of being a priest—never had a moment of altar boy fervor—no inclination—nothing—not once.

"Yes."

"C'mon. This isn't for guys like me. That's for someone else. You create those guys. You know from beyond time that they're going to be priests. You put them into a wonderful family, they come out the altar boy chute, and then—boom—they're priests."

"I know what I'm doing," he said, and then he turned and walked away.

To read Fr. Rick Wendell's entire story of conversion, see *Of Men and Mary: How Six Men Won the Greatest Battle of Their Lives* (www.QueenofPeaceMedia.com/of-men-and-mary).
Also see Fr. Rick give his full testimony on
Queen of Peace Media's YouTube
Channel: http://bit.ly/2m3kA7d

Jesus:

Write this for the benefit of distressed souls; when a soul sees and realizes the gravity of its sins, when the whole abyss of the misery into which it immersed itself is displayed before its eyes, let it not despair, but with trust let it throw itself into the arms of My mercy, as a child into the arms of its beloved mother. These souls have a right of priority to My compassionate Heart, they have first access to My mercy. Tell them that no soul that has called upon My mercy has been disappointed or brought to shame. I delight particularly in a soul which has placed its trust in My goodness.

~Diary of Saint Maria Faustina Kowalska, #1541

DALE RECINELLA

A High-Powered Lawyer without a Defense

In early March, 1986, Susan and I met with Ms. Maxine and the builder at our new property. The closing would take place on acceptance of the completed house. We had designed it ourselves, through modifications, to a basic plan he suggested. It was time to break ground. I handed him the fifty-thousand-dollar cashier's check required by the contract for him to start work. We were on our way in Tallahassee. We would celebrate with dinner later that night, after attending the Saturday evening vigil service at our new parish, Good Shepherd Roman Catholic Church.

Since the change of law firms in Miami in February 1984, my work hours had exploded. The intense spiritual focus that was giving gravity to our lives in 1983 seemed to have waned as the pressures of children and career dominated our schedules and our daily resources. It couldn't have been anything of our making that caused us to step into church on the very night of signing the contract for our dream house, only to be confronted by the Gospel reading of the rich young lawyer in Mark 10:17-25:

> As Jesus started on his way, a man ran up to him and fell on his knees before him. "Good teacher," he asked, "what must I do to inherit eternal life?"
>
> "'Why do you call me good?" Jesus answered. "No one is good-except God alone. You know the commandments: 'Do not murder, do not commit adultery, do not steal, do not give false testimony, do not defraud, honor your father and mother.'"
>
> "Teacher," he declared, "all these I have kept since I was a boy."

Jesus looked at him and loved him. "One thing you lack," he said. "Go, sell everything you have and give to the poor, and you will have treasure in heaven. Then come, follow me."

At this the man's face fell. He went away sad, because he had great wealth.

Jesus looked around and said to his disciples, "How hard it is for the rich to enter the kingdom of God!"

The disciples were amazed at his words. But Jesus said again, "Children, how hard it is to enter the kingdom of God! It is easier for a camel to go through the eye of a needle than for a rich man to enter the kingdom of God."

Although the story had been read at church many times before, we heard it that night for the very first time. The dinner afterward to celebrate the contract on our new house was not going as planned.

"Do you think He meant what He said?"

"Who?" Susan was not picking up my thread without some context. "The builder? Did the builder mean what he said?"

"No." I was unfairly impatient. "Not the builder . . . Jesus. Do you think Jesus meant what He said?"

"What did He say? What do you mean?"

"What He said in the Gospel reading tonight."

Susan had the thread now. She set down her fork and looked at me intently.

"Do you think Jesus meant what He said tonight in the Gospel?" I leaned forward to speak softer, intuitively aware that anyone in the restaurant who heard me ask such a question would think I was nuts.

Susan shrugged. "Does anybody think He meant that? Does anybody take it literally?"

"Well, I guess priests and nuns do," I conceded in acknowledgment of the well-known assumption by Roman Catholics for centuries that the literal Gospel only applied to those called to the so-called religious life—priests, brothers and nuns. "But the guy He was talking to in the Gospel tonight was not religious. He was like me. He was like us."

"And . . . ?" Susan left both her words and her fork hanging midair.

"And so the question is, did Jesus mean what He said?"

"I don't know." Susan instinctively lowered her voice, too. "I've never heard anyone discuss it."

"Me neither."

"Maybe we should find out."

At first, we began reading the Gospel to each other in the evening. We were so stunned at the challenge of Jesus's actual words that we decided not to even try to discuss the question for at least six months. Instead, we separately prayed and studied His words, searching for an answer. By the end of September 1986, weeks after moving into our spacious new Tallahassee home, it was time for us to sit down and compare notes.

"Well, I'm not sure what to do with my answer, but I have my answer." Susan leaned back in her chair opposite the fireplace in the alcove that made up a portion of our 1,200-square-foot bedroom.

"Me too." My nod and shrug in a single gesture indicated that I was stuck in the same predicament. "Who should go first?"

"I'll go first." Susan leafed through her Bible to the gospel of Matthew and found the end of the Sermon on the Mount, Matthew 7:24-27:

Therefore everyone who hears these words of mine and puts them into practice is like a wise man who built his house on the rock. The rain came down, the streams rose, and the winds blew and beat against that house; yet it did not fall, because it had its foundation on the rock. But everyone who hears these words of mine and does not put them into practice is like a foolish man who built his house on sand. The rain came down, the streams rose, and the winds blew and beat against that house, and it fell with a great crash.

"I don't know what everybody else thinks." She closed the book with her finger between the pages, like a bookmark that would prevent those un-preached, un-thought-of, and un-discussed words from disappearing forever if she needed to refer to them again. "But, obviously, Jesus thinks He means what He says."

"That's where I come out, too. So, what do we do with this?" My right hand swept outward in a gesture that symbolically took in our monument of a house, 22 ceiling speakers and all. "And with this?" My left hand

136

held up the book of God's Word.

"Dale, I haven't a clue."

"Me neither."

The fire crackled loudly into a spray of sparks as the top log fell behind and rolled to the bottom.

"Sounds like we better pray, Dale. This is not going to be easy."

Susan had never spoken truer words. For weeks, in addition to prayer, we brainstormed ways to begin making ourselves available for service to God's Kingdom. The same obstacle kept asserting itself, the unyielding limit of time. There was not enough time. All our resources of time were committed to the needs of earning and maintaining our affluent lifestyle.

It is said that the blessing of limited resources is what makes human beings moral creatures. Limited money requires us to prioritize. Limited energy requires us to choose between the greatest good and inferior goods. And limited time requires us to pick between the things of the Father and the things of the world. If money and energy and time were unlimited, no choices would be necessary.

Each one of us could do everything. But they are limited, and we must choose. We kept praying for God's direction.

In November of 1986, I woke with a scream from a dead sleep, pouring sweat from a profound nightmare. Susan bolted upright in the bed next to me, scared awake by my sounds of terror.

"Dale, what happened? What made you scream?"

"A dream. A horrible nightmare." The sheets and pillow on my side of the bed were soaked. I pushed myself up by the elbows and turned on my back to lean sitting up against the brass headboard. "It was incredibly real."

"Tell me about it." Susan sounded very clinical, with a voice that would usually irritate me, but not tonight. This dream had to be shared.

"I am outside our bedroom here, on the west side of the house, raking leaves with the kids. It is late afternoon, very pleasant. Everyone is in a good mood. I am thinking how lucky I am. Then . . ." I paused, groping for words.

"Then what happened?" Susan's hands rotated toward herself in a circular gesture as though trying to reel out the words from somewhere inside me.

"Then I hear a voice. It is more than a voice, more than music—music is not descriptive enough. It is the sweetest, most beautiful sound I have ever heard in my life. It is coming from the direction of the setting sun. Everything in me knows I must follow it. So I start walking toward it. But I can't. I can't walk toward it because something is holding me back."

"Dale, what was holding you back?" Susan spoke with a gentle sharpness that was rare for her.

"I cannot move my left leg. I look down, and there is a huge chain on it. Massive steel links in this chain running from my ankle back to the house. The chain is embedded into the bricks of the house, right into the outside of the chimney for this fireplace." I waved my hand toward the bedroom alcove that we knew was essential to our happiness.

"What did you do, Dale?"

"I try to tear off the chain. I try like a madman to break the steel links, even to break my leg to get it off, but it will not budge. And then . . ." My voice fails as the desperation and despair in the dream leeches back into my senses. '"And then, the voice starts to fade. I can't get to it. The voice is going away. I am filled with terror because the voice is going away. It isn't just about wanting the chain off. It is all about the voice. It is so beautiful that I cannot imagine not running to it, not being with it.

I try to pry the chain out of the wall. I even try to pull the whole blasted house behind me. But it is futile. As I stand there trembling and weeping, the voice fades, the sun sets and, finally, it is completely dark. The voice is gone. The cold is absolute. In the dream, I know that there will be no second chance. I have lost it forever. I scream and wake up."

Susan seemed oblivious to the sweat and tears that were erupting anew with the recounting of my visit to personal hell. She was holding me close and praying softly.

"Sweetheart," she finally whispered so low that I can hardly hear her. "I think God may have given us our answer. Maybe we can't have all this and His Kingdom. Maybe we have to choose."

It is hard to describe the interior swirl of emotions unleashed by moving from the fear that Jesus may have meant what He said in general, to the shock of thinking that He may have meant it for us personally.

A year and a half later, God would visit me again. As a transplanted Yankee, I had never heard the warnings against eating a raw oyster, in a month without an *R* in its name. Yet the moment I bit into that raw oyster, I knew something was wrong. It did not taste right.

"Mr. Recinella . . . Dale." He cleared his throat. "It's over. You cannot survive the night. You cannot live more than another ten or twelve hours. You will not see tomorrow morning."

Susan was absolutely rigid, except for the squeezing of her hands wrapped around mine. I knew he was going to say it. I had not thought I would ever hear it. "Mr. Recinella, you need to get your affairs in order."

The children had visited in the afternoon. Susan's mom was minding them at home. Our pastor came for the last rites. Before losing consciousness, I kissed Susan good-bye. She was crying. She was staying. She would be there through the end. She was on *death watch,* though we had not yet heard the term.

The fever spiked tremendously high. I could not keep my eyes open. I wanted to, but was unable to. My last visual moment was Susan, sitting next to my bed, looking at me as though the strength of her gaze could hold me here. It could not. The fever had its way. My eyes fell closed. All was darkness.

Suddenly, at some point in the night, I found myself standing in the center of a room. It was not my hospital room. It was dark, except for the illumination pouring from the person in front of me. I recognized Him immediately. It was Jesus. He looked exactly like His picture that hung in my bedroom as a child. He glowed with a heat that defied description, both warm and luminescent, radiating out, penetrating the whole room and even my body. He was gazing at me intently, but He was not smiling. He was deeply saddened. There were tears on His face. He was weeping softly.

"Dale." His arms stretched out toward me as His head shook gently with sorrow and disappointment. "What have you done with My gifts?"

The lawyer in me responded by defensive instinct, "What gifts?"

As He listed my skillset, He did not look angry or perturbed, just sad, very sad. I would not be able to wriggle off this hook. He detailed every aspect of the intellect, education, upbringing, personality, and temperament that was part of my worldly success. I still did not get it. The moment did not feel like a judgment. But every response that came into my mind was defensive. "I have worked hard. I have made sure that my children go to the best schools." Even as the words spilled from my lips, it occurred to me that I was talking code for upper class and expensive.

"We live in a safe neighborhood; my family is safe." There was that sensation again. While my mouth was yet moving, in my thoughts I heard the same code being expressed.

"Our future is financially secure." There it was again, the voice in my head, code for "We have filled all our barns and are building bigger ones." Only this time the thought came with a memory  of Jesus's words in Luke 12:16-21 about fools who fill their barns.

"I have taken care of my family, just like everybody else does." The overt defensiveness of my voice made me realize that I was arguing with somebody. Who? He was not arguing back. Who was I arguing with? Myself?

Finally, His hands dropped to His sides. His expression was not one of condemnation. Rather, it was like the look of dismay of a parent who has told their teenager something a thousand times and is beyond the point of belief that the child still has not heard it. He spoke with a pleading that bordered on exasperation.

"Dale, what about all My people who are suffering?"

In that moment, it was as if a seven-foot-high wave suddenly and unexpectedly broke over me on an ocean beach. I was not at a beach, and the wave was completely transparent, invisible but tangible. I could feel its substance, and it was acidic-corrosive in the extreme. I felt that my very being would be dissolved in it.

Somehow, intuitively, I knew in the moment that the acid was shame, the shame of the selfishness and narcissism of my life. My family was an excuse for taking care of only me, my ego and my false sense of importance. I struggled against the sense of dissolution penetrating every cell of my being, trying to muster a coherent response.

"Please!" I summoned the energy for my last plea as Jesus was still tearfully before me. "Please, I promise You. Give me another chance, and I will do it differently."

That was it. That was all. The wave was gone. He was gone. The room was dark.

It was about six-thirty when I opened my eyes the following morning.

Susan had been sitting next to my bed all night, waiting for me to die. I shuddered at the reality of my last visual thought before the night, my mind's last picture of her in this world.

"I'm not dead, am I?" My voice betrayed its surprise at hearing itself again. There was a long moment before she responded.

"Well, you look pretty awful." Susan smiled with the full irony of her very long and rough night. "Obviously, you are not dead." There was another long moment of silence.

"Uh-oh." My sigh bore the full weight of having no clue as to what I had promised Jesus I will do.

There was no more fever. The bacterium was gone. The doctor said it was truly impossible. Three years later the bacteria would be identified as vibrio vulnificus, a flesh-eating bacterium that causes deadly food poisoning and wound infections. It is overwhelmingly fatal with external exposure. I swallowed it.

Nonetheless, my prayer was answered. I saw myself, my choices, and my life as God sees them.

Jesus meant what He said.[ix]

The full story of Dale Recinella can be found in his excellent book, *Now I Walk on Death Row*. Dale and his family experienced a radical change of life after his encounters with the Living Word. He went on to live a life of little money, few possessions, and a great love of God, which led him to minister to men condemned to die in prison.

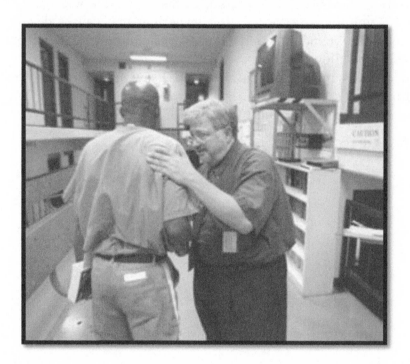

Jesus:

My daughter, faithfully live up to the words which I speak to you. Do not value any external thing too highly, even if it were to seem very precious to you. Let go of yourself, and abide with Me continually. Entrust everything to Me and do nothing on your own, and you will always have great freedom of spirit. No circumstances or events will ever be able to upset you. Set little store on what people say. Let everyone judge you as they like. Do not make excuses for yourself; it will do you no harm. Give away everything at the first sign of a demand, even if they were the most necessary things. Do not ask for anything without consulting Me. Allow them to take away even what is due you—respect, your good name—let your spirit rise above all that. And so, set free from everything, rest close to My Heart, not allowing your peace to be disturbed by anything. My pupil, consider the words which I have spoken to you.

~Diary of Saint Maria Faustina Kowalska, #1685

CHRISTOPHER WINTERS
God's Film of a Video-Journalist

I am a video-journalist from Cranberry Township, Pennsylvania. One day, a friend of mine, who had noticed I enjoyed telling people's formative life stories in my productions, suggested I visit a shrine in Western Maryland, called the National Shrine Grotto of Lourdes. The proposal didn't go over well. "Why do I need that religious stuff in my life?" I retorted. Patient, but persistent, my friend politely re-invited me over a period of months to see this place and the Monsignor who ran it. To appease him and silence his requests once and for all, I finally relented.

When I arrived at the shrine, the Monsignor said, "I think you're an answer to prayer. I have been looking for someone to do a video about this place and asked the Blessed Mother to send someone."

The thought startled me. "Monsignor, I don't think I'm your guy."

"Why not?"

"Because I know that Mary is the Mother of God, but I don't know anything more about her, and I wouldn't wish to do her story poorly."

He paused, then smiled. "You're perfect for this."

"I really don't think so, Monsignor. This is a beautiful place, but I think there are others more qualified to do this story."

"Are you uncomfortable being here?" he asked kindly.

"No, I just haven't been close to the Church, so I'm probably not where I need to be spiritually in order to do this production."

"Are you angry with the Church?"

"No, it isn't anger. Probably just apathy and laziness more than anything else."

He looked at me for a moment, and then responded, "That's fair enough. I'll make you a deal. Why don't you go up into the grotto and kneel down in the little chapel up there. That's where Mother Seton used to pray. Don't try to remember any formal prayers, just say whatever is in your heart. When you're done, come back to me. If you still feel the same way, I'll give you my blessing, and you can go on your way. No hard feelings."

Figuring I'd just found my way out, I agreed. "Fine."

It was late summer heading into fall, and the warm evening air filled with sounds of insects and birds ending their day. As the sun drew low on the horizon, I made my way to the grotto. I particularly remember the loud, rhythmic buzzing of locusts, the beautiful grounds, and the fantastic smells. All of my senses seemed more alert than usual, and a powerful, distinct, and very relaxing, almost comforting sense of peace pervaded the grotto and pervaded me.

Time was approaching closing, and I was the only person inside the shrine, as far as I could tell. On my unhurried stroll toward the chapel, many of the symbols of the Church surfaced in my memory, though I hadn't been to Sunday Mass for ten years or better. Like many, I had focused on building a family and career, unconcerned with the non-issue of God and His role in my life.

The chapel itself was much like an old-style, one-room school house, but made of stone and rimmed with vibrant, stained-glass windows. The few pews within it seated but fifteen to twenty people, and behind its central Tabernacle, stood a statue of the Queen of Heaven holding the infant Jesus.

I knelt down before the Tabernacle and pondered my life and the concept of God. I believed there was "something" out there somewhere but didn't know if it was Jesus, Buddha, Muhammad, or whomever. Was any one religion right? Were they all partially correct, and nobody had a monopoly on God? Was He even called "God" or by some other name?

At that point in my life, I was suffering through difficulties with a business partner and in my marriage. I started pondering my troubles, including my poor heath, lamenting how I was in emergency rooms on a regular basis, as often as two to three times per week. Then my eyes focused on words that were written on the plaque beneath the chapel's crucifix: "You are now in front of the Lord God of all Creation. What would you say to Him?"

For some reason, that question floored me. If there really was One God, and only One God, and I could say one thing . . . just one thing . . . what would I say? I started making a "wish list," almost wishing things aloud, one by one, that I wanted from this God for my family, for my business, for myself. But then I stopped myself and said, "No." Leaning back toward the crucifix, I said, "If I could say one thing and only one thing to the Lord God of all of Creation, by whatever name He is known, I would simply say, 'Thanks. Thanks for allowing me to be. I'll take the good with the bad. Thank you for allowing me to ever be at all.'"

A beautiful fragrance quickly filled the air of the chapel. I thought this was odd and reminded myself to ask the Monsignor what flowers could still be in bloom this late in the year. Then I was suddenly aware of a presence in front of me, about an arm's length away and slightly to my right, on the right side of the Tabernacle, although I didn't see him or her. Since this "somebody" was small and seemingly harmless, I wasn't afraid and didn't mind if he or she wished to stay. The atmosphere was pretty, the smells were terrific, and I remained peaceful and relaxed.

After a brief time, all of the bugs and birds ceased their noise instantaneously, as if on command. Now all was dead quiet—more of a respectful silence than a forced hush. Then there was another presence in the chapel on the other side of the Tabernacle. This one had power and authority and was a man. He was looking, not at me, but through me. Without warning, he began to call to mind every decision I had ever made and reviewed them all with me. This happened at a blinding speed, but I could recall in perfect and clear detail every decision, every conversation, from years ago, some long forgotten. He was calling out to something inside of me that was answering him. I was simply a spectator on this journey, helplessly observing the same things he was watching—but through his eyes, not mine. I soon realized that this was truly the Lord God of All Creation, and He was going to make a "judgment" about me when He was finished. I also understood that His decision would be permanent, without appeal, and forever.

The process was terrible to endure—truly horrific—and I am quite certain that it would kill many, not because of any condemnation, ridicule, or accusation on His part, but due to simply seeing the terror of truth.

I was failing this test miserably. Before me passed a life pattern of decisions far from where they needed to be in order to gain eternal life. I was not going to make it to heaven. God was going to throw me out, and I agreed with His assessment.

Through the eyes of the Lord, I perceived for the first time how much I had offended Him, even in the tiniest of ways; the things held up in front of me were sometimes so very small. In seeing myself as God viewed me, I didn't like what I witnessed and began to cry with a heartfelt sorrow. *"My Lord, I am sorry,"* I sobbed, and I meant it. At that moment, the review ceased. There was a pause, as He considered my fate. My heart almost stopped. I knew his decision would be forever.

Then He spoke one sentence and only one sentence. "My dear child, your sins I shall remember no more." And they were gone. I felt it happen. I was physically different. Cleaner. Lighter. Much, much different.

As difficult as my life review was to watch, I can say with honesty that a tremendous, extraordinary sense of peace and calm emanated all the while from the Lord, the Source of endless and unconditional love, Who has waited from the beginning of time to impart His Heart to anyone wishing to receive it. This is a love, like I never thought possible, and a peace that the world can't give. All of my questions about Him and about where I stood with Him were gone. That night I slept like I never had before.

I stood up to leave the grotto in an entirely different state than when I entered. Elated and surprised, I noticed that every one of my senses seemed more alert than usual. As I got about halfway out of the shrine, suddenly my body was no longer able to move, as if it were frozen. Then I heard two sentences, "Be not afraid," and "Prepare ye the way of the Lord," as an enormously strong sensation overtook me, much like an electrical charge or the ding of a funny bone—only it didn't hurt. The powerful current began in the bottom of my feet and worked its way up, healing and "fixing" me, as it went.

Simultaneously, a rush of Scripture flashed through my head at lightning speed, starting with the Old Testament, traveling through the New Testament, and ending with the Book of Revelation. Suddenly it all made sense. With sin no longer upon me, I could see Scripture's timeless, eternal, and beautiful Truth clearly for the first time. The love wrapped around the power of the Word was enough to melt me into tears of joy.

The passages highlighted the fire of the Holy Spirit. Until that moment, I had thought of the "Holy Spirit" only as a metaphor, like "The spirit of the law"—certainly not a person. I was wrong because this was Him. This was the same fire that destroyed Sodom and Gomorrah, the fire of the burning bush that spoke to Moses, the fire that came to rest upon the apostles at Pentecost. And it was now upon me.

There was a distinct personality to this fire, separate from me, but working in conjunction with me. It made me feel very safe, like a protective blanket or coat of armor, and I could see and hear its thoughts and emotions. I could work with it, under the authority of God, but not control it, for it wasn't mine. There was a beautiful peace, almost a playfulness about it. It feared nothing. It was the controlling force of all creation.

The second the Scriptures ended, so did the feeling of electricity in my body, but the presence of the Holy Spirit remained. He spoke again, "You shall travel the world telling the story of the Blessed Virgin." Until a few moments earlier, I did not know the story of the Blessed Virgin. Now I did.

After that day, I received a series of "lessons" about Scripture, which lasted for several months. The Holy Spirit taught me more of what God was saying through the Scriptures, about how He wanted to be followed, about what He had in store for us, and about how very, very much He loves us. But there were difficult words, too—words like "chastisement" and "purification." They must happen. And they will. But the world has been granted a time to prepare and to change. That time is now upon us.

Shortly after my experiences at the grotto, all of my children were baptized, and my family started going to church again. I took up praying the Rosary, which I hadn't once recited as a child. Praying it became a burning desire, for reasons unbeknownst to me, and when I did, I often felt a terrific peace again and received many insights and inspirations.

I started a video production company in the 1980s, called Faith Films, dedicated to the Blessed Virgin and the Lord Jesus Christ. That company—represented by either myself or people I hired to work with me—has been in some twenty foreign countries, telling the story of the Blessed Virgin Mary. We must do now what the Virgin Mary has asked of us in her many apparitions. We cannot ignore her.

A new sense of serenity and love has stayed with me, in larger and smaller degrees, ever since I walked out of the National Shrine Grotto of Lourdes. Even through the toughest of times, the words of the Holy Spirit, "Be not afraid," return and echo peace and safety in my being.

All will ultimately face this "judgment," and some of us will face it twice—once in the flesh and again at the end of our lives. I happened to have a miniature version of my judgment in this lifetime, while I still have time to make changes. But when we face this judgment separated from the flesh, which is fated for all of us, we will no longer have any opportunity to convert.

Why God gave me this great gift of the illumination of my conscience, I am not sure. But it taught me that we are all called to be good examples in this lifetime, and every day is an opportunity to fulfill that calling. Take time to make friends. Say, "Please" and "Thank you." Appreciate the little courtesies and overlook the offenses. Be grateful that God ever permitted you to be at all.

Many have called what I experienced, "The Warning," as reported by the children of the apparitions at Garabandal. I don't know if I would call it that. Perhaps, if one isn't grateful to the Lord, it would be a warning. For me, it was the finest gift from God that I have ever received.[x]

Jesus:

[All those] who will proclaim My great mercy, I shall protect them Myself at the hour of death, as My own glory. And even if the sins of souls are as dark as night, when the sinner turns to My mercy, he gives Me the greatest praise and is the glory of My Passion. When a soul praises My goodness, Satan trembles before it and flees to the very bottom of hell.

~Diary of Saint Maria Faustina Kowalska, #378

RHONDA L'HEUREUX

Never the Same

One night around 3 a.m., Dad woke up my twelve-year-old brother, eleven-year-old sister, and nine-year-old me, and brought us to the kitchen table. "What do you want to do with your life?" he asked. I could tell immediately that he was drunk. Digging nervously for an answer, I remembered how I loved my teachers and animals, so I blurted out, "I want to be a veterinarian or a teacher."

With a rageful stare, he slammed his fist on the table. "That's not good enough! You need to do something better with your life!" I froze, terrified. I wanted to escape, but no one dared to run away from my dad.

Just a few years earlier, I had been Daddy's little girl. He was quiet and funny. I relished his company so much that I followed him ice fishing and froze. It was no matter. I was with Dad. I especially loved praying in church on Sundays in my polished shoes, alongside my father, with his head bowed and eyes closed in sincere communion with God. My parents taught us always to give thanks to the Lord because at that time, we didn't have much in our modest home in our in our small Canadian town, but we were happy.

Mom was Catholic because when her mom (my grandma, "Nan") married my grandpa ("Pa"), Nan's mom (my great grandmother) said that Nan could only marry Pa if she promised that her kids would be baptized and go to Catholic school. So Nan went with Pa every Sunday to Mass to be with her husband and kids, and that's how my mom grew up in the Church. But Nan never became Catholic: "I am United Church of Christ, and I'm going to stay that way." Curiously, she never stepped foot in her own church, and the only religion she ever practiced was Catholicism, but she stubbornly held back.

Dad's mom, on the other hand, was a very devout Catholic who wanted her son to be the same. But when I was five, we stopped going to church.

Each week, my siblings and I would ask my parents if we were going to Mass. "No," the answer always came back. Eventually, we stopped asking. My wholehearted desire to receive my First Communion was crushed. Church was replaced with parties that involved drinking, and more drinking. . .

We didn't know why Dad started to get so angry. He ran downstairs one day and kicked to pieces the wooden Barbie house that Pa had lovingly made for my sister and me. One Saturday morning, Dad whipped my thirteen-year-old brother with a belt for telling him a statue had been broken, even though my brother did not break it, and then struck my mother when she tried to intervene. My brother ran down the street in his underwear, making his escape, while my sister and I cowered in fear behind the bathroom door.

Dad worked as a paramedic and Mom as a nurse, and every day for a couple of months when I was eleven, I cut my hands and forearms with hospital scissors I found in their pockets. Watching my skin bleed gave me an odd sense of relief from my anguish. If my sister caught me in the act and threatened to tell my mom, I don't know if I would have stopped. Around that time, I turned to God with the first deeply personal prayer I had ever said to Him: "Make Dad leave. Make him go so we can all be safe."

By age eleven, I had learned through the grapevine that my father had never been faithful to my mom, who was a loving woman with a heart of gold and a mind in denial. She didn't believe others who told her of his affairs. She didn't allow us to talk about Dad's outbursts with extended family, especially not Nan and Pa, the loving bedrocks of our family. Even when Mom had a black eye, she told us to tell her parents that she'd had an altercation with a cupboard door.

When I was twelve, Dad entered into an affair with my mom's best friend, Wendy, whose daughter was my best friend. Worse yet, they lived just behind our new four-story house in Medicine Hat, Alberta. My prayer would soon be answered. One afternoon when I returned home from school, I saw that my siblings weren't home yet, and I walked into the backyard. My dad was sitting in a lawn chair. Near him sat my mom and my extended family—both sets of grandparents. Sensing an enormous, invisible cloud of pain hovering in the atmosphere, I looked around and realized everyone was crying. Seeing my dad dissolve in tears for the first time overwhelmed my emotions. All of my anger and disappointment disappeared. Suddenly, I was Daddy's little girl again. I walked over to him, sat in his lap, and started crying, wondering what was happening. But I knew I couldn't ask.

My dad's mother knelt in front of him . . . us, with a look of bitter anguish. Wiping away the tears streaming down her cheeks, she said: "You are no son of mine. I don't know where I went wrong with you. I wish you would have died at birth." For her firstborn son to have committed adultery was more than she could bear. My dad said nothing. He just cried. That was the end of their relationship.

At that moment, Wendy leaned over the fence and called out to me, "Hey, Rhonda, you don't need to hear all this. Come on over here to be with me and my daughter." Pa went over to Wendy, took her arms off the fence, and pushed her back angrily. "Get out of here!" he barked. "You're the reason why this is all happening!"

"No, just let Rhonda go," my mom said between sobs. "She doesn't need to hear this." I went next door. I just wanted it all to stop. I had heard enough: a separation had been announced. My dad was leaving.

After that, my sadness turned into anger, which turned into sin. I didn't go around looking for a fight, but if someone got bullied, I stepped in to help the underdog. Once when I saw a girl start picking on a friend of mine, I grabbed her, shoved her face down in a mud puddle in the school playground, and told her she needed to drink from it. When I was thirteen, a girl a grade below me didn't like one of our female gym teachers who was pregnant and grew extremely upset with her. Someone told me that this girl was threatening to punch the gym teacher in the stomach to kill her baby. So I went up to the girl, threw her up against the wall, and told her not to lay one finger on the Phys Ed teacher or there'd be hell to pay. When the teachers found out why the confrontation had happened, they gave me no repercussions. The Phys Ed teacher actually came to me, teary-eyed, and thanked me. But my defense of her just seemed normal to me—anyone would have done it.

In general, I hung out with guys, and if any of them showed interest in me, more than as just a friend, I would punch them. I gravitated towards people with difficult pasts, and together we formed a tightly knit group of friends. One of our group activities was making our own tattoos, using a safety pin that we stuck into the end of an ink pen, heated up, then burned into our skin. I still have an "L" and an "F" on the back of my hand, scars which once read, "LIFE SUCKS." By thirteen, I had taken up smoking, drinking, skipping school and homework, going to parties with my sister and her friends, and trying a few magic mushrooms—all the while lying to my mom about everything.

THE WARNING

The darkest turning point in my life happened that year when my fifteen-year-old sister invited me to a basement jamming party. Surrounded by smoke and the smell of alcohol, I sat down on a couch, feeling shy and quiet, in a dim, unfinished room. Singing teens playing drums and guitar fancied themselves a little band. A boy named Rob, five years my senior, sat down beside me and started to make conversation. An hour passed easily. He slid closer to me. Another hour passed. Then time seemed to stop. I let him kiss me—the first time I'd ever been kissed. I let him because he knew how to talk to my heart. He was gentle, not aggressive in any way. He made me feel something I had never felt before. He made me feel good about myself.

It was 10 p.m. when I suddenly became aware of my surroundings. I had to get home. Rob invited himself along for the ride, hopping in the back seat next to me. I didn't mind. As the band Boston played loudly on the cassette stereo, we kissed the entire ride home.

This started an ongoing sexual relationship for six years. I stayed on the birth control pill and never got any satisfaction physically from our escapades, which grew more frequent when he got his own place. I desired affection, while Rob wanted sex. Fornication fueled Rob's extreme jealousy, which I saw as love; he loved me so much that he didn't want me to talk to other guys. Rob ended up cheating on me repeatedly. He was a lot like my dad.

When I finally broke up with Rob, I embarked on a long–string of casual sexual relationships. After my graduation at nineteen, I started working as a hostess at a restaurant, then at twenty-one, as a bartender at a popular nightclub, where I stayed out far past closing time to have a couple drinks or more. Some nights I'd pick up a guy at the bar and go home with Eric . . . James . . . Sean . . . the names began to blur.

When I was twenty-two, a young man named Travis, whom I had known for years as a friend, invited me home with him one night and tossed some respect my way by letting me choose my response—something I had never experienced before. It threw me right off, causing me to pause and think for the first time. Sex had always been just a given. But I then shrugged off my hesitation and said, "Yeah, sure." That night, while still on the pill, I got pregnant.

Travis worked on an oilfield rig and left to work up north for a month. I was staying at my sister's apartment, where she lived with her boyfriend, when I learned of my pregnancy test results. The idea of an abortion shot through my mind for a brief, chilling moment, but I soon rejected it. I had always wanted to have children, and underneath my debilitating fears, I desired to get my life together for the child I was carrying.

The news of the pregnancy, coupled with my rejection of Travis's marriage proposal, sent him over the edge and onto a path of drinking and drugs. He would phone or come over when he was drunk, but I told him I would only talk to him if he was sober. Then he went away—I didn't know where—and we didn't talk again for another thirteen years.

The day I learned I was pregnant was the day I started to pray. With my whole being, I called out to God, "I can't do this alone, I need your help!" Shortly after that, I noticed I had no fear. Even though I lacked financial stability and a clear future, I felt an overwhelming, gratuitous assurance that everything would be okay.

For years I had never been willing to go to church, been willing to change, and now suddenly, I wanted an intimate relationship with Jesus. This I can only attribute to grace, since it made no sense for me to swing so wildly and quickly into His arms. I felt Him softening my heart, calling me close, and began to chat with Him even more than with my friends. I asked Him to make my kid healthy, adding, "And make him very smart in math because that's my worst subject."

Only one month into the pregnancy, I started to attend RCIA, the Rite of Christian Initiation for Adults program, at our parish. A powerful stirring was growing within me to know what Catholicism really was, what the sacraments meant, what the Church taught and why. The eagerness and yearning for Holy Communion, which was stolen from my childhood, returned. Without hesitation, I entrusted to God my future.

Five months into the pregnancy, I met my husband-to-be, Rick—a tall and handsome Canadian soldier with a strong build and beautiful blue eyes, which I noticed immediately. Within five minutes, I could tell that he was respectful, polite, and funny. He asked me out, oversized belly and all. Rick and I moved in together one month after my son, Devon, was born, and not until Devon was three months old did we become intimate. Still talking to Jesus, I muted my Catholic leanings for fear of losing Rick.

In 1995, Rick was sent overseas for six months to Bosnia during the Bosnian war. When he came home, he wouldn't talk about it, and when I tried to pull information about his time there, he clammed up. Five years later, when he went back again for his second six-month tour of duty to help pull out troops after the war, he came home with a full-blown case of PTSD—post-traumatic stress disorder. Rick was no longer the man I had married.

I finally gleaned from him that on his first tour to Bosnia, he had struggled terribly with seeing the horrors of war, especially mass grave sites with emaciated orphaned children wandering among them, children with no home and no one to care for them. Feelings of extreme helplessness and pain overtook him and gripped his soul. He was a man who could fix things, who could protect people, who could make everything better—yet he had to leave children alone, with dead parents, to starve.

Rick fell precipitously into depression and thoughts of suicide. He had to go on antidepressants, which helped little, and I grew deeply concerned for him. His brother and biological mother had committed suicide; his dad's first wife had shot and killed their baby and then herself; and his dad was an alcoholic up until Rick was in his later teens. I feared to know what "ghosts" were haunting him.

One of the few silver linings that offered Rick brief moments of peace came from our conversions back to the Church. When it came time to help Devon prepare for his First Communion, Rick and I, together with Devon, received our First Communion and the Sacrament of Confirmation. In 2001, six years into our relationship, we finally married in Pa and Nan's backyard. Then two years after our backyard wedding, our union was blessed in the Church.

Rick found solace in the Holy Mass on Sundays, but during the week, life proved a bitter struggle for him. Meanwhile, I began attending adult catechism classes and felt drawn to a life of penance, obedience, and service. Each homily preached by our pastor, Fr. Ray, seemed tailor-made for me, as the Lord reached out through his words, leaving me feeling like the only person in church. Once again, I threw my heart open wide to Jesus, and He filled me with His love. I would need it for what was to come.

One night in 2008, I was kneeling and praying my Rosary beside my bed, as I did every night. Devon was asleep, and Rick was still at work. I started to feel a little lightheaded and sad. Then, without warning, I was suddenly plunged into the stark realization of my own sinfulness.

Overwhelmed with wrenching sorrow and shame, I felt that I was the worst person in the world. I was able to clearly sense deeply within myself all the ways that I had been horrible, from the time I was very little to the present moment. My unworthiness and my nothingness without God, were no longer mental concepts but visceral realities. My heart and soul were being crushed. Strapped into a rollercoaster ride of pain, I was made to experience all the hurt and disappointment that I had caused Our Lord and others through my entire life. And I knew that Jesus was in charge of the ride.

This unbearable agony lasted for four hours, and all that my senses could do to cope was sob constantly and uncontrollably. I didn't see my sins, but I felt them through an internal life review. It began with lying to my parents when I was just three years old, and grew more intense as I approached age eleven. More selfishness . . . more things I did for my own reward and pleasures without regard for others' emotions or wellbeing. Oh, the damage I inflicted in people's lives through my attitude, which was all about me and what I wanted. Adamant in my opinions, there was no changing my mind, and if people thought differently, then they were wrong. Now I was experiencing exactly how they felt.

As the minutes passed, the sins of my life grew more intense and serious: the drinking, the smoking, the sex with Rob, the lying, the manipulations, the belief during my school years that because of my fearsome reputation, I was my own god. People now had to listen to me or deal with me. By creating fear in the hearts of others, I was enjoying a sense of control over them, making sure they felt less empowered than I.

It seared my soul to feel the hardship I caused my mom by piling more pain, grief, stress, and neglect onto her already bruised heart. The nights I didn't come home, the ways I wasn't there for her, my chronic deception—it all fit into an overarching pattern of selfishness. My mom had let me know her standards: she wanted me home by curfew time; Rob had to stay downstairs if he slept over; no big parties at the house; and no sex before marriage. But ultimately, she let me make my own choices, and I betrayed her trust.

Three quarters of the way through this experience, the worst of it came. The depth of my self-gratification intensified. I had repeatedly disrespected and abused the body God had given me by using it for my own pleasures, rather than treating it as a temple of God. The boys and men with whom I'd had sex were using me just as much as I was using them, but I felt the Lord's agony more intensely over the way I had harmed their souls and caused them to fall. It wasn't they, but I, who initiated the sin. I was the one in pursuit for most of my life.

On top of the excruciating harm I'd caused, I sensed all the ways I could have helped people and didn't. At times, I'd even made life harder for the very people whose situations God was calling me to improve. I simply wasn't loving enough, forgiving enough, selfless enough. Souls had been seized in the very grip of Satan because of my actions and my neglect.

I felt nearly paralyzed. Leaning over my bed, I buried my face in my hands, barely able to breathe. I thought I was dying, literally, and my overwhelming feelings of shame made me want death. I had never in my life felt such severe torment in my whole being. It was like seeing your worst nightmare come true before your eyes, and there's nothing you can do to stop or change it. It was like seeing somebody's precious child ripped out of their arms, causing devastation and helplessness all around, and you know it's your fault; yet there's nothing you can do but feel everyone's agony. One painful truth after another played like a horror movie that wouldn't stop, and I was the villain.

For a full hour I believed I was at hell's door. Would I enter? My hands were shaking, and my insides were trembling with fear. Jesus revealed to me that had I stayed on the same path without finding Him, I would have ended up in eternal fire.

Not a drop of my goodness was present. I felt so confused. I didn't understand what was happening or why, but I knew the Lord wanted me to feel the effects of my offenses against His holy will. I had been going to the Sacrament of Reconciliation regularly for a year by this time, and knew all my sins, but I quickly learned that it is one thing for us to confess and quite another to feel the Lord's pain over our wrongs. Plunged into deep remorse, all I wanted to say was, "I'm so sorry." I couldn't apologize enough and begged the Lord repeatedly for His mercy.

As the experience moved into more recent years, I still felt shattered and cried copious tears, but the fear of hell left me. Then as I was guided into the present, the pain lessened, and then finally was gone. When I realized I had been brought back to normal, my heart swelled with a huge sense of relief. I felt like Ebenezer Scrooge after he had been taken against his will on an eye-opening journey by the Ghosts of Christmas Past, Christmas Present, and Christmas Yet to Come. When I returned to this present existence, I was a transformed person, overjoyed to have a second chance at life.

How much time had passed, five minutes or ten hours? Had I left my body or remained? Only when it was all over did I regain any concept of time or place. After four hours of kneeling, my knees weren't a bit sore or stiff, and for the rest of the night, the Lord flooded my body with supernatural warmth and peace, igniting my soul with the fire of the Holy Spirit.

Before the Illumination, I loved our Lord and sought a close relationship with Him. Afterward, I felt as though He resided in my house and walked beside me. I lived and breathed Him in a way I never thought humanly possible.

I would need the Lord with me in this way. That same year, our family entered into the worst of Rick's mental illness. His PTSD symptoms began to flare uncontrollably. He grew rageful and verbally abusive with Devon, in particular. If Devon's shoes weren't placed in the right spot, or his room wasn't cleaned to Rick's specifications, he would yell at Devon and bring him to tears. Rick would try to unleash his anger on me too, but I always stood up for myself and for Devon, who responded with silence.

Through it all and by the grace of God, I was always able to love Rick and stay with him. I believed with everything in me in the Sacrament of Marriage, prayed for Rick every day, and put our lives in God's hands. I was clinging to the hope that when Rick retired from the military, he would get the proper help with good doctors, and I would again have the man I fell in love with. The primary reason, though, why the option of leaving my husband never entered my heart was because I sensed Jesus telling me to stay.

In order that I might have the strength to do this, the Lord gave me an extravagant grace. In addition to the divine intimacy I received after the Illumination of Conscience, the Lord never allowed me to feel the real pain in my surroundings. I don't know if it came because I was going to daily Mass, going to Adoration, praying a daily Rosary and Divine Mercy Chaplet, helping out with RCIA and the parish council, cleaning the church for free—or simply because I needed it. But from the moment I entered the Catholic Church, Jesus lavished upon me an overwhelming sense of His unconditional love and indescribable peace . . . such peace. Not once did He leave me, not once was I ripped away from the comfort of His bosom.

Devon, especially as he grew older, revealed through his behavior that he, too, must have been protected to some degree. He found his voice and began to defend himself, pointing out where Rick was unfair. While he went on to suffer, at times, from migraines, sadness, and anger, he never fell into a depression. He enjoyed his time with friends, became captain of his lacrosse team, and kept his marks up in school. Math, as it turned out, was his best subject.

When Devon was thirteen, Rick was posted to the town of Suffield, a half hour's drive outside of Medicine Hat. In July of 2009, our whole family returned to the area where I'd grown up. We moved in for a time

159

with Nan and Pa, and the joy and excitement of being with family attenuated Rick's depression.

One morning at Nan and Pa's, when my mom had also slept over on the couch, she woke up at 7 a.m. and walked upstairs to see my grandma sitting on the side of her bed, looking disheveled and distraught.

"What's wrong?" my mom asked.

"I don't know," Nan said. "I've been up all night. I haven't slept. All I've been doing is crying. I've seen stuff from my past . . . all the hurt. I don't know what's wrong with me."

"Oh, mom. You need to go wake up Rhonda."

Nan was in such a stupor that she could barely move, so my mom walked downstairs to wake me: "I think Nan just had the same thing you had. She is upstairs crying and has been up all night. She saw things from when she was a little girl."

Suddenly wide awake, I rushed upstairs, sat on the side of Nan's bed, hugged her and asked, "What happened?"

Through a flood of tears, she said, "I don't know. I don't know what's going on. I saw so many things from my whole life throughout the whole night. I don't know what's going on."

"Nan, you had what's called an illumination where Our Lord shows you all your past sins, and now you have a chance to confess them and to be forgiven for any ways you've hurt others, yourself, and the Lord. You've been through a miracle." She slowly calmed down and began listening to me very attentively. "When did it start?" I asked her.

"I went to bed. I was doing my night prayers and saying blessings for our family, when I started to feel sad and to see all these images of when I was little girl—things I did wrong. And it wouldn't stop. All I could do was cry. I couldn't get out of bed, couldn't call out to anybody. Rhonda, it was horrible. It just wouldn't stop."

"You've been awake all night?"

"I haven't slept a wink. I've been crying the entire night."

One month before Nan's illumination of conscience, a Catholic nun from the local parish came to visit my grandparents, and she brought Fr. John with her. Nan started telling Fr. John about how she never converted, and he said to her, "Would you like to receive Communion, Dorothy? You are more Catholic than a lot of Catholics out there. Do you want to convert? At your age, we can do that quickly for you." Surprisingly, my grandma said she would love to, and she received our Lord in Communion for the first time at age eighty-three. My Nan, all five-foot-one of her, was a very strong lady with a stoic temperament, but upon receiving her First Communion, she dissolved into tears.

After Nan's illumination, everyone could tell she was doing a lot of thinking. She was quieter and kinder. She wasn't nearly as agitated and snappy with grandpa as she had been for decades. Within only a couple months, she slid quickly into dementia. The Lord had gifted her with illuminating her conscience while she still had the mind to grasp what was happening. Not even a year later, after suffering from congestive heart failure, she lay in a hospital bed, on morphine, completely unconscious. She was slipping away.

After Nan received the Anointing of the Sick, I held her in my arms and prayed for Jesus to protect her and bring her into heaven. All of a sudden, she woke up, stared right at me and through me. Three seconds later, her eyes looked upwards, focusing intently on somebody or something just above me, and then she closed her eyes and went limp in my arms. The Lord's presence was palpable. When He came to take her, it was the most beautiful moment of my life.

Soon after Nan's funeral, my small family moved out of Nan and Pa's into our own place. After a couple months, Rick came to me and said, "I'm not doing well." He wasn't eating. He wasn't sleeping. He was quieter and stayed in bed or lay on the couch for hours. By Christmas of 2009, he was so far gone that, even though we both had incomes, he thought we'd soon be destitute. He grew paranoid and didn't even want me to spend any money on Christmas presents. Slow and lifeless, he opened his gifts and just stared at them.

On January 8, 2010, Rick took our futon mattress and propped it against the wall. Pulling out his military ID and driver's license, he placed them on the kitchen counter. He unlocked the front door and set a note beside the futon that said, "Call my wife," with my work number on it. Then he phoned 911, told the emergency workers of his plan, gave them our address, and hung up. They couldn't keep him on the line. Then he stood with his back to the futon, took a loaded pistol, and shot himself in the head.

At that same moment, I was in the middle of my busy job as a clerk at a bistro. I stopped in my tracks, looked at my manager, and said, "I have a feeling something is wrong."

"Why?" she asked.

"I don't know. I just have an overwhelming feeling that something is wrong."

"Why don't you take a break and get a cup of coffee," she responded. I finished washing the dishes, grabbed a coffee, and sat down. Not five minutes later, a cop came in the door along with Devon.

"Are you Rhonda L'Heureux?"

"Yes."

"You need to come with me."

I looked at Devon and asked, "What did you do?" thinking he had done something wrong.

"Mom," he said, "I got home from school, and there were four cop cars and two ambulances outside our house."

Tears welled in my eyes, and Devon looked terrified. In our hearts, we both knew. The policeman took us into a little board room at the academy of learning around the corner from the cafe, and said, "You both need to sit down. I have some bad news."

"It's Rick, isn't it," I said.

"Yes."

"He didn't."

"He did."

"He isn't."

"He is."

Rick died just a few months after Nan, and not long after his funeral, the uncanny grace that kept my heart protected in every situation vanished. Whereas before, I couldn't fathom why I didn't feel any hurt, now I couldn't understand why I was feeling every emotion possible. I wish I could have savored that divine gift forever, but became an ordinary human again, just like everybody else.

Today I'm still in Medicine Hat where all my temptations began, and yet my illumination of conscience has sustained me, not just in chastity, but from drinking, gossiping, vanity, pride, materialism—the world around me. Without it, I believe I would have fallen in many ways. One of the greatest gifts it brandished on my soul was a heightened sense of obedience to Our Lord. The experience of feeling the agony that my sins caused Him has stayed with me. The pain of my illumination was a hundred, perhaps a thousand, times more excruciating and life-changing than the suicide of my dear husband.

Now, as soon as I become aware that I have done something wrong or refused to do a good, even if it is a small offense, the pain doesn't just hurt, it is unbearable. I experience more than remorse. I sense Jesus's suffering. It feels as though I have taken a sharp nail and pounded it straight into His hand.

The illumination has also given me a heart of love and forgiveness for everyone, and my eyes have been opened to see the good in people. I am keenly aware of people's feelings and try to be understanding of others. Judging people used to be a habit, but now judgment has left my soul. I truly don't sense it. My heart has also been opened wide with gratitude for every little gift of goodness: the warmth of the sun's rays, the sounds of the birds' chirping—and I don't take anything for granted because all I have is free from the Lord's hand. Life, I have realized, is not so much about what happens in this world as what happens within our souls.

Today I am a single mom with no support system and no friends who share my fervency of faith, but I still have complete trust in God. Some days are a struggle, but those happen when I get caught up in the world and don't pray as much as I should. When I do pray, the spiritual fruits are manifold. Since coming back home, I have seen many conversions happen to family and friends because the Lord has worked through me, helping me to share the right words with them. My mom has since gone back to church and wonders why she ever left. When I asked her that question, she grew teary and apologized, saying she felt horrible denying her children a life in the Catholic Church. But she never really gave me an answer as to why we left. I believe that had we stayed, I would have given my life to the Lord, perhaps even joined a convent; I had such undying love for Our Lord once I entered the Church.

Devon is seventeen now, and our relationship is good. Some days, we share how we miss Rick, not the craziness and the verbal abuse, but the Rick before and underneath his illness, who loved us with all he had. One night recently, while lying on his back in bed, Devon started talking to Rick, telling him how much he missed him, when all of a sudden on his ceiling appeared an image of Our Lady of Guadalupe. Overwhelmed by her loving presence, he broke down and cried, sensing that our Blessed Mother was with him and that everything was going to be okay. "Mom," he told me, "she looked exactly like the picture downstairs above the fireplace." That moment changed him, and after a few years of being away, he too has come back to the Church.

Not long ago, I received an illumination of my soul quite different from the illumination of conscience. Sitting in the front pew of my church, praying close to the Tabernacle, I was immediately consumed, body and soul, by the Lord's beaming heart, as He expressed, one by one, all the ways He was pleased with me. I sat there for an hour, and all I could do was cry. But this time, each tear was filled with joy.

St. Faustina Kowalska:

When I see that the burden is beyond my strength, I do not consider or analyze it or probe into it, but I run like a child to the Heart of Jesus and say only one word to Him: "You can do all things." And then I keep silent, because I know that Jesus Himself will intervene in the matter, and as for me, instead of tormenting myself, I use that time to love Him.

~Diary of Saint Maria Faustina Kowalska, #1033

CHRISTINA GEORGOTAS

Through the Eyes of the Soul

In 1981, my mother gave birth to my older brother, who had to be rushed to a neo-natal center because he was not breathing. The doctors had no explanation for my brother's condition and did not know if he would live. Threatened with the possibility of losing her first-born child, my mom fell to her knees and prayed from her depths to the Blessed Virgin Mary. Although very devout, she didn't have a particular devotion to Our Lady, yet felt deep pleas rising from her soul, begging for Mary's intercession as a Mother.

After a week in intensive care, my brother recovered as mysteriously and suddenly as he had taken ill, and with no apparent explanation. He was released from the hospital on the Feast of the Presentation of the Blessed Virgin Mary. Because of this miraculous incident, my mother consecrated both my brother and me to the service of Our Lady when we were born.

I grew up going to church every Sunday and loved God in my childish ways, but as I got older, I found myself drifting away from that connection. In my teenage years, our three-hour Greek Orthodox service seemed endless, and I often hoped for Sunday traffic on the car ride from New Jersey into New York so we could miss as much of church as possible.

In high school, I had an intelligent and motivational teacher whom I admired. He often challenged us to question the status quo: "Why do we believe the things we do? Do we really believe them, or are we just following what others tell us to believe?" He used this reasoning to challenge our prejudices and stereotypes, but in a subtler way, called us to question all of our beliefs, including religion.

I began to internalize a lot of his rhetoric. It made sense. I was Christian because I was raised that way. If I had been born in another part of the world, I might have been Buddhist or Hindu. People of other religions were convinced that their religion was also correct, so how could Christians claim to have the truth, but not others?

This teacher quoted Karl Marx's famous line, "Religion is the opiate of the masses." I started to believe it. Maybe people just needed a way to cope with death and created a story to ease their fear of the unknown. By the end of the year, not only did I question Christianity, but the concept of God became so abstract for me that it seemed implausible that He could really exist.

Despite my disbelief, I wasn't a negative youth. In school, I was funny and people liked me. Academically I excelled and chose to attend a "Top 25 University" in the "Bible Belt." I'm not sure why, but I chose to go to a pre-school program at the college that was centered on faith. Somewhere inside, I must have longed reconnect with God, even though I wasn't aware of Him. I even took an "Intro to Christianity" class my freshman year and attended a few Bible studies on campus. But with each attempt to rediscover my faith, I felt increasingly distant, disappointed, and discouraged. The more enthusiastic and "over the top" people were about Jesus, the more I mentally rolled my eyes.

I graduated from college a semester early in order to start working as a personal assistant to a celebrity couple in New York—a dream job. I became a neurotic workaholic, and within a couple years, the hard work paid off because I was promoted to an executive level development position at the couple's newly founded production company, where my job was to come up with concepts for new Reality TV shows. The first TV show I pitched in Los Angeles sold to a major network, and I moved into a spacious downtown Manhattan apartment with friends. From a worldly point of view, I had climbed to the top.

On October 12, 2008, I came home for the weekend in order to travel to Boston with my family for my cousin's daughter's baptism. On that day, I was hardly thinking about God, Jesus, Mary, or any religious subject, for that matter. Actually, I was thinking about an off-color Saturday Night Live sketch that my coworkers and I used to play in the office. My mom called me over to the living room to show me a YouTube video she had found online—something about Our Lady appearing to children in Bosnia. I had no idea what she was talking about and hadn't heard of Marian apparitions before.

To humor her, I walked over to look at the screen. In the video, a blonde woman was in a large hall, surrounded by hundreds, maybe

166

thousands of people, and everyone was reciting the Rosary. Completely focused in prayer, the woman began to breathe heavily and clutched her heart. Then she looked up, and the expression on her face was like nothing I had ever seen in my life.

That moment is one that, to this day, I cannot fully describe. When the woman's face beamed with wonder and ecstasy, a very strong and sudden awareness came into me. The first thing I understood immediately was that God exists. I knew this as an undeniable fact. I also knew that Jesus was real and that He was God. At the same time, God revealed to me that what was taking place in the video was real, that this woman was actually seeing and conversing with the Blessed Virgin Mary.

In the same breath, I was given the grace to see myself in absolute

truth—not how I pictured myself, but how I really was. Suddenly, and down to the smallest detail, I saw all the ways I had offended God. Never before or since have I felt so deeply, painfully sorry. I started sobbing. I felt appalled by all the ways I had mocked and denied Him, for the many times I had hurt other people through my actions. Even things I had never thought about, like sarcastic jokes, had aggrieved God because they made light of people's suffering.

Except for my crying, my mom didn't know what was happening to me. I just kept repeating, "This is real, this is real," it took me so by surprise. Until that point, I had always seen myself as a good person. Now I became painfully aware that I was not as upright as I had viewed myself to be. I was much different in God's eyes than in my own. How could I have been that way? I felt so distraught that I could not stop bawling, and

I cried for many weeks after that.

This experience was like a mini-death for me, a taste of what I would face at the end of my life, if I continued to offend God in so many of my thoughts and actions. At that time, I didn't know what had happened to me. It wasn't until years later that I heard of the term, "Illumination of Conscience." I do believe that this is what I experienced on that day, sparked by the video of what I soon learned was the visionary, Mirjana Soldo, seeing an apparition of Our Lady in the holy site of Medjugorje, Bosnia-Herzegovina. Quite fittingly, one of Mirjana's missions, given to her by the Blessed Mother, is to pray for the conversion of nonbelievers.

I watched the video a few more times and continued crying and processing what I'd been shown. All the Christian fanfare I had mocked was now very real to me. I turned to my mom and said, "I want to go there—to Medjugorje." Being that I was twenty-three and this would involve a trip across the world, my mom gave me her classic, "Let's see! Maybe one day," in a tone that meant, "There's no way I would allow you to go to Bosnia on your own."

That night, my mother gave me a book to read about Medjugorje, which she'd had for many years. I had never seen it before: *Queen of the Cosmos*, a short book of interviews with the six visionaries of Medjugorje. I had managed to get through the education system by scanning CliffsNotes and wasn't much of a reader, but I consumed that book, cover to cover, and somehow knew that everything the visionaries were saying in it was true. The next day, as I rode to Boston with my family, my mind was consumed with all of this new information.

When I entered the church in Boston, the beautiful scent of roses wafted by me. But there were no roses in the church. I didn't know that Mary sometimes makes her presence known through the smell of roses. Everything around me looked different than the world I'd known. Suddenly, the icons of saints adorning the church represented real people, not make-believe caricatures. I didn't want to escape. I wanted to stay for every minute of the service.

As we sat in one of the front pews, my cousin came over to me, just as the baptism was about to begin and said, "I don't know why, but I have this strong urge to ask you to be Nina's Godmother." In lieu of the night before, it was an extremely meaningful last-minute request. I sensed Mary reaching out to me directly, and as my goddaughter received the waters of baptism in the name of the Father, the Son, and the Holy Spirit, I felt as if I was renewing my own.

The next couple of months, however, were very difficult. I was a totally different person inside, while everyone and everything in my environment were exactly as before. I didn't want to tell my friends about what had happened to me, and I wasn't sure what I would say, if asked. Surely, they would think I had lost my mind. For many weeks, I slipped into my room to be alone, to cry, and to pray.

Once back in New York, I became acutely aware of the presence of evil. Just as suddenly as I had understood that God existed, I was made aware that Satan existed, as well. Now I started to see his mark all around me. It seemed as if everything in New York City had been created as a distraction to keep us from seeing God. People were bombarded with a million different messages, advertisements, superficialities, pop culture icons, movies, bars, strip clubs, satanic images, obsessions, fears, lusts, jobs, money. . . Satan was trying to lure and distract humanity in so many ways, and people were oblivious to his tactics—slaves to this fake world around them.

I got the distinct feeling that this world we have created around us is not real. I sat on the subway and listened to so many meaningless conversations, so much talk and focus on trivial, unimportant things, so much gossip, so much negativity. I, too, was guilty of all of these things, but now I felt remorse for it. I also felt very sorry for these people. I walked around Manhattan overcome with tears.

Every week, my friends and I would watch a vampire show called "True Blood" on HBO. Before, I'd never thought anything of it, but now I became so disturbed that I had to turn my eyes away and stare at the ground to avoid the images on the screen. In just the opening credits, there were so many blatant and subliminal attacks on religion, so much darkness. It was satanic. I couldn't believe I had never seen this before. The direct attacks on Christianity in advertisements and on mainstream TV were manifold. I would call my mom, overwhelmed: "What am I supposed to do with all this information?"

I was drawn to the Bible and began to read it with interest for the first time, starting with the New Testament. I was captivated by Blessed Mother Teresa—now Saint Mother Teresa of Calcutta, and her writings. I devoured everything I could find about Medjugorje. Fueled by a strong desire within me to do charitable works, I signed up for an organization called NY Cares, which allowed me to volunteer at soup kitchens with the elderly and the homeless, almost any day of the week. Some days, I would wake up at five in the morning to volunteer before work.

I didn't want to speak badly about anyone ever again. I didn't want to be part of the superficial world of TV production anymore. I didn't want to go out to dinners with my friends and make meaningless conversation. I wanted to be totally focused on God every minute of the day, and I found myself thinking about Him and Our Lady from sun up to sun down.

After some months, I began to struggle through different trials. Strong temptations assailed me, and I felt Satan battling for my soul. He let me know that he was not at all happy about my coming to know and love God, and he wanted to win me back. Over the course of the next year and a half, I never stopped believing in God, but I experienced many enticements to pull away from Him.

On June 24, the anniversary of the first day Our Lady appeared in Medjugorje, I woke up to the sound of my phone ringing. I answered with a groggy, "Hello?" My beloved father had died. Quickly and without warning, he passed away from a heart attack. He was retired and had been away visiting his sister in Greece for a few weeks when it happened. The date on which he died and the place in which he died turned out to be no coincidence.

Some months after my dad's death, my mom was online and found the speaking schedule of one of the Medjugorje seers named Ivan Dragicevic. He was going to have an apparition and give a talk at a small chapel on the campus of MIT. The two of us drove there early, and to our surprise, arrived at the chapel before anyone else. A priest kindly invited us to sit up front. When Ivan entered, he walked forward and knelt next to us.

I could hardly believe I was right next to Ivan and would soon be inches away from the Blessed Mother. I felt as though I had been transported to the other side of the screen of the video that changed my life. When Ivan lifted his head and began to converse with the air slightly above and in front of him, I froze, overwhelmed with emotion. I didn't move the entire time. When Ivan came out of apparition after a few minutes, he went back to his seat and passed sets of Rosary beads to me— one for myself, and one for my mother. Being Greek Orthodox, I had never prayed the Rosary on my own before.

At the end of the night, a woman named Carol who booked Ivan's speaking schedule in Boston, came over to us and mentioned that she ran pilgrimages to Medjugorje. Her next group would be going during the anniversary of the first apparition, and she asked if we would like to join. I wanted to go! My mom explained that we would be in Greece on that date for memorial service of my father, but she took Carol's card in the event we could go another time.

The next day, my dad's sister called from Greece and asked if we could move the memorial service back a week. Suddenly, June 24 opened, and my mom called Carol to coordinate a stopover in Medjugorje with her group on our way to Greece.

That pilgrimage to Medjugorje was only three days long, but it had a profound impact on me. Many miracles took place when I was there, but the greatest one of all took place in my soul. I went to Confession for the first time in my life and felt such peace! I came home with a new strength, and I began to live Our Lady's messages of prayer, Confession, reading the Bible, going to church, and fasting on Wednesdays and Fridays. I also started praying the Rosary. Now I was armed with the most powerful weapons against Satan.

Only two months later, I returned to Medjugorje, this time alone and with my mother's support, in order to discern what God wanted me to do with my life. During this trip, I got the overwhelming desire to tell everyone in my life about Medjugorje and to share Our Lady's messages. I began to feel a specific call to make a documentary in order to introduce Medjugorje to nonbelievers and to people who had never heard of it. I believed that if I could be changed, so could others who were struggling with faith.

I knew it would be necessary to leave my job in order to pursue what God wanted of me, so when I returned to Manhattan, I put in my notice to be out by Christmas. I began telling my friends and family about Medjugorje, but I had a very difficult time describing it to people, especially secular, non-Catholic friends unfamiliar with Fatima or Lourdes. Nothing I said ever properly conveyed what was happening there, and I found myself directing them to the YouTube clip that I had seen, thinking naïvely that it would have the same impact on them as it did on me.

On Christmas Eve, I packed up my desk and moved back home to New Jersey. By New Year's Eve, I had come down with a bad flu. As I sat at home on the couch with cough medicine and Dick Clark, my mind began to spin: "Did I just make a huge mistake by leaving my job? How am I going to support myself? How will I be able to interview the visionaries? I don't know the visionaries! I don't know how to film anything. I don't even know how to edit video. How the heck am I going to make a documentary?"

Thankfully, Our Lady made her presence known to me every step of the way. Doors opened during the filming that should have been sealed shut. Although there were many difficulties in the making of it, in just over a year's time, I had a completed project. Two days after consecrating myself to Our Lady on August 15, 2011, I had my finished DVD in hand, called "Queen of Peace."

Since its release, I have received messages across the country from people who have watched the film. Family members and friends who were once skeptical, believed and were brought to tears. Some decided to go to Medjugorje—even entire families have decided to travel there together. The feedback of viewers has brought me great joy. I feel blessed beyond words. (See www.medjfilms.com)[xi]

It is my ongoing prayer that "Queen of Peace" be used as a tool in the hands of some of the millions who have been to Medjugorje and wish to share Our Lady's messages with those in their lives who have never heard of Medjugorje, or with people who are struggling with their faith, or with their parishes and prayer groups.

Through Medjugorje, Our Lady is giving us all the tools we need to walk the difficult path of holiness and leave the path of the world. Without her intercession, I don't know if I ever would have turned and traveled down the right road. I am forever grateful to Our Lady for bringing me back to her Son, and I pray that my life and my film are signposts that continue to point people toward their eternal home.

They say a picture is worth a thousand words, but I can tell you from experience: one simple video can be worth a million.

Jesus:

When you reflect upon what I tell you in the depths of your heart, you profit more than if you had read many books. Oh, if souls would only want to listen to My voice when I am speaking in the depths of their hearts, they would reach the peak of holiness in a short time.

~Diary of Saint Maria Faustina Kowalska, #584

CARTER SMITH

A Passion Play

In grade school, I watched a couple of movies about Christians martyred by lions, and I have wanted to give my life to God in an all-consuming act of love ever since. From age seven to nine, I would lose the day's hours reenacting the Passion in my backyard sandbox. With the crosses of the two thieves, stuck side by side into the top of a mound, I'd march my tiny Jesus with his cross of twigs on his back through the Via Dolorosa, traced by my fingers in the sand. Then I would mount Jesus on his cross and imagine myself there with Him. The crucifixion fascinated me, and as I grew up and learned of the stigmata—the wounds of Christ appearing on the hands and feet of saints—I greatly desired to undergo that, too.

In my teen years, I attended Mass and prayed often to Our Lord and the Blessed Mother, but my shy, insecure nature blossomed into anxiety, neurotic fears, and a crushing lack of confidence. Adding to my confusion, a latent homosexual orientation began to surface, and I experienced conflict and guilt around feelings of same sex attraction. In my junior and senior years of high school, my guilt wasn't strong enough, however, to prevent me from initiating sexual activity with other boys who were unsure of their own sexuality and experimenting. Sometimes I felt badly after an encounter, and sometimes I didn't. Yet for some reason, I always felt guilty after sex with myself, which conflicted with my faltering Catholic beliefs.

In my sophomore year at the University of San Francisco (USF) in 1969, my friends lived in a commune in the Haight Ashbury district, where I was introduced to the countercultural hippie movement and its mind-altering bedfellows. When I first dropped acid in a park with my friends, they were amazed at how natural I acted on the drug. In an unhealthy way, it seemed to suit me. But when I wasn't on a "trip," I was anxious and worried about every little thing. During my time in college, I got high on mescaline, opium, hashish, and a steady intake of marijuana—and I dropped not just acid, but also the Holy Mass, and out of college after my second year.

I just didn't know what I wanted to do with my life. I was seeking something much deeper and not finding it. My parents wanted me to go to junior college, so I enrolled for the fall semester at age nineteen, and then promptly dropped out of that, too. When my folks found out, my mother, always flamboyant with her emotions, became outright hysterical. Beside herself with disbelief, she began screaming at full lung capacity. Then she frantically walked into the kitchen and got a carving knife, started waving it around, and charged at me with it, chasing me around the dining room table. My father stood nearby, watching the mayhem and didn't try to stop her. I darted toward the front of the house, with my father following, trying to grab me. As I lunged toward the front door, he gripped my shoulder, but I wrestled myself free and made it out the door, while my mother plunged the knife at me, just missing my shoulder.

I walked into the bitterly cold night in my pajamas. Flashlight beams flickered through nearby trees in the park next to our home, and I knew my parents were looking for me, but I stayed hidden. That night, I slept fitfully on the park grounds, a half-block away from my house. When I came home the next morning, things had settled into a loud silence.

I continued living at home, careful to keep quietly to myself so as not to ruffle any parental feathers. After a couple of bad drug trips, I decided to stop taking mind-altering substances. Although I wasn't going to school or working, to the displeasure of my parents, they recognized that I had stepped away from drugs and back into church, so they loosened their reins.

During this time, I started to accept myself as I was, especially concerning my sexual orientation, but I had no sexual activity with others. With free time on my hands, I dove into the mystical roots of Christianity, and in particular, St. Teresa of Avila and St. John of the Cross. One day, while praying alone at the Cristo Rey monastery in San Francisco, I met a man named Joseph Lancaster, a third order Carmelite. We decided to meet on occasion to discuss Christian mysticism, particularly within Carmelite spirituality, which piqued my interest even further.

Around this time, music also began informing my soul, and I would listen, repeatedly, to an inspiring recording of a Renaissance Mass. For me, it represented a soul travelling through spiritual stages of development into the heights of heaven. During those months at home, I began to notice a holy and sacred presence living within me—and loving me. It wasn't long before I entertained thoughts about the monastic life, and at age twenty-one, decided to enter a Trappist monastery in Vina, California. There, I began living an austere life of poverty and prayer.

My third week living with the Trappists, on the feast of the Sacred Heart, I felt a desire to walk out in the fields after Compline prayers. At twilight, I covered almost a mile on foot. The colors of the landscape, paint-brushed by God with the fading light of the sun, looked stunningly beautiful, and as I turned to walk back, the next thing I knew, Our Lord was on my right side. I saw Him as the crucified Jesus, wearing the crown of thorns and a loincloth, walking slightly in front and to the right of me.

It wasn't imagined, nor was it an apparition. It was an intellectual vision, as described by St. Teresa of Avila. At the same time, I saw the twelve apostles and Our Blessed Mother walking before us, about twenty feet ahead, leading the way toward the monastery. This gave me a comforting feeling of family, all walking home together.

My first thought was, "Jesus is closer to me than I am to myself." In the moment He appeared, I sensed a pure, divine, warm, and all-consuming love rush over me. The feeling was intoxicating, and His love was beyond expression. When I turned my head toward Him, I could see, in tragic detail, every wound on His body. "My gosh!" I gasped. "Did I cause all these wounds on You?" Awestruck, I thought, "What am I going to say to Him? He's right here!"

The Lord's head bowed slightly, as He gazed forward. I saw everything: His eyes, His broken body, His blood dripping down His light brown skin. His wounds from the crown, the scourging, and the nails looked so fresh! It seemed as though He had just come down from the Cross to walk with me.

I turned toward Jesus and began to sob, pouring out to Him my heart's innermost desires. "Jesus," I cried, "I want to be a great saint. I want to reach the spiritual heights, like your great followers have, but I don't want any of the ecstasies, or the visions, or extraordinary experiences." Humbled by His presence, I felt unworthy to even ask to reach so high, so I added, "Let me go through the dark night, the dark trials, and carry heavy crosses. That is the way I want to attain the heights. I want to soar like an eagle in the heavens, to be a saint in Your eyes only, and be small and unknown in the world."

After I spoke, truly meaning all that I said, Jesus responded to me, not with words, but through an imprint on my soul. He turned His head toward me, looked into my eyes and said, "Yes."

"My gosh," I gasped, "You're going to grant this." Then I saw a lance of His fiery love plunge into my heart, and I fell into a swoon, an ecstasy of love that filled my whole being and took away my breath.

Then He wasn't there anymore. I was left by myself, trying to regain my balance. Yet a fierce love for Him remained, burning in the center of my chest. Within a short while, it turned into an actual physical pain, which lasted for two or three weeks and brought me great joy.

My novice master expressed his support of my experience and confirmed that I had received a very special grace from God. I entered the Trappists and stayed at the monastery a good six or seven months, but ultimately the superiors felt I was too young and naive to make a commitment to their way of life. "Go out into the world," they said, "gain experience, and then decide whether or not you have a vocation." They suggested I join the service, and I chose the Navy, because I liked the ocean.

I became a hospital corpsman and received training to become a nurse. Despite my mystical encounter with the wounded Lord, the extreme hardship of boot camp broke my spirit, and the worldly aspects of life in the Navy dulled my conscience. I fell from grace. Hard. Succumbing to sexual temptations with myself, I started to feel guilty going to Mass on Sunday. It didn't seem right to me to be a Sunday Catholic while continuing to sin. Slowly but steadily, as my soul wrestled with compromise and conflict, my desire to go forward in the Christian life waned.

I struggled to stay in the Navy for over a year and a half and then received an honorable discharge. Glad to be out, I drove to my family home in San Carlos, California, sat down with my parents, and told them I was gay—pointblank, no commentary. They surprised me by making me feel comfortable and causing no backlash. They knew all along.

Wanting to continue my education, I moved to San Francisco, where I went to nursing school for a year in an area close to a gay neighborhood. Loneliness and longing for companionship began to press on my heart, so I decided to look for a one-on-one lover. The gay scene never attracted me, though. I found it to be a superficial and shallow world of wayward philosophies, multiple lovers, physical beauty, showy parades, and crazy partying, which conflicted with my spirituality. So I danced around its outskirts. I never initiated any sexual activity. Others did. And I was very passive.

"These are my weaknesses," I figured, "and they don't bother me much." I didn't feel bad at all about my sexual encounters. In fact, they felt very natural and guiltless. But I also thought that one should try to follow Christian values and the commandments, if one attended church— so not wanting to compromise or go half way, I removed myself completely from the Mass. When inner conflict arose in my heart, I would visit the Blessed Sacrament, alone, in silence.

In my late twenties, I got a job as a nurse at the Veterans Administration hospital, and while working there, an ad in a gay newspaper caught my eye. The man wanted to meet someone who was worthy, a good person. At least, that's how I read it. A couple weeks later, after I met the man, I glanced again at the ad and noticed it didn't say, "worthy," but "wealthy." I would never have answered it had I known.

Thus began a long-term, one-on-one relationship with a man from India. Actually, the relationship was one on one, plus a whole family. He was married with a wife and two children: a baby boy and toddler daughter. The marriage was ruined before I walked in because neither person had had any say in the arrangement. The wife knew of my relationship with her husband and was very accepting of me. I became one of the family—a friend to the wife, and an uncle to the children. At one point, when my lover's sister, her husband, and a couple of family friends visited from India, they too openly embraced me. Yet I always thought, "One day, I'm going to leave this man for God."

After five years of being together, my partner went back to his home country with his family, and I returned to San Francisco with a broken heart. I resumed nursing work and passed several months in pining and loneliness—my Achilles' heel. Unable to keep it sealed, my heel ripped wide open for the next seventeen years in an on again, off again, dance of extremes.

My next lover was Japanese, and my spiritual leanings had become more Eastern than Western through my Indian immersion. But after three years together, I broke off the relationship because I felt my soul losing itself in Eastern encounters with "nothingness," while sensing God prompting me to make some significant changes. Knowing the Catholic Church to be rich and fulfilling, I turned back to my roots and started going to Mass, Confession, and spiritual direction with a couple of Jesuit priests.

Change didn't come easy. As I reached for my spiritual roots, my drama with men catapulted to Shakespearean heights, and my soul became glaringly divided. Unwilling to stop looking for love in the world, I succumbed to occasional liaisons with my visiting Indian friend, and answered a personal ad for a committed relationship. This led to my involvement with a doctor who came from a well-known cotton plantation family in the Deep South. After two or three years of exclusivity with him, he wanted to have a threesome with another man. "No thank you and Good-bye!" I huffed.

Now forty-eight, I moved to live near the ocean in San Francisco and met another doctor—this time, a very wealthy Jewish one from Marin, who was in a loveless marriage. We stayed together for eight months. Toward the end of our relationship, an old Jesuit priest at St. Ignatius Church in San Francisco said to me in Confession, "If you continue this, you will both go to hell." Somehow, I knew what he was telling me was true, and I accepted his words immediately; but before he said it, I had never thought once of the eternal price of my sins.

God was calling me to Him alone, and I knew it. After looking into different monastic orders, I finally entered an Eastern Rite monastery in Redwood Valley, California. In that setting of structured daily prayer and contemplation, the fire in my heart for Jesus rekindled and burned so brightly in the center of my chest that my holy desire of old was renewed.

The liturgies of the Catholic Byzantine Rite helped me to live deeply in the Lord, especially during Holy Week. After a Seder meal on Holy Thursday, not unlike the one the Jewish people celebrated, the monks followed a strict fast of no food, not even water, until the evening of Good Friday. On the day of the Lord's death, all the lights went out, and a shroud was laid over a burial tomb in front of the altar. The warmth and closeness of Jesus's last supper had cooled into the stark emptiness of His crucifixion—but would reemerge for me in a spectacular fashion on the day of Christ's Resurrection.

When I entered the church for midnight Mass on Easter Sunday morning, amidst hundreds of lit candles, ringing Easter bells, and twirled chandeliers, I was transported into the infinite majesty of God. Everywhere I looked, it seemed as though I was seeing eternity. The uncreated, inexpressible light of God was shining through everything— formless and limitless, timeless and eternal. People were singing, "Christ is Risen," and I was speechless, trembling. As I stood in the sanctuary next to the monks' choir chairs, facing the altar, I felt suspended in a state beyond time and space.

Then Jesus made Himself manifest within me. His heart seemed to beat in rhythm with mine to the pulse of an exquisite peace. Then through Jesus, I experienced God the Father inwardly, yet also as a separate Person. Melting into union with Him, I knew without a shred of doubt that all of creation was in His hands.

When the monks began to chant the Easter gospels in multiple languages, I felt the Holy Spirit, the third person of the Trinity, rushing out to cover everyone in the church, and then from there, the whole world. Then I felt Him rushing back to the altar, drawing all things back to Jesus. He was like a sacred wind, an incomprehensible mystery. The words "Holy Spirit" do not do justice to Who He Is.

This mystical experience lasted from midnight until the very last blessing of the Easter liturgy at 4 a.m. And when it ended, I felt like I had been reborn. God had dressed me with new robes, and I never wanted them taken away. Nowhere else had I ever experienced God so intimately. The Byzantine monastery became my new home, and I planned to live and die there.

But the devil doesn't sleep. After one and a half years of living as a monk and finding great peace and satisfaction in the mystical nature of liturgy of the Catholic Eastern Byzantine Rite, the monastery disbanded.[86]

Disillusioned and profoundly wounded by the experience, I relapsed into an affair, knowing full well that I was offending God, but I couldn't seem to help myself. At age fifty-three, I joined a flailing monastic community on the east coast, which turned out to be run by an off-kilter monk. Disappointed yet again, I returned to San Francisco and fell into the temptation of sex with myself, followed by three visits to my Jewish former partner, in an attempt to ease my crushing loneliness.

The following year, I thought, "What am I doing? I need a spiritual director." I started to see a spiritual director who affirmed my great love for Jesus. She helped me see that I had sinned for so long in the area of my sexuality that I had opened myself to temptations, which would likely be a battle for the rest of my life. But with a firm desire to please God and with the ongoing grace of the Eucharist and Confession, I could be strong.

I wondered if my sin of masturbation was cutting my soul off from God because I knew of the three conditions in which a sin was mortal: full participation of the will—I was not coerced; knowledge of my sin—I knew; and grave matter—masturbation had certainly opened my soul to

---

[86] The monastery is called Holy Transfiguration Monastery, and it has since been "resurrected."

deep loneliness and paved the way to my seeking sinful pleasure with others. Looking up what the Catechism of the Catholic Church said about it, I read:

By masturbation is to be understood the deliberate stimulation of the genital organs in order to derive sexual pleasure. "Both the Magisterium of the Church, in the course of a constant tradition, and the moral sense of the faithful have been in no doubt and have firmly maintained that masturbation is an intrinsically and gravely disordered action. To form an equitable judgment about the subjects' moral responsibility and to guide pastoral action, one must take into account the affective immaturity, force of acquired habit, conditions of anxiety, or other psychological or social factors that lessen or even extenuate moral culpability." (CCC #2352)

I was guilty. How guilty exactly, only God knew. At least, I thought only God could know. Never could I have imagined that soon I, too, would know the extent of my guilt. I put the Catholic Catechism back on my shelf and went to St. Patrick's Church in San Francisco. Arriving early, around 10:00 a.m., for a Mass that started at 12:10 p.m. and was preceded by confessions, I began my normal routine of a thorough examination of conscience. Around 11 a.m., as people began to cue up for the Sacrament of Reconciliation, I stepped behind the first person in line and got down on my knees to pray as a penance for my sins, which were weighing heavily on my heart.

I looked inward and suddenly, within a split second, I could see God inside myself. I met Him in the divine spark of my being. While still retaining all my senses and acutely aware of all that was happening, I also saw my own soul. It appeared to me as a pure white light, infused and intermingled with the light of God. My true nature within God was revealed: I was closer to God than to my own inner self.

Then I saw all those places where I had embraced what was wrong and how this had separated me from the Lord. There they were before me, my mortal sins: pitch-black, circular blotches casting an ugly darkness over my soul and causing a complete severing from my true nature. Consent to lustful thoughts ("adultery with the heart"—Matthew 5:28) and masturbating had completely blocked out the divine light of God within me! My venial sins also appeared as multiple grey spots, letting through only the partial light of God. In choosing darkness, disguised on earth as light, I had given myself over to the evil of the world. So many times, I

181

had stepped into the realm of the deceiver, the Prince of Darkness, into a delusional reality of who I was. When I did this, I was not fully in control of myself. Satan was.

I received a profound awareness that even one mortal sin causes us to be completely blocked off from the light of God. We start living in death. We are alive, but dead, and don't know it. When God reveals our souls to us in this life during a collective Illumination of Conscience, which I believe will happen, or surely after death in our particular judgment, those of us in mortal sin will know of its effects through every fiber of our being. This is so. It is inescapable. The truth and the reality of it all will be pushed before our eyes, and we will have no choice but to see.

In His mercy, God gave me the exact knowledge of what each blotch on my soul meant, and because I felt true contrition for my sins, my entire soul hadn't blackened, like hard coal. Lighter or darker, greater or smaller, the blotches represented a tendency within me, a collection of a certain type of sin. Consent to lustful thoughts and sex with myself had caused the larger, darker circles. The scattered grey circles revealed my lying (even white lies), overindulgence of food (not even to the extent of gluttony) and drinking of alcohol (not even to the point of getting drunk), uncharitable thoughts, judgment of others, and gossip.

There were also my sins of omission: God had given me great graces, and many times over, I had rejected them. He had inspired me to pray or do a good work, and I did my own thing instead. All my little sins, all my little moments of selfishness throughout the day, which seemed so minor and to which I gave little consequence, were there in the light of truth, and I had no way of hiding from them.

God not only gave me direct knowledge of the state of my soul, but presented me with a choice. I could continue on my journey of conversion or not. I could choose to follow God or follow Satan. By making me more aware than ever of the consequences of my thoughts and actions, and by showing me the pitch-black invasion inside of me, God was inviting me to deeply repent—especially of my mortal sins. Those were the dangerous ones.

In that mystical encounter, I said emphatically, "I choose you, Lord." Twenty minutes had passed while I was on my knees in the confession line, staring into my own soul. Others must have walked around me, wondering why I hadn't moved. I stood up and walked into the small Reconciliation room, shared the sins revealed to me, and added, "May all the sins I have forgotten, all the sins of my life, be forgiven."

The priest made the sign of the cross and spoke the heavenly words of absolution: "I absolve you from your sins, in the name of the Father, and of the Son, and of the Holy Spirit. Amen." Shaken and grateful, I walked back to a church pew and knelt to pray. Again, God illumined my soul, but this time it shone spotless and pure white, without a trace of sin. It was my true self immersed in God, the living Spirit within me. I was seeing the greatest reality there is of the human person.

The illumination helped me to feel a great repugnance toward my own sin and plunged me into a personal purgatory—a deep and brutally painful purification, beyond my normal sense of contrition—which subsided only gradually over time. The special gifts the Lord had bestowed upon me, especially during my time in monasteries, had placed upon me a greater calling and responsibility of faithfulness to Him. Yet I had traveled in between desire for the things of the world and desire for Him. My falling back, time and again, had broken Jesus's heart and gouged His wounds.

A week or two later, I fell into sexual temptation again, and the following morning as well. With two mortal sins on my soul, I could sense a complete distancing from God. Sick inside, I felt His life and grace leave me. That day, I went to Confession, and after absolution, God bathed and cleaned my disfigured soul with His pure, unblemished light, leaving me renewed and at peace.

While at home in my room that afternoon, I received another profound illumination. This time, God gave me a focused look into my past and infused me with greater knowledge of the ugliness of sexual sin. I had considered myself a real Casanova. I had felt completely comfortable with what I was doing. But God showed me how corrupt and rotten I actually was. Not only did I see the effects of my sin within myself, but also the scandal and sin I brought to my fellow human beings made in God's image. Had I died during my long period of habitual sexual sin, I would have fallen into the fires of hell and burned in eternal torment, raging at the very One for Whom I had pledged to become a great saint.

For me, the worst of this revelation was learning that had I continued along my wayward path, I would have become a complete sexual deviant, an apple rotten to the core, with little other desire than to please myself at others' expense. The fact of how easily this could have been me was mortifying. I had been born into this world to bring God's light, but would have become like walking scum, an ugly being of degradation, headed for everlasting shame.

Sorrow, pain, and remorse, even more penetrating than before, seized my heart, calling me to an even more profound choice. I simply could not continue falling anymore, due to masturbation and impure thoughts. I decided, that day, with every ounce of my will, to stop. Never until that moment, did I become so committed to my Lord and so horrified to fall and cut myself off from Life, because Life is God. There is no real life at all outside of Him!

In 2014, I retired from working as a nurse for many years, and I now live in a low-income retirement apartment complex in Ukiah, California. Here, I spend my solitary days, like a monk, much removed from the world. Every two-to-four weeks, I go to Confession. And every day, I pray the Rosary and the Chaplet of Divine Mercy, attend Mass, read the Bible, say morning prayers when I rise, and evening prayers before I retire at night.

My sole desire is to suffer for Jesus in order to help Him rescue souls. I know this is hard for anyone to understand because it flies in the face of human reason. Why would anyone want to suffer? Perhaps I can explain. *"The message of the cross is foolishness to those who are perishing, but to us who are being saved it is the power of God"* (1 Corinthians 1:18). Jesus showed us the perfect path. He said, "Take up your cross and follow me," and it is through His excruciating, unbearable suffering and death that we are saved.

We are called to be like Jesus, and when we choose to join in the Lord's suffering, we help Him save souls. This is why suffering, offered up in love, is never in vain. It explains why there are victim souls in the world, why people receive the stigmata, the wounds of Christ in their own body. St. Paul, who accepted his own unrelieved suffering, spoke of this reality: *"I want to know Christ and the power of His resurrection and the fellowship of sharing in His sufferings, becoming like Him in his death"* (Philippians 3:10); and *"Now I rejoice in my sufferings for your sake, and in my flesh I am filling up what is lacking in the afflictions of Christ on behalf of his body, which is the church"* (Colossians 1:24).

The Diary of Saint Faustina Kowalska, the Saint of Divine Mercy, gives even more clarity to redemptive suffering. In it, Jesus says: *"There is but one price at which souls are bought, and that is suffering united to My suffering on the cross. Pure love understands these words; carnal love will never understand them"* (Diary #324) . . . *"Every conversion of a sinful soul demands sacrifice"* (Diary #961) . . . *"I have need of your sufferings to rescue souls"* (Diary #1612) . . . *"Suffering is a great grace; through suffering the soul becomes like the Savior; in suffering love becomes crystallized; the greater the suffering, the purer the love"* (Diary #57).

Nowadays, I want to be a living sacrifice. May nothing be left of me, but love. When I leave this life, I long to approach my Lord's throne in purity and whiteness, to be that sparkling soul He showed me I truly was.

"I love you, Jesus! I love you! Let me be a living holocaust for You!" is the constant cry of my heart. The deepest, most sincere desire of my heart, ignored for so many years, is now coming true. The "Yes" that Jesus gave me at the Trappist monastery long ago, when He appeared at my right side, and I told Him I wanted to carry heavy crosses, has come to be. I have felt the crushing weight of His cross for many years now, as my soul has been submerged in darkness, every moment of every day.

This bitter void is not depression, but the cross I choose to bear. I am not hopeless. I eat well, sleep well, and my mind is alert. I have suffered from moments of depression in the past, and while the loneliness I feel is normal, the experience of the absence of God that I feel is entirely unique. In these long years of darkness, God has taken control and is leading me along an obscure path of redemptive suffering by the difficulties that I go through in everyday, ordinary life—spiritual, physical, financial, social, and familial. Through a relentless stripping away of my life into the emptiness and nothingness of living in the world, I am completely bereft of any felt sense of spiritual consolation or closeness to God. It is very painful at times, indeed! God has taken away everything that I most cherish and hold dear to my heart, on all levels of my being. I am now in a place which is the opposite of home.

I wish to gather lost souls into my arms, like flowers from a vast meadow, and present them to Jesus in a magnificent bouquet. So I live in this void, in this dark night, in order that others in danger of losing their souls may someday live in the fullness of light. If it pleases the Lord, I will suffer this for an eternity, just to know that I gave Him everything and kept nothing for myself. My constant prayer is to be consumed like a holocaust offering, to take on His wounds, His agony, His abandonment, and be mounted in union with Him on the Cross. And when it comes my turn to die, I pray that I can shed my blood for Jesus in an ultimate act of love, just as I desired to do as a small child, playing in my sandbox, in the backyard.

St. Faustina Kowalska:

"O my God, how sweet it is to suffer for You, suffer in the most secret recesses of the heart, in the greatest hiddenness, to burn like a sacrifice noticed by no one, pure as crystal, with no consolation or compassion. My spirit burns in active love. I waste no time in dreaming. I take every moment singly as it comes, for this is within my power. The past does not belong to me; the future is not mine; with all my soul I try to make use of the present moment.

~Diary of Saint Maria Faustina Kowalska, #351

MARINO RESTREPO

A Saint Paul for Our Century

I was born in a small Colombian town called Anserma, high in the Andes mountains. Both my fraternal and maternal grandfathers were powerful patriarchs who owned large coffee plantations, so my immediate and extended family members are coffee growers. My parents had ten children, eight of whom are living, and I am number six; my two older brothers died very young. My uncles and aunts were even more prolific with fifteen to twenty children each, which gave me ninety-two immediate cousins. Our family is more like a tribe, and our Catholic faith extends back in time many generations, so I never had to search for God or for a friend.

When I was fourteen, I was sent to Bogotá, the capital of Colombia, to finish my high school education. It was the 1960s, and a lot of my friends were walking away from the Catholic faith. So did I. It was easy to leave, and there was no one telling us to do otherwise. At sixteen, I fell in with a group of young American hippies visiting Colombia for three months. One of them was a blue-eyed American girl named Donna, who introduced me to marijuana, to "liberation" from the "establishment," and to everything she knew about sex—and I stopped believing in God.

From marijuana, I quickly graduated to LSD, mescaline, PCP, and mushrooms, and then to dealing all of them. I also dove headfirst into eastern paganism, gurus, tarot cards, metaphysics, occultism, magic, divination—all of the spiritually poisonous currents that eventually came to be known in the 1970s as the New Age movement.

In the course of four years, I had affairs with innumerable "Donnas," who were visiting from all over the United States, and with a similar number of "Marias" from my own country. In the late 1960s, I ended up staying together with a Colombian girl for a full year without having other relationships, something abnormal for my new lifestyle. She and I seemed to be meant for each other. When I was twenty, I got her pregnant. Most of her family was involved in politics, working for the government and living a lifestyle that our younger generation hated. Her family, in turn, considered us to be the trash of the world. Only because we both had Catholic parents who demanded it, did we get married in a Catholic church in Bogotá; but we didn't believe in marriage anymore. A few days after the ceremony, my bride's relatives suggested we move to Germany, where they would help us find work. The truth was, they wanted to send us far away from them so we couldn't damage their reputation.

In Germany, I studied at the University of Hamburg and became an actor and musical composer. We lived there a little over six years, and my wife gave birth to two sons. By the end of our stay, the only pastime my wife and I shared as a couple was our outings to expensive rock 'n roll concerts, which we attended after feeding our babies. This left us without adequate funds for everything else, but we didn't care.

Little by little, although we cared for one another and knew each other intimately, the life and union between us changed. She started to feel nostalgic for her roots, and I became increasingly involved in my artistic, psychedelic world. In 1976, we decided to return to Colombia. A few months later, we separated.

I left for the United States and spent some time in Florida and New York doing theater. With a heart riddled with anxiety, due to the separation from my children and wife, I immersed myself into a confused and troubled world of bars, cocaine, and women as decadent as I was. Two years later, my artistic connections and acquaintances in New York led me to Hollywood. The same spirit that had baptized me into Donna's world through sex, and handed me my first marijuana joint in 1967, continued to guide my life with force. For the next twenty-nine years, I worked in the entertainment industry as an actor, director, producer, and composer, roving within a Hollywood mecca of drugs, lust, and the New Age.

In the mid-70s, while living in Hollywood, I was signed to CBS Records in New York and travelled to many countries with a band, promoting music and producing records. I had money, fame, and power, and truly believed I was the coolest guy in town. A slave to the New Age, I decorated my home using Feng Shui, an imported Chinese tradition. My sofa faced north, my bed faced south, and my mirror next to the front door reflected a crystal to the right so that everything could correctly channel "universal energy." I cultivated "powers," "knowledge," and other "cosmic forces" through candles, astrology, horoscopes, psychics, and so on . . . in addition to following all the superstitions I had brought from my culture . . . plus those I had picked up from the countries I had visited. All was gain in my eyes.

The evil one, being very astute, made sure that everything I touched turned into worldly success so that I would think my esoteric spiritual practices must be right and good. When I visited my Catholic relatives who were suffering financially, I would counsel them: "Do what I'm doing, use these crystals. . ." Their response was to cross themselves and run. "These people are so funny," I'd think. "They are living in the dark ages."

But I was the one living in the dark, while believing I dwelled in the brightest light. Lucifer, dressed as an angel of light, was impossible for me to detect because I was walking right with him. The only person able to bring a perspective of God to my life was my mother. When she flew to California every year or two to visit me—making up for my infrequent visits to Colombia—she would always tell me, "I'm not very impressed with your money or your success. I'm very concerned about your soul. If you die living the type of life you're living, you're going to be condemned." It was inconceivable to my family that I had lost my faith and didn't believe in Jesus, so upon returning home my mother would simply say, "Pray a lot for Marino."

My mother's warning rang deep within me, but I wasn't about to obey her because I had too much on my plate. Besides, Catholics were an outdated breed who had to learn from me. How could they still believe in such things as hell? What a superstitious, dehumanizing, and absurd concept! Whenever the subject came up in conversation, I made sure to voice my views, loudly.

A few months after I had signed the contract with CBS Records (now called Sony Music), my wife arrived from Colombia on a surprise visit to tell me that she had cancer. The news of her diagnosis brought me great sadness. In spite of our separation of several years, we had always enjoyed mutual concern and a close friendship because we knew each other's lives so well. No secrets existed between us.

Not long after her visit, we decided it would be better for our boys, now teenagers, to live with me permanently. My first years back together with my boys were very difficult because of my frequent music tours, but this new responsibility forced me to abandon many of my destructive habits, except for my occult practices, which I saw as harmless. Never mind how all the superstitions I'd adopted meant my surroundings could suddenly turn menacing. I feared much more than just walking under a ladder or a black cat crossing my path. I had turned into an idiot.

In 1992, I entered a period of loss. That year, my wife died after much suffering. In 1993, my youngest brother died in a boating accident off the island of Antigua—his body was never found. Six months later, my father passed away from a brain hemorrhage. In 1996, my last living brother shot himself to death during an argument with his wife, after consuming alcohol at a party in Bogotá. At the time, my mother was critically ill, emaciated and worn from all the family tragedies. Two months later, she died in my arms, following a three-hour ecstasy during which she relived and narrated her entire life.

One year later in 1997, I returned to Colombia to spend Christmas with my four remaining sisters, all practicing Catholics. At the pace our family was going, it seemed as if God might take the rest of us pretty soon. One of my sisters, who had fallen ill, was convinced she was next. She asked if we could go to church to pray the Christmas novena to the Infant Jesus of Prague,[xii] a special devotion that was once widespread throughout the Church, and still continues in countries such as Colombia and the Philippines. The novena began on December 16 and would end on December 24, with the Baby Jesus laid ceremoniously in the church manger.

Thirty-three years had passed since I had last stepped foot in a Catholic church, and I didn't believe in any of it. I went just to please my sisters, especially the one who believed she would die soon. As part of the priest's introduction to the novena, he said, "For the one who prays this novena with devotion and faith, the Baby Jesus will grant a grace." That caught my greed's attention. "Maybe I can get something out of this child," I thought to myself, so I asked the sister sitting next to me, "So, how powerful is this baby?"

She shared with me many testimonials of miracles that occurred because of the novena, so I said, "Sounds good to me." This Baby Jesus, in my perception, was like magic—yet another "power" that would offer me good luck and fortune. I had long ago lost any understanding of grace.

"I'm going to ask the Baby Jesus to change my life," I decided. Keeping my plan to myself, I asked Him to give me the opportunity to retire with a lot of money and live the rest of my life like a king with at least three women, on an island in Indonesia that I'd seen in pictures.

"Do it with a lot of faith," said my sister.

"You bet. You bet," I responded.

I felt convinced that the Baby Jesus would answer my petition. Little did I know I was actually talking to God and that He would answer my prayer to change my life—His way. I finished the novena the evening of Christmas Eve. On Christmas Day, after partying with friends and relatives, I got into my Land Cruiser at midnight with one of my nephews. Off we drove to my uncle's coffee ranch plantation in order to spend the night. My uncle always kept the entrance gate open when he was expecting me, so I was surprised to see it closed when I arrived. Stopping the car, I asked my nephew to step out to open the gate.

All of a sudden, six hooded men holding machine guns jumped out of the darkness. Throwing open the car doors, they pushed my nephew into the rear seat, yanked me out of the jeep, and tied my hands together behind my back. After putting a cloth hood over my head, they shoved me into the back seat with my nephew.

All six of them piled into the jeep, and the driver zoomed out of town at a dangerous speed. When we stopped, four of the hooded men stepped out of the car, bringing me with them. The remaining two drove off with my nephew. Later, I would learn that they abandoned my car and my nephew in a sugar camp plantation that same night. He was safe, but I went on to fear the worst for him.

Moving quickly, the men tied a cattle rope around my waist. One of them held the rope from the front and another from the back. Then they forced me to run through the mountains throughout the entire night, with my hands still tied behind my back and with the suffocating, acrylic hood still covering my head. When we finally stopped, I was dumped in what sounded from the echo like an abandoned farm room. At sunrise, still tied up and hooded, I was shoved into a car and spent the next few hours suffering a bumpy ride, without hands or sight to help brace myself. "We have to change locations," I overheard them say, "because the police and army are looking for him."

Then I was forced to walk again for several hours through the night. This time, I could hear the frightening sounds of the jungle, which added to my sheer panic. The car ride had left my body bruised and bloody, the humidity was making it difficult for me to breathe through the hood, and lack of circulation was causing shooting pains in my back and arms. The alcohol I had consumed for the last three days of Christmas partying had also sapped my energy, and each step felt like one move closer to a heart attack.

When this terrifying odyssey through the jungle ended, one of the men threw me into a cave. As my body hit the floor, I heard a commotion of fluttering and quickly realized I was surrounded by hundreds of bats. I didn't know which was worse, the smell of the cave or the showering of bat excrement that covered the rotten floor. Every time I moved an inch, the bats were disturbed, and their excrement rained on me. Adding to this horror, thousands of bugs began crawling out of the excrement and into my clothes, biting me from head to toe. Soon, my whole body was covered with various kinds of insect bites. Some felt like electric shocks, some produced great patches of inflammation, and others caused terrible itching, which I couldn't scratch with my hands still tied behind me.

On the third day, I started to call for my captors, thinking that they might remove me from the cave, and once outside, I might have a chance to escape. I shouted for them, but my voice almost failed me from fatigue. After some time, one of the men came, dragged me out of the cave by my feet, and yanked my hood off, leaving me lifeless on the ground. "Do you want something to eat?" he asked. I didn't answer. My eyes, with lids swollen from bug bites and blinded by many days of complete darkness, took time to open and adjust to light, and when they did, I became even more afraid.

Sitting up, I stared into the cave and saw what looked like a macabre stage of vast spider webs covered with a greenish slime. Slowly, I began to observe the largest and hairiest spiders I had ever seen. They seemed to know I was looking at them. Horrified, I noticed I had made a big hole in one of the larger, thicker spider webs, where I had been laying for the last three days. All I wanted to do was run. I didn't care if I got shot. But I couldn't even stand up, my blood circulation being so poor. Then the man hooded me and shoved me back into the cave.

Once a day, one of my captors would offer me food, but I refused to eat it because I desperately wanted to die. He explained that they were giving me what they found in the jungle because the group that was supposed to pick me up hadn't arrived yet. He didn't say whom they were waiting for or what they were planning to do with me, and I didn't dare ask any questions.

Every day, I was growing weaker, angrier, and more desperate. I only wanted to kill those men, or find a way to escape, or just die. Eventually, I decided to try to regain some energy and started to eat and drink the wild fruits, roots, and jungle water they were giving me. On the fifteenth day, they took me out of the cave (I kept track of time until the twenty-first day of my kidnapping). I found myself in the midst of nearly eighty Marxist guerrilla rebels in military uniforms, between the ages of around fourteen to twenty-one. They were members of the FARC revolutionary group and claimed to have an ideology, but were regular criminals. Immediately, I realized that the army had stopped looking for me because these rebels were now able to move about openly without needing to hide.

The FARC commander of the camp, about thirty years old, started walking around in circles, making a show of his power, declaring how I had been purchased from my first captors and that I was to pay his group a high ransom (money I didn't have). This, he claimed, was just a small amount of my fortune. They must have assumed I was rich because I had been on TV and in movies and was the relative of prominent coffee plantation owners, whom they had harassed for years.

This caricature-like commander knew where my sisters were and went as far as to show me a list of their names, addresses, and telephone numbers. If I refused to give them the money, my sisters would be killed, one by one. I knew that human life meant nothing to them, and they wouldn't hesitate for a second to follow through with their threat. Everything the commander said was celebrated with laughter by the pack of malnourished, preying jackals surrounding me. In this absurd trial in the jungle night, my emotions oscillated wildly between anger and fear, bravery and painful despair.

My initial kidnappers belonged to a well-known family from my village, who had failed in the drug-trafficking business and were paying off their debts by kidnapping people. The FARC commander stated that those kidnappers wanted me dead after the ransom was paid since they came from my same town and feared I would go after them. Because I had seen their faces, my sentence was death.

The commander ordered my return to the cave, and the guerrillas put my hood back on. This time, they tied my hands together in the front, which provided only the slightest relief. Back in that cave, I felt utterly demolished, with no hope whatsoever of making it out alive. I thought of my boys who were fearing for my life—who no longer had a father. I thought of my sisters—my entire family, now in danger of being killed. I had literally lost everything. My existence had turned to ashes. I had hit below bottom, if there was such a place.

I tried desperately to conjure a power, a guide, anything to sustain me through this agony. I groped for help from the eastern philosophies I had cherished as things so deep and wonderful. But the magic formulas, the metaphysical knowledge of the occult, the mantras, the crystals, the mystical amulets from around the world—all these things that I lived for—were offering me nothing and leaving me spiritually bankrupt. My mind then travelled back to my early years, as I tried to recall the prayers

I had said in church and in school, but I couldn't even remember the "Our Father." Nothing.

My Illumination of Conscience

It was at that moment, when I was completely destroyed as a human being, that God walked into my life. Throughout the night, for about eight or nine hours, the Lord held me in a mystical embrace. I was taken through an illumination of my conscience, which was followed by an extraordinary infusion of His teachings—bits of which I will include as I relate what happened during the illumination. (Although I will often use the words, "the Lord showed me," when describing the illumination, only after it ended did I understand the Lord to be its source, for at the time, I didn't know who the Lord was.)

While still maintaining a grip on reality, aware of being present in the cave, I entered a mysterious, infinite state, with no sense of time or space. In this realm of vivid awareness, I reviewed my entire life of sin. Suddenly, I was seeing myself at age three, speeding a tricycle around the old Spanish-style terrace of my childhood home in Colombia. With a stick in hand, I was whacking the decorative plants and damaging the potted flowers. In the background, I could hear the voice of someone, perhaps a maid, telling me to stop. "Maybe, I'm going insane," I thought. "At forty-seven, I'm reliving my life at age three."

Petrified, I reconsidered, "For three hours before Mom died, she talked about her whole life, and so I must be dying, like my mother." Then the thought came, "No, maybe I'm hallucinating because I've been bitten by poisonous insects for fifteen days." Something deep within was telling me otherwise, but the answer was too mysterious, too big. None of my rationalizations could withstand my unfolding experience, so I gave up trying understand it. My mind was far from thinking that the illumination was coming from God.

As I witnessed scenes from my childhood, I saw how, step by step, I grew increasingly attached to the external world, abandoning my relationship with the Holy Spirit, Who had permeated my entire existence. I saw how profoundly my attachments developed to my environment, to material possessions, and to the people in my life. The culture into which I was born had also exposed me to unbridled sexual impurity, and early on, I began to engage in intense sexual activity with myself. I lost a sense of joy, security, and love, and gradually turned into a person who constantly depended on human affection, with an appetite geared toward the senses and instincts.

As I witnessed my happiness fade, I watched my tongue turn into a weapon.[xiii] As early as elementary school, I committed a terrible offense against a schoolmate who was being teased by our classmates. The worst nickname he received was the one I gave him: "gallo," which means rooster. He carried this nickname throughout his life and had to endure humiliation and persecution from most everyone, which caused him great anguish. This boy grew up suffering from isolation and extreme loneliness, which purified his soul in a precious way. His purification through suffering caused enormous damage to the souls of all those who contributed to his holiness, including myself. This may sound confusing, but it is exactly the way I saw it take place.

One could argue that as a schoolboy, I was too young to know better and didn't yet have a fully formed conscience. On the contrary, this would be a rationalization because the Lord later shared with me that wisdom rings in the soul at the moment of birth, when the soul first becomes perfectly independent from the mother's womb. This precludes us from feigning ignorance to justify committing such an act. The soul feels the pain of sin at the very moment sin is being committed, or is even consented to in one's mind. Therefore, I had no excuse.

By the time I was seeing my life at ages eleven, twelve, thirteen, fourteen, I began to experience a spiritual pain that was excruciating. For the first time, I was feeling the agony of sin. This suffering penetrated so deeply into my heart that I would never be able to describe it—and I was only approaching my teens. As a forty-seven-year-old man in a cave, who didn't believe in sin, I was suddenly feeling all the pain of the wrong I had already committed by my early teenage years. The older I got during the experience, the more devastating the agony, for I had spent the last thirty-three years of my life steeped in mortal sin.

Not only was I witnessing my sins, but every consequence of every sin. To explain this reality, I will share a particular scene that I later faced before the Lord:

I was shown a group of people lined up in front of a bank teller early one morning. For some reason, the teller was working very slowly. One of the people in the line became restless and started to complain, cursing the bank, its employees, and then the government. Other people in the line became agitated and began to grumble, too, so that when they eventually met the teller face to face, they also insulted him. Consequently, the teller lost his temper and behaved badly for the rest of the day. The chain of events that developed in the bank spread to other parts of the city, causing a rise in hostility and violence, and then across the ocean through the telephone, generating an incredibly long radius of evil actions. By the end of the day, acts of extreme violence were being committed as a consequence of one person's reaction to a teller not working quickly enough.

If I was the one who started a fire of sin, I was also accountable for its spreading. To see all of my transgressions passing from one soul to another, like a terrible plague, was beyond devastating.

I saw how the relationship between me (a creature) and my God (the Creator) broke down the moment that I believed I had control of my own life. By age fourteen, I was encased in such an edifice of vanity, pretentiousness, and pride that I dropped the Sacrament of Reconciliation because I thought it was ridiculous to confess to another human being.

I started making fun of the Church and leading others to do the same. I watched myself put forth the most absurd arguments to demonstrate how unnecessary it was to be part of the Church. I belittled all Christians, but especially Catholics. "Look at those priests! They're a wreck. I'm not going to tell them anything. Who needs a middleman anyway?" . . . "Hell? What a joke that is! It can't be possible. God wouldn't create us to go to hell. He would never do that to us." I saw all of the souls I was meant to serve and evangelize, had I stayed in the Church. For the next thirty-three years, I would abandon all of them. I had received the great blessing, coupled with the great responsibility, of being raised Catholic, and I did nothing with it.

God also highlighted one particular moment in 1966, when I was fifteen years old. I saw myself in the kitchen of a house in Bogotá in the company of a maid about my age. I had a macho attitude inherited from my ancestors, and it manifested through my cruel, arrogant, and abusive actions toward those over whom I had authority. I spoke to her harshly, while holding an object in my hand that she was supposed to have cleaned. She was staring at the floor, her face flush with misery. She neither protested nor showed a single gesture of resistance or disgust. My soul was torn apart when I saw this. I saw how she was in one of the most delicate states of her spiritual and emotional life, and my actions led her into deeper pain. She had recently been taken from the countryside where she was born. She was separated from her parents and transferred to the big city where she was placed in the service of strangers who felt no love or charity toward her, causing her greater suffering and despair.

I could see how spiritually handicapped I was at sixteen, due to the extensive roots I had developed in the world. As a result, my existence was absolutely drab and filled with anxieties and the desires of nature. With infinite sadness, I witnessed how my sinful actions caused my separation from the grace that was given to me at birth.

Then at seventeen, I entered the territory of the truly fallen, descending into a cavern of impurity at the consummation of my first sexual act with Donna. The Lord later revealed to me that through fornication, I lost the grace of my baptism and fell back into original sin, as if I had never been baptized.[xiv] Not only did I enter into the consequences of my own serious sin, but I received the iniquities of my ancestors who had likewise engaged in fornication.[xv] Instead of reserving virginity and chastity for sacramental matrimony between a man and a woman, with its abundance of Christian graces, my ancestors and my culture had chosen the path of carnal pleasure prior to marriage. Now, so had I. I was therefore left without a spiritual compass and continued multiplying these sins—this horrible curse—for future generations.

From that first act with Donna, my entire life began to function in the flesh and away from the spirit. I saw how my eyes changed and hungered to penetrate the deepest abyss of sexuality. Like sponges, they sought to absorb every detail along the way. As a result, I lost countless graces and the treasure of peace.

If only Our Lord would allow you, the reader, to observe for an instant what I witnessed concerning what the arrival of Donna represented in my life and vice versa. To see this would be an intense warning as to the seriousness of the battle being fought for our souls.

With horror, I followed the growth of my carnal appetite, which brought serious consequences to my life and to those around me. I grew convinced that sex was like breathing. But the Lord would later explain to me that sexuality is not a need but a function. A human can survive without a sexual life. He may not be able to procreate, but he surely will not die or become atrophied, physically, emotionally, or spiritually. Sexual impurity, He said, is one of the fastest routes to separate us light years from His presence, a path that gravely compromises us with its diabolical realms. Every sinful sexual act is an internal metamorphosis, gradually emptying the human being of its spiritual existence. This can only lead the soul to a premature death—turning it into a walking corpse, driven by the evil one toward an eternal burial.

That first relationship was the beginning of a long sequence of infernal events in my life. Through Donna, two different venoms were injected into me: one of hallucinatory drugs and the other of promiscuity, whose poisonous flames were fanned by my intergenerational inheritance and history of sexual activity with myself. Uniting with Donna ignited a fire that would not be extinguished for decades.

The devil prepared me well for the coming of my second affair with another visiting American named Cindy. After establishing a fountain of corruption within the two of us, Satan used us as his tools to ensnare those with whom we would come into contact. Cindy and I caused the destruction of many souls. Through us, they were initiated into LSD and a spontaneous, casual sexual life. To see all this was so painful. Cindy, herself, died of a heroin overdose back home in San Francisco.

The Lord later explained to me that the evil one knows the gifts and talents that God has given us, and he wants to capture all of these capacities for his territory early on in our lives. Otherwise, they will become weapons used against him. The devil gave me decadent talents to cultivate the opposite sex, and I was captivated with ease by women's invitations of carnal passion. Without effort, I could seduce others and could be seduced even more easily. I saw how I even took on the mannerisms and gestures of the demons working through me. Donna and Cindy and I, however, were not just puppets of Satan. We were fully conscious of acting against everything addressed in the moral law of God.

After reviewing the truth of my contact with Donna and Cindy, I witnessed the evil one using me for many more years, taking advantage of my vitality and artistic inclinations. From a very young age, I had an affinity for the arts, and every artistic talent that I possessed was used by evil to increase the venomous influence of my actions.

It was terribly difficult for me to learn in this revelation of my conscience that the key to heaven was not power or comfort or sensuality, but renunciation. The world I had created for myself was oriented toward avoiding pain and attaining pleasure at any price. My version of reality made it all the more impossible, as each day passed, to conceive that the path of purification toward absolute union with God was paved with suffering, pain, and tribulation. Moreover, I was chasing happiness in this world—an impossible task because there cannot ever be full realization of the eternal in that which is not permanent. It is like trying to build a house on the waves of the ocean.

At least a thousand times during this illumination of conscience, I noticed the way my eyes were riveted on crosses in so many places. With every gaze at a crucifix, a burning call stirred deep within me but could never reach my heart since I was immune to the movements of the Holy Spirit.

The more sins I committed, the more tormented I became, and the more desperately I went out in search of lost happiness. In the midst of my distress, I ended up doing certain things that part of me most detested. God also allowed me to see how, in the midst of my most intensely sinful activity (when I thought I was enjoying the most pleasure physically), my soul was bleeding rivers of internal pain that consumed my entire being. My eyes looked like windows of sadness, covered in carnival makeup, fooling no one.

I also saw the eyes of those who had sinned with me. They, too, were undergoing an interior anguish, with the exception of those who seemed to be consumed by the darkness. In the midst of all this pain, the Lord later showed me that He was there in every action, no matter how dark, to alleviate the weight of sin from our tormented souls, which recognized something was totally wrong.

There is no way I can describe to you the spiritual torture I went through in this awakening of my conscience. I'm not sure how I lived through it. I know that if someone in a state of ongoing mortal sin were to undergo what I experienced, they would most likely die.

My Personal Judgment

Throughout this review of my life of sin, I was mysteriously aware that I was still present in the cave. I still possessed a grip on reality. But then that grip was gone. All of a sudden, I was taken into another dimension. Whether I fainted, died, or fell asleep, I do not know. I found myself immersed in the freshness of a very friendly field, face down in beautiful grass, which covered the plateau of what appeared to be a high mountain—but one unlike any on earth. I was amidst the most incredible and immense silence—what I will call, the perfect silence. I could also see my body in that cave in another dimension. My first thought was, "I just died." And yet I had never felt so alive. My entire being was weightless, free from all anxiety or pain and permeated with a pure sense of joy.

Before me in the far distance, I noticed another even higher mountain, disconnected from the one I was on. Through a distant mist surrounding the mountain top, a spectacularly beautiful city began to slowly appear. I was in a perfect state of knowledge, understanding everything I was seeing. As I began to explore that city (I could see it inside and out, though it was far away), I knew perfectly well that my soul was supposed to have ended up there, but it did not make it.

Then I heard the voice of the Lord speak to me. I knew it was God. His voice sounded so majestic, so immense, that it seemed to come from everywhere in the universe, while at the same time, from inside of me. All of the beauty in the world could not begin to describe it. I was experiencing the most magnificent, loving, forgiving, compassionate voice; but in my pride, I felt so ashamed of being who I was in the presence of this awesomely magnanimous God that I wasn't able to accept His mercy. I wanted to sink into my shame, but the Lord kept holding me up. He was trying to save me from myself. The more shame I experienced, the more mercy and love He showed me, in a back-and-forth symphony for my salvation.

The unconditional love and extravagant mercy in the Lord's voice was burning me. I didn't want to hear it, so I turned it down. People have a hard time thinking that we human beings could ever reject God, Who only wants to save us. But we can. It happens if we die and appear before the Lord without love. When I rejected the Lord's voice, He immediately stopped talking to me. I fell into an indescribable loneliness. The silence was no longer perfect, but instead, became the total absence of love. I knew that if that voice did not talk to me again, I would be destroyed, because that voice was my life.

Then everything vanished: the grass, the mountains, the city of light. I was now floating on top of a terrifying abyss, above what appeared to be an ocean of fog. I began to sink into it, and as I descended, I noticed that it wasn't fog at all. Every particle was a condemned soul, a demonized person. Each horrifying figure still possessed traces of being human; I could see the resemblance of an arm, the piece of a face. But every being was totally deformed by sin, and I was perfectly aware of exactly what type of sin had inflicted what type of deformity. At the same time, I also knew and felt the origin of every one of my own terrifying deformities.

As I looked deeper into this frightening abyss in the bowels of the earth, I saw that it became increasingly complicated because there were infinite levels of condemnation, and all of the condemned human souls were connected to demonic hierarchies far below. Those hierarchies were formed by fallen angels.[xvi] Each hierarchy was ruling a different territory of sin, and I could see how the souls were eternally enslaved to the hierarchies of demons that corresponded with their sins. It was as if the souls were wired to them, and I was wired to them, too. My sins were perfectly connected to millions of evil spirits in different dimensions of the abyss. All at once, I saw the horrifying faces of the demons I fornicated with and committed adultery with—I saw the evil, twisted faces of my violence, my dishonesty, my greed, my gluttony.

Most people who are living in mortal sin, as I was, argue that God is so merciful, therefore there is no hell. Well, I was wrong. There is a hell. Surrounded by abominable creatures beyond my wildest imaginings, I experienced the most excruciating pain of my whole human existence. I felt as though my soul was stolen, raped, and trampled on. The worst part was recognizing that I had voluntarily caused this. Even though the word "rape" might sound exaggerated, I truly sensed a violation of the inner recesses of my soul. I could see the different angles in which evil worked in me and how it had invaded the spaces of my inner life, gradually erasing the minutest details of the presence of God within me.

This was my moment before the "Judgment Seat," the "Holy Tribunal," of God. The spiritual presence of sin before the Holy Tribunal is the greatest pain a soul could ever suffer. It is unspeakable and beyond compare. I found myself in a territory of evil so great that I lost all hope of seeing the light ever again. In God's Holy Tribunal, I experienced my own personal judgment, and my sentence was eternal damnation.

In His Presence

At death, when the soul faces its own personal judgment, it will find nothing that is unknown. Self-knowledge has already been infused in the person through the workings of the Holy Spirit. It is sin that causes this wisdom to lie dormant. In the presence of the Lord, the soul knows truth instantaneously. The only confusion the soul experiences at the moment of physical death is the encounter with its relationship with evil. This takes it by surprise.

If we knew with clarity while on earth when we were standing in a hierarchical territory of sin, we would never allow ourselves to be deceived or manipulated and turned into such absurd puppets of Satan. There is no half way before the Judgment Seat of God. We cannot say we were sort of good or sort of bad. The dividing line disappears, and we are left either on one side or the other, destined for purgatory or heaven—or for hell.

I stood on evil ground. The devil had been my master, and on his terrain, I was to render an account to my Lord. In the Divine Presence, I was like a married man caught by his wife in his lover's embrace, unfaithful and in bed with the evil one for thirty-three years. I assumed that I would be in hell for an eternity, never to see the light of God again.

Suddenly, I found myself back on the mountain with my face on the grass. It seemed as though I'd never left this place of perfect silence—never experienced hell; yet I knew I had. Then the Lord began to speak to me again. As I was looking around, trying to discover where His voice was coming from, I found myself submerged up to my waist in a small lake. Besides being acutely conscious of my presence in three different states—in the cave with the bats, lying down on the grass, and now in the lake—I was also made keenly aware of the relationship between each. I know that this will seem as inconceivable to the reader as it seemed to me.

With my attention present in the dimension where I stood waist-deep in the lake, I looked up with my arms outstretched. There, in front of the lake, appeared an immense and precious golden rock—impossible to describe. It seemed to be as big as the universe. While unimaginable in size, my intellect could still fathom it.

In that same instant, I was made aware of the presence of myriads of evil spirits that were in the lake. Then my guardian angel appeared on top of the rock. He was dressed in a pale ivory tunic, of the same color as his face, as if it were part of his body. With perfect knowledge, I knew everything he was saying without "hearing" him. "You are standing in the territory of all of your sins," he said. "You lived your life against the commandments of God Almighty." As he stared at the spirits of evil around me, his eyes were like torches of fire.

I was then shown my guardian angel's presence throughout my life, along with the presence of many other angels—the guardians of my relatives, or of people I had hurt—and I saw how the actions of those angels had been negated by my sins. I watched their spiritual struggle against the fallen spirits. It was devastating to see how many graces I had wasted and how much of my life I had spent with demons, and with so little awareness of them!

There was something even greater in this grand apparition, and I knew what it was: the Lord, Himself. Having only heard His voice up to this point, I understood that I was about to see Him. In shame, I wanted to disappear into the lake. But He gave me the strength to look up at the pinnacle of the rock. Very softly, smoothly, the Lord Jesus began to take shape as a person, transparent and immersed in majestic light. This revelation astounded me because I hadn't thought of God as a divine person for decades, only as a universal, cosmic "energy," or nirvana.

I melted into His Presence; His aura penetrated me so completely that I felt as if I were united to Him. No words can describe my encounter with our King. I saw all of my life in Him. I saw all of creation in Him. I would have expected to see Him dressed in a tunic, but I can only say that He was dressed in the most precious light. At the same time, the most spectacular spectrum of colors as could delight the eyes appeared within Him, presenting Him in different accents of light. These colors were like living creatures because of the enormous animation in which they existed. There is no comparison between the light and the colors I saw and what we see in the material world.

Jesus's hair was shoulder length and appeared in various shades of gold, from the darkest to the lightest. I was seeing Him older and younger—all at the same time—with a face that was eternally beautiful, wise, powerful, and filled with infinite love. I couldn't help but submerge myself completely in His eyes, which embodied unbridled love and compassion. They changed from yellow to blue to green, colors that caressed, bringing the greatest relief that a soul could desire. To see the eyes of Jesus Christ is to find the absolute realization, the ultimate fulfillment, of our existence.

Our Lord was the resplendent mansion through which I could see heaven. Within Him, I was witnessing an amazing, endless ocean of purity—a vast expanse of exquisite green. As my eyes focused on one particular spot, I realized that, like a green field is made up of millions of blades of grass, so was this ocean comprised of great numbers of individual angels and saints.

Then in the midst of the most colorful light, as if coming from the hearts of all the angels and saints, emerged the most splendid of all creatures, the Blessed Virgin Mary. She was precious and young and filled with such regal authority of abundant humility and grace that I was not able to stare at her. Then I found myself like a child in her womb, connected to her through a spiritual umbilical cord. In the embrace of her being, I felt such tender nourishment that I was afraid to lose her.

Together, she and all of the heavenly hosts began praising and worshipping the Lord in a single choir, which cannot be described in human terms. The presence of such perfection can only produce in the soul a state of sublime ecstasy.

My initial understanding of Jesus and Mary was so poor that every discovery was a profound one. I had never learned my catechism or paid attention in my religion classes. For me, it was the greatest of all revelations to learn that Jesus Christ was God. Moreover, to discover that I had a Mother in heaven filled a profound maternal emptiness in my soul—a void I wasn't aware of until the moment I saw her. While nestled as a child in her womb, I also remained waist deep in the lake. She spoke to me with profound love, in words I didn't "hear" but understood perfectly: "You have to trust in your Lord Jesus. You have to open your heart to let Him in. Jesus loves you. He forgives you." In my heart, however, it still felt impossible to accept the Lord's forgiveness because I was not able to forgive myself.

When I was with Our Lady, I was shown a large valley of loneliness, packed with millions of souls, which looked like a great body of fire, yet was as cold as ice. It looked like hell, but my guardian angel told me I was seeing purgatory,[xvii] far below the earth. The souls in this state, he explained, had made it to salvation, but not to sainthood, so they had to be purified.

The souls there were suffering because they were separated from God, Whom they loved. In their spiritual senses, they were experiencing the extreme sensations of fire and ice, for it was either too hot or too cold. The levels of purification in purgatory that I saw were so many and so large that if a hundred people were to die suddenly and go there, they wouldn't be able to see each other, as they would likely end up on different levels, according to their greater or lesser sins. Our Lady, the Queen of purgatory, was feeling great compassion for each soul and never stopped interceding for them. She, my guardian angel, and other angels of the Lord were showing me how all of the souls I was seeing possessed a beautiful and real assurance that they were saved. They accepted that they could not yet attend the banquet of the Lord because they were not properly dressed in virtue, and they took great comfort in God's promise to them of heaven. The Blessed Mother and the angels wanted me to accept that same mercy and hope for myself, but I could not.

I felt so unworthy that I turned my head away and looked down at the lake. Gently pursuing me, Mary met me on the surface of the water.

Alongside her reflection, she pointed to the spirits of my sins and said in a voice of the sweetest tenderness, "They are not you."

Finally, I was able to allow the Lord's mercy to envelope me. It was then that He began to lead me through extensive teachings, bits of which I have included in the telling of my illumination of conscience. Jesus spoke about my life, humanity, the Church, the seven Sacraments, the Ten Commandments, the Blessed Mother, the saints, heaven, purgatory, hell, demons, angels, eschatology, salvation, the capital sins, what He called the "soul's economy," and so much more. The state I was in is very difficult to describe. The only way I can think to express this phenomenon would be to say that everything He spoke of materialized in front of my eyes and was infused into my heart.

Words do not allow me to even approach the perfection, peace, and absolute wisdom in which His teachings took place, and I will never be able to measure them. If I were to live another hundred years, I would not be able to convey even the minimum of all the Lord shared. I had never studied or read anything of what He taught me in books or heard it from the people around me. Everything was new.

Back in My Body

My entire mystical experience lasted throughout the night for about eight or nine hours. Then the Lord returned me to my physical body. As I reentered the prison of my flesh, it went into convulsions. Outwardly, I was back in the same living nightmare. Inwardly, I was an absolutely changed human being.

For the next five months, I lived in captivity. Daily, I suffered physical and psychological torture from the rebels, who were trying to get money out of me and my family. During those long months, I went through great suffering and desperation. Never did I dream of making it out alive. I would look at those young men, knowing that they were prisoners of the devil. They were attacking me, physically and mentally, and they didn't know why. I felt so bad for them.

Every day, I offered each suffering I endured for the reparation of my sins. I now fully believed in God's mercy, but I was afraid of myself, of what I was going to do in the presence of the Lord again when I died. I begged Him to send me someone who could give me Confession, even if it was a priest who had been kidnapped.

By the fourth month of my captivity, I had given the FARC guerrillas every penny I had ever saved, though it was much less than they were seeking. I was then informed that they were awaiting instructions for my execution. For the next couple of months, I lived waiting to be killed. Whenever I saw one of the men carrying a rope, it meant they were going to hang me. When I caught one sharpening a knife, I braced myself to be stabbed to death. If one was cleaning a machine gun, I anticipated getting shot to death. At least two times a day, I experienced, emotionally, my final moments of life.

One day, a guerrilla rebel told me to ask the commandant to kill me on the road so that my family could find me. I followed his suggestion and approached the commandant. "Could you kill me on the road?" I asked secretly.

"No," he said. "I have to kill you in the jungle. We have no time to take you to the road."

So I anticipated being murdered at any moment in the heart of the jungle. One day, at 2:00 a.m., in the midst of torrential rain, I was untied from the tree to which I had been bound and ordered to follow four of the guerrillas. Through the early hours of the morning and the rest of that weary day, they led me through one of Columbia's western rainforests— a dark, mountainous, and forbidding jungle. By this point in my kidnapping, I was as thin as a rake, with a beard down to the center of my chest, and wore the same ripped clothes that had sat in bat excrement six months earlier. For an entire half year, I hadn't slept in a bed or taken a shower.

After the sun had emitted its last rays, we approached an unpaved road. The date was six months to the day of my kidnapping. Without any explanation, one of the guerrillas told me, "Walk straight and don't look back." So I set forth with difficulty, my legs almost paralyzed by fear— with each step awaiting the ominous sound of a rifle shot piercing me and the dark, silent night. I begged God to let the bullet hit me in the head so I could be killed instantly, rather than left to suffer an agonizing death, mortally wounded on a lonely, secluded road.

It was the longest walk of my life. Petrified, I walked . . . and walked . . . and walked . . . and nothing happened. Approaching a curve in the road, I mustered the courage to glance behind me. Utterly confounded, I saw the four men climb back up the mountain in the direction of the woods from which we had come. Could I dare hope? Would I be intercepted further down the road? My heart beat rapidly as I scanned the horizon in the faint moonlight, looking for rebels. But none appeared.

I had been kidnapped for so long that I didn't know what to do. I had lost my will. I actually started hoping that the criminals would come back to tell me where to go and how to manage. After what felt like hours, I heard a far-off car engine. Along the dirt road came an old bus, which passed by on my left and stopped a few meters ahead of me. A woman stepped off onto the dirt road and walked into the woods, so I realized she was one of the guerrillas. Filled with adrenaline, I rushed to get to the bus door, which was shut in my face because I looked like a caveman. Shoving my elbow and knee in the crack of the door, I pried it open and stepped inside.

Everyone on the bus immediately turned their heads to look at me. Eyeing the empty, far-rear seat covered in broken glass and dust, I walked to the back of the bus and sat squarely in the center of the seat. Through his rearview mirror, the driver stared at me, undoubtedly expecting me to do something terrible; and I stared back at him. Everyone on the bus had swiveled their heads, continuing to look at me. "Are they guerrillas?" I wondered. "Is this whole thing a set-up?" Even though I didn't know where I was, I didn't dare ask anyone anything. Yet somewhere in my fear, I began to hope.

After a while, I made it to a town, then to another. The police came around and my sisters eventually picked me up. Our reunion was dramatic. They were ecstatic, and at the same time, pained to see me because I couldn't handle their expressions of love and affection. After being crushed and beaten, tied up with rope, and undernourished for six months, I had become paranoid. There was no strength in me to receive a hug or a look of love because I had been punished every minute of every day with no conceivable end in sight but my murder. Cruelty was all I knew, so when my sisters came toward me, I felt scared. When they tried to grab me, my body shook and trembled.

My sisters took me home, and I spent fifteen days locked in a bedroom. Unable to sit with anyone, I would inch my way to the table to eat on my own, making sure no one was around. When I needed to bathe, I could scarcely make my dash to the shower and back. My sisters offered me psychiatric help, but I didn't accept it. Only slowly did I begin to take little steps back into the world. It was easy, however, for me to pray . . . and pray. I knew that the Lord was going to heal me.

After I recuperated a little, both physically and emotionally, the first thing I did was to go to Confession at a monastery in my sister's town. After standing in a long line, I found myself face to face with the abbot, a holy Franciscan with a long beard, who listened kindly to my interminable confession. Because we were in a room empty of furniture, the echo travelled everywhere, and the ladies waiting outside in line could  hear my sins. I imagined they were petrified, thinking, "Whoah! We're doing OK."

Finally I reached the end, and the priest said, "I'm going to give you absolution now. . . God, the Father of mercies, through the death and resurrection of His Son has reconciled the world to Himself and sent the Holy Spirit among us for the forgiveness of sins; through the ministry of the Church, may God give you pardon and peace, and I absolve you from your sins, in the name of the Father, and of the Son, and the Holy Spirit."

Feeling incredibly light and deliriously happy, I walked out of that confessional waving at everyone. I could have confessed my sins in front of a million people because the Lord told me that sin is the devil and that we are all sinners. Since I understood what had just happened mystically, I rejoiced in having hauled the devil off to jail. I could almost hear him and his legions being burned, one after the other. Not only that, I was practically healed of all my paranoia and of every emotional and psychological consequence of my trauma from the kidnapping. It was the greatest sense of relief and deliverance of my entire life.

Shortly after that, I moved back to California, to my home in Los Angeles. There, the first thing I did was go back to Church. My first experience of Communion was a glimpse of heaven. Jesus overcame me in a way that is impossible to describe. How in love I was with the Lord and the Church—with the Scriptures, the Catechism, the liturgy, the stories of the saints. Everything confirmed for me what I had learned through my mystical experience in the cave. To know that I was in the Church of the Lord, the House of God, made me feel so safe. Every day, I made sure to attend Mass, and I went to Confession often. I was home.

At Church, I felt very shy around people because I was a Catholic who didn't even know the "Our Father." When standing next to people in conversation about the faith, I would bend toward them to listen in. Sometimes they would get intimidated by this leaning stranger and stop speaking. "Darn!" I'd think. I joined prayer groups but kept silent about my mystical experience, never telling anyone, not even my sons. I figured it was a big secret between me and God, one that meant God was giving me another chance. I never considered that anyone would believe me anyway.

Though spiritually fulfilled, I still felt exhausted and devastated, physically and mentally, from the kidnapping and the beatings. I didn't think that I would live much longer. All I wanted to do was move to a small town in northern Italy, retire, and live out my last few days in a simple, little, humble existence. My family and friends were worried about my "strange" behavior because I had stopped most of my former activities and was always in Church. "He's going back to his old life one day," they'd say. "He's just traumatized and needs to see a shrink." Little did they know I had left this realm.

At age forty-nine, after living in Los Angeles for two years, I made a trip back to Colombia during Holy Week. On Palm Sunday, I attended a noon Mass that was so packed I didn't make it inside. Through the main doors of the church, I peered above a sea of people and focused on a gigantic crucifix, hanging above the altar. As I stared at it, I began to feel dizzy, as if I might faint. Then I realized that the Lord was bringing me into another mystical experience.

He manifested Himself again, this time from the crucifix, in the same way that He had appeared to me in the rock. Whether I entered into the crucifix, or the crucifix entered into me, I don't know. In this inexplicable state, the Lord showed me that my mission in this life was just about to begin. He said He was going to take me all around the world and that all the knowledge He had infused into my soul was for me to share. He would support me and express Himself through my testimony, using natural means—my speaking style, culture, and the languages I knew. He told me that He had already chosen every place I would go, and chosen by name every person who was going to listen to me, adding that they would be responsible for everything I would tell them. The Lord's only immediate request of me was to be faithful, to pray, and to read the Word of God.

I didn't understand a thing He was communicating to me. "No way," I told Him. "So, a sinner like me who's lived such a decadent life, persecuted the Church, and laughed at Christians and priests . . . I'm supposed to speak to a congregation and say, 'Hey, I sinned against the Lord, and then the Lord spoke to me.' I'll be greeted by tomatoes and rocks!"

Walking away from that Palm Sunday service, I thought, "Now I've really lost it." But the Lord had a plan. Recalling the holy abbot at the monastery who had heard my confession two years earlier, I went to him again for Reconciliation. I told him what I'd just heard from the Lord, and for first time, I disclosed my mystical encounter in the cave. After spilling my entire experience before him, he said, "Well, if everything you told me is from God, don't worry. Just go back home to California, and He will take care of it."

"What?" I thought and left there even more confused. I was hoping for a manual. But the abbot was right. A mysterious mission opened up before me. Though I had no idea that people gave testimonies in churches, I began to share my story in prayer groups and little gatherings. That ignited a fire. Word of me went everywhere, and I grew very scared. People started looking for me, and when I gave talks, they would pull out recorders and cameras, which I found disturbing. "Why on earth are they doing that?" I wondered suspiciously. I felt a little upset about a lot of things I didn't understand.

Little by little, the Lord started to take all my time. My two sons were independent, grown men, and my estranged wife had died long before in 1992, so I had no excuse not to follow God's call. The Lord never let me make my money back in Hollywood. He kept me as I was after my release from the kidnapping—poor and stripped.

Invitation after invitation poured in, though I never promoted myself. I became an international lay Catholic missionary, and at the Lord's request, founded a mission in 1999 called Pilgrims of Love, with the Archdiocese of Bogotá. I have ecclesiastical approval from the Church, as prescribed in canon law.

The first year of my mission was difficult. I lived out of a suitcase, traveling from place to place, diving headfirst into the incredible ocean of the Church. Within four years, the Lord had sent me to twenty-one countries. As of today, I have spoken in five continents: in parishes, retreat centers, universities, high schools, seminaries, religious communities, lay communities, Protestant churches, and so on.

When I first set out, I wondered, "How on earth am I going to support myself?" But I have never lacked anything, even at the eleventh hour, when I had no idea how the Lord would provide. I have never and will

never charge for my talks. I live as St. Paul did, on people's generosity. St. Paul built tents and I develop materials, writing books and recording my talks. I live on faith.

As of today, I have written nine books and developed over a thousand different topics covering little windows of my mystical experience. Because the Lord walked me through so many different areas of the faith, I haven't been able to scratch the surface of what He infused in me. I never studied theology or the religious sciences. I never prepared myself for this life. When I am about to give a talk, I never think ahead of time about what I will say—I leave it up to the Holy Spirit. I don't speak out of intellect or memory. If that were so, I would have been too tired to continue long ago. Everything that the Lord infused into me flows back out of me.

I am not special. You have read who I am. I was one of the most terrifying sinners. So why did the Lord pick me? Because of His great mercy, and because He wants to make sure that those who hear or read of my experience know that the teachings I speak of come from Him, not me. How could I ever speak of these things when I never studied them? It is the Holy Spirit Who shares them. It is as simple as that.

For me, I am begging the Lord not to let me die until I walk the last mile trying to repair all the damage I caused when I was living in mortal sin. Even if God were to give me one hundred more years to do His work, I wouldn't feel completely at peace and ready to see Him. No matter the obstacles (health, spiritual warfare, etc.) that present themselves, I will continue the mission He has entrusted to me. To speak and rescue souls from going to purgatory, and more importantly, from ending up in hell—a destination I wouldn't wish for my worst enemy—is my desire until the day that the Lord calls me.

The World Today

We are living in the darkest spiritual age humanity has ever experienced, and the Lord told me it is going to get darker. But the world has also never been as bright as it is now, and it is going to get brighter. The Lord is shining on us more than ever because our world is losing its light.[xviii] Still, we don't understand that love.

Because of advances in medicine and the health sciences, there have never been as many physically beautiful people as there are today; but there have never been as many ugly-looking souls. The Lord said that the world now is inhabited by billions of undernourished souls who are so concerned about feeding the flesh that they neglect to feed the spirit. Undernourished souls are not able to love, to have compassion. They cannot forgive and are filled with such self-centeredness that they reject the love of God when they die.

Even faith has become superficial. "There is no hell," some Christians say today. "There is no judgment." So it is vital that we live up to what we were given. If we have been gifted with the Catholic faith, we have to be real Catholics. How can we do this? Besides living the commandments and the teachings of the Church, we must study our faith, learn the Catechism of the Catholic Church, and read about the saints and mystics, which prepares us to talk to our neighbor. Lack of knowledge, of faithfulness, of courage, and of love is why so many people are taken away from the Church. We have to live the truth and die telling the truth.

The Lord shared with me that while there has never been a greater risk on earth for a soul to go to hell as there is today, there has also never been a greater opportunity for a soul to attain sainthood while in the flesh. We are living in a glorious time for those who are obedient to God.

Today we are in the apostolate of the end times. The Lord told me that we are at the very end of the very end of the end times. Yet, as St. Peter said, a day for the Lord is like a thousand years.[xix] Pay no attention to all these "prophets" who say, "The end of the world is next month! It's in May!" Then May comes around and nothing happens, so the "prophet" says, "Thanks for your prayers. It's gonna be May of next year." We can't let ourselves be fooled. The devil is the only one who makes us concerned about the future.

We can see signs of apostasy even now. If you tell someone today, "I've decided to become a saint," they will likely laugh at you. People think that reading the life of a saint is like reading that of an alien. And

yet we are all called to sainthood.

We see people studying for eight, ten, fifteen years to become doctors or specialists in their field, sacrificing their time, their whole family. They suffer through and accomplish the most incredible things to do something that is going to die with them. But how many people do you see working hard enough to be with God eternally— to be a saint? How many people truly love God and love their neighbor: the stranger, the poor, their enemies? Very few.

Especially during this period of human history, the evil one is rapidly developing the artistic talents of ambitious people to the highest levels. In this way, he can captivate and capture millions of souls in our flesh-centered culture. The Lord told me that there are no talents that attract Lucifer more than the arts. More than ever before, we see an ever-increasing number of young stars climb the artistic stage, cloaking themselves in human power, wealth, and fame. Their high profile and influence provide the devil a platform to corrupt the masses, because he knows that people emulate the decadent and worldly behavior of the stars.

As for the world and its future, the Lord said it will become even more industrialized—a godless world centered in materialism. Religion is going to be a private activity that cannot be publicly expressed and will be watched and controlled by the governments. The true Church will live practically underground, as in the beginning of Christianity.

The Lord told me that the conversion of Israel has to take place before Jesus will come again. He explained to me how the Jews are the chosen ones of the Lord. Catholics are grafted into the tree of the chosen as their adopted children, and the Jews are our elder brothers. We have to acknowledge the Jews, even if they don't believe yet. He said that just as the Jewish people were chosen for the incarnation of Jesus, they have also been chosen for the Second Coming. The Jews are the ones who will prepare the way for the Lord when He comes again.

At the very end, the Jews will convert massively to Catholicism. An anointing from the Holy Spirit will call them back. This will happen nearly overnight, in much the same way the Berlin Wall fell. Once the conversion begins, there will be much confusion among Jews, and many of them will kill each other. When the Jewish people flood into Catholicism, it is the final bell ringing, "Jesus is coming." They will rescue the Catholic Church from a great apostasy. These are the signs the Lord said He will give.

In the next few years, however, many people will fall away from the Catholic faith. The Lord is cleaning His house, and a lot of dirt is going to be uncovered—what was hidden will come to light. The Church will become smaller, but it will become a Church of real believers. It will not be possible to endure the times we are facing without a faith that is radically centered in love and perfect obedience.

It is absolutely vital in our times that we learn how to really love. We must look around and ask ourselves if we truly care about the salvation of those around us, or are they simply shadows? Before I give a talk, I beg the Lord to give me His love for all who come to listen, and to help me speak from no other place than a pure desire for their salvation. I want everyone to make it home. Each one of us on earth is extremely important. If I don't care about my neighbor, then my works and prayers will be empty.

When we care deeply for strangers and allow their presence to touch our heart, even if just for the moment that they pass by, then we are truly able to love. If we are standing at a busy street corner, smiling at people at the grocery store, speeding by others on the highway, and we know in our hearts that they are immensely important creatures born of God's love, and we cannot help but deeply care about them and their salvation— no matter their looks, beliefs, or behavior—then we know how to love.

If we do not learn how to love this way, if we do not pray with our hearts for the conversion of all sinners because we care about everyone, then we will have to learn this lesson in purgatory. The Lord may ask us when we see Him, "Do you remember this person who was standing next to you for an hour . . . for thirty minutes . . . for five minutes? This person needed your love and your prayers. Did you notice her, or was she another passing shadow? Did she mean nothing to you because you were so into yourself?"

Our life is not a game. It is very serious, and it only happens once. What does it matter if we win in this life but lose our soul?[xx] We have to be awake. We have to be concerned about every little thing we are doing: what we are thinking, saying, touching, feeling, and desiring. We have to be conscious of everything we are listening to and participating in. The truth is that eternal life begins when we are in our birth mother's womb. We are standing in eternity right now, and everything we do reflects upon and will be seen in eternity.

Our life is a journey that will never end. It is important for us to think beyond flesh and bones. Being in this body is just the very beginning. We are in step one, and things will get so much better if we are faithful to the Lord. If we only knew what awaits us, we would be smiling, even when we are hurting and our lives are upside down. This is all going to be over very soon, and the joy that awaits us far surpasses our greatest imaginings of happiness.

People ask me, "Do you wish your kidnapping had never happened?" I tell them that I wouldn't change a thing. I would relive every excruciating moment, if it meant that I could be in heaven for eternity. I've been with Jesus, and He is the fulfillment of all human desire.

By choosing a terrible sinner like me as a mouthpiece of His grace, the Lord is inviting us to trust in His mercy more than the merits we seek. My life is a witness to His forgiveness and compassion. We have a mighty God, an incredibly loving God, a God Who is all good and all just. We should be very, very happy, but we should be very, very holy. There is no other way.[87]

---

[87] Today, Marino Restrepo is hailed as a new St. Paul for this century. Since 1999, he has travelled globally as a Catholic lay missionary, preaching the Gospel message. Marino has produced many pivotal and inspiring DVDs, CDs, and books, and his talks

Brothers and sisters:
We are always courageous,
although we know that while we are at home in the body
we are away from the Lord,
for we walk by faith, not by sight.
Yet we are courageous,
and we would rather leave the body and go home to the Lord.
Therefore, we aspire to please him,
whether we are at home or away.
For we must all appear before the judgment seat of Christ,
so that each may receive recompense,
according to what he did in the body, whether good or evil.

~2 Corinthians 5:6-10

The book, *Winning the Battle for your Soul: Jesus' Teachings through Marino Restrepo, a St. Paul for Our Century* contains of the most extraordinary teachings that Jesus has given to the world through Marino—teachings that will profoundly alter and inform the way you see your ancestry, your past, your purpose, your future, and your very salvation.

"I most willingly say, this book should be widely disseminated, all for God's glory!"
—Archbishop-Emeritus, Ramón C. Arguelles, STL

"This little book is AN AUTHENTIC JEWEL OF GOD."
—María Vallejo-Nágera,
one of the most widely read authors in all of Spain and Latin America

can be found on YouTube in English and Spanish. He is the founder of the lay missionary association, Peregrinos del Amor (The Pilgrims of Love), approved by the Church. See www.marinorestrepo.com.

St. Faustina Kowalska:

Today the Lord said to me, "Daughter, when you go to confession, to this fountain of My mercy, the Blood and Water which came forth from My heart always flows down upon your soul and ennobles it. Every time you go to confession, immerse yourself entirely in My mercy, with great trust, so that I may pour the bounty of My grace upon your soul. When you approach the confessional, know this, that I Myself am waiting there for you. I am only hidden by the priest, but I Myself act in your soul. Here the misery of the soul meets the God of Mercy. Tell souls that from this fount of mercy souls draw graces solely with the vessel of trust. If their trust is great, there is no limit to My generosity. The torrent of grace inundates humble souls. The proud remain always in poverty and misery because My grace turns away from them to humble souls."

~Diary of Saint Maria Faustina Kowalska, #1602

APPENDIX

BIOGRAPHIES AND WORDS OF THE PROPHETS OF THE WARNING

SAINT EDMUND CAMPION, SJ
ENGLAND (1540-1581)
Priest and Martyr

St. Edmund Campion, born in 1540, was raised Catholic during a time of great Catholic persecution in England. Under King Henry VIII, then later under Elizabeth I, the Catholic Church had been usurped by the Church of England, and Catholic priests and laity were being arrested and killed for their faith.

Edmund, the son of a bookseller, had such a powerful and flamboyant intellect that at the age of fifteen, he was given a scholarship to St. John's College, Oxford, and at seventeen, was made a junior fellow. In 1566, Queen Elizabeth I visited Oxford with her advisors, Robert Dudley, Earl of Leicester, and Sr. William Cecil, one of the principal architects of the Reformation in England. Edmund was assigned to give a welcoming speech to the Queen, explaining the movements of the tides, the moon, and the planets, which he did—in Latin, after first praising the Queen. The Queen had hoped to find talented scholars who would agree to be ordained as Anglican priests and lead the new church. Enthralled, she recommended Edmund to an equally impressed Dudley, who offered to become Campion's political patron and help him build a powerful career. A flattered Edmund became an Anglican deacon in 1564 and took the required Oath of Supremacy acknowledging Elizabeth as head of the church in England.

Doubts about Protestantism, however, increasingly wracked Edmund's mind, and in 1569, he went to Ireland where further study convinced him he had been in error. He eventually returned to his Catholic roots and to England, where he was in danger of being captured. Campion fled to France, and when Cecil learned of it, he stated, "It is a great pity to see so notable a man leave his country, for indeed he was one of the diamonds of England."[xxi]

Edmund felt the calling to be a Catholic priest and went to seminary in France, then set off to Rome, barefoot on pilgrimage, where he entered the Society of Jesus in 1573. As a novice, he was sent to study in Brunn, then part of Austria, and later in Prague. In Brunn, while in a garden, Campion had a vision of the Blessed Virgin Mary who told him that he would be a martyr for the faith. He was ordained a Jesuit priest in 1578, and in 1580, his superiors asked him to join fellow Jesuit, Robert Parsons, in leading a dangerous mission to England. He accepted the assignment joyfully. The night before his departure from Prague, one of the Jesuit fathers wrote over Campion's door, "P. Edmundus Campianus, Martyr."

Back in England, a disguised Fr. Campion preached one to three times a day, mentally preparing his homilies while traveling on horseback across the English countryside, administering the sacraments and winning many converts. Queen Elizabeth had spies everywhere searching for priests. Fr. Campion's notoriety and the publication of his pamphlet stating his case if he were captured, titled Rationes Decem (Ten Reasons) but labeled by Protestant refuters as "Campion's Brag," made him the object of one of the most intensive manhunts in English history.

Shortly after dawn on July 18, 1581, Edmund Campion was found in a Catholic home, huddled behind a secret wall with two companions. The cry went out: "I have found the traitors!" Fr. Campion was thrown at the Queen's command into a dungeon in the Tower of London, and when he refused to publicly renounce Catholicism, Cecil and Dudley ordered Campion to be tortured on the rack. He was tied by his wrists and ankles to a frame that was then stretched until his limbs were dislocated. In intense pain, Campion blurted out the names of a few people who had sheltered him. He was then forced to participate in four formal conferences to debate with six high-ranking Anglican ecclesiastics who demanded answers regarding his pamphlet. Without notes or preparation, weakened from torture, he brilliantly refuted their accusations. He was then brought to trial at Westminster Hall on a made-up charge of a plot to assassinate the Queen. Terribly weak after months of imprisonment and torture, he could not even raise his right arm to swear his oath at his trial. A fellow prisoner kissed Campion's arm and held it up for him.

At age forty-one, Fr. Campion was found guilty and sent to the gallows. Executions in Elizabethan England were gruesome affairs that attracted large crowds of spectators. Those convicted of high treason were sentenced to be hanged, drawn, and quartered. Fr. Edmund Campion was first hanged until almost dead, then cut down while still conscious, and disemboweled. Finally, his limbs and head were hacked off. Addressing the crowd right before his death, Campion forgave the council for condemning him. He also asked forgiveness for any harm he might have caused by giving names under torture. With his last words, he prayed for the Queen and wished her a long and prosperous reign.

Though Elizabeth and her advisors hoped Campion's death would lead to the end of Catholicism in England, it had the opposite effect. His martyrdom on December 1, 1581 sparked off a wave of conversions to Catholicism, and strengthened many Jesuit priests to follow in his courageous footsteps. Edmund Campion, SJ, was declared a saint by Pope Paul VI in 1970.[xxii]

WORDS ABOUT THE WARNING:

"I pronounced a great day, not wherein any temporal potentate should minister, but wherein the Terrible Judge should reveal all men's consciences and try every man of each kind of religion. This is the day of change . . ."[xxiii]

~St. Edmund Campion, SJ

BLESSED ANNA MARÍA TAIGI
ITALY (1769–1837)
Wife, Mother, and Mystic

Blessed Anna Maria Taigi was born in Siena, Italy, on May 29, 1769. Physically beautiful, she caught the eye of a handsome porter with dark curly hair, named Domenico, and they were wed on January 7, 1790. In the first years of her marriage, the working-class Anna Maria was more worldly than godly. Given to vanity, she enjoyed adorning herself with pretty dresses and jewelry, and one day while strolling in her fashionable attire around St. Peter's Square, she accidentally bumped into Fr. Angelo Verandi, a Servite priest, who immediately received an inner locution: "Take note of that woman, for one day, I will confide her to your care, and you shall work for her transformation. She shall sanctify herself, for I have chosen her to become a saint."

Soon after, Anna Maria felt contrition over her way of life and went to Confession to a priest she didn't know: Fr. Angel Verandi. She left the confessional overcome with remorse and once home, beat her head against the floor with such force that she caused herself to bleed. Her fancy clothes and accessories were replaced with plain dresses from that moment on, and she lived with a great spirit of penance and renunciation. In time, she would experience ecstasies and locutions and told Fr. Verandi that she was "to be a victim of expiation for the sins of the world." She often received personal counsel from the Lord and the Blessed Mother, the latter of whom told her, "Know well, my dear daughter, that here

222

below, you will have for every one good day, a hundred bad ones, because you must be like my Son Jesus. You must be devoted above all to doing His will and submitting your own constantly to His. . ."

Anna Maria's holiness lay in her daily and difficult work of wife, mother, and managing a household of over a dozen diverse family characters, including her difficult parents, and a priest of some importance, Msgr. Raffaele Natali, who served as her confidant and secretary. In addition to her burdens, her husband, Domenico, had a volcanic temper, and while Anna Maria made sure dinner was made for him when he came home, he once yanked the tablecloth off, sending her fully served meals flying. Nevertheless, she never regretted marrying him. Oftentimes, she prayed and worked until the wee hours of the morning and rose early for Mass. Without overburdening her children, she kept them busy, believing that "laziness is the mother of all the vices." She made sure prayers were said every morning and evening, and the Rosary was said on everyone's knees before dinner. Her crosses were numerous: constant infirmities, diabolical attacks, malicious gossip, penances, and an ongoing fast. Sadly, she had to bury four of her seven beloved children.

Anna Maria quickly became known as a living saint and received a stream of visitors, who sought her counsel. Jesus had told her: "I destine you to convert sinners, to console people of all sorts and conditions: priests, prelates, My very Vicar, himself. All who listen to your words will be granted signal graces at My hands." She was also given the gifts of healing and prophecy. Monsignor Natali, the secretary of Pope Pius VII and a close confidant of hers, said she spoke of a future time of tremendous strife in the Church and the world. ". . . Then entire nations would return to the unity of the Church, and many Turks [Moslems?], pagans, and Jews would be converted and their fervor cover with confusion the original Christians. In one word, she told me that Our Lord was intending to cleanse the world and his Church for which he was preparing a miraculous rebirth that would be a triumph of His mercy."

Anna Maria's most remarkable spiritual gift was one that has never been repeated: a glowing light, like a small sun, that remained always by her side. Cardinal Carlo Maria Pedicini, who knew her for thirty years, said in his deposition for the cause of her sanctity:

For forty-seven years, day and night, at home, at church, in the street, she saw in this sun, which became increasingly brilliant, all things on this Earth, both physical and moral; she penetrated to the depths and rose up to heaven, where she saw the eternal lot of the dead. She saw the most secret thoughts of persons nearby or far off; events and personages of bygone days. . . She had only to think of a thing, and it presented itself in a clear and complete manner. . . A mere glance at this mystic sun, and she entered, at will, into the most secret council-rooms of kings. She penetrated into the prisons of China and Arabia. . . where confessors of the faith, slaves, and prisoners languished in agony. . . In this way, did she exercise an unbounded apostolate, won souls to grace in every part of the globe, and prepared the way for missionaries; the entire world was the theater of her labors.

On June 9, 1837, Anna Maria, nearly blind, died at the age of 68. After her passing, marks of instruments of penance and a hair shirt were found on her body. When her coffin, sealed for eighteen years, was re-opened, her body was found incorrupt. Later, in 1920, when her holy remains were once again examined, they were at that point subject to the normal processes of decomposition. Blessed Anna Maria Taigi's body, with a wax covering placed over her face and hands to preserve her resemblance, still lies today in the Chapel of the Madonna in the basilica of San Chrysogono in Rome. Her Memorial feast day is celebrated in the Church on June 9.[xxiv]

WORDS ABOUT THE WARNING:

"A great purification will come upon the world preceded by an Illumination of Conscience in which everyone will see themselves as God sees them."[xxv]

~Blessed Anna María Taigi

Blessed Anna Maria also indicated that this Illumination of Conscience would save many souls because many would repent as a result.[xxvi] In her beatification process, published in *Analecta juris Pontificii*, the following circumstance was deposed upon oath by Cardinal Pedicini. He said that one day, "Anna Maria, while shedding a torrent of tears, prayed and offered her actions and sufferings for the conversion of sinners, for the destruction of sin, and that God might be known and loved by all men. Then God manifested to her the horrible sins of persons of every condition, and how grievously He was offended. At this sight, the servant of God experienced a profound sorrow, and sighing, she exclaimed: 'Dearly beloved! what is the remedy for this disaster?'

Jesus Christ answered:

'My child, the Church, my spouse, my Father, and myself shall remedy everything. For after a punishment . . . . those who shall survive shall have to conduct themselves well.' At this point she saw innumerable conversions of heretics, who will return to the bosom of the Church; she saw, also, the edifying conduct of their lives, as well as that of all other Catholics."[xxvii]

BLESSED POPE PIUS IX
THE PAPAL STATES (1792–1878)

Pope Pius IX was born in Senigallia, Italy in 1792, the ninth child born into a family of nobility. He had a disease, not well diagnosed, which some called epilepsy, and his childhood was marked by little voluntary mortifications and an intense religious life. In 1815, St. Vincent Pallotti predicted that he would become Pope and that the Virgin of Loreto would free him eventually from the disease.

Serving from 1846 to 1878, he held the longest and one of the most difficult pontificates in Church history. (St. Peter's pontificate is traditionally listed as twenty-five years.) He governed the Papal States at a time in history when the Pope acted not only as the head of the Church, but as the monarch of a series of territories in the Italian Peninsula (from the 8th century until 1870). Shortly after his election, he began rudimentary political reforms in the Papal States. He freed political prisoners, removed many of the restrictions on Jews, and tore open the gates of the Jewish ghetto in Rome.

Bl. Pius IX was immensely popular throughout much of the Catholic world, and affectionately called Pio Nono—a pun on Pio Nove ("Pius the Ninth") which means "Pius Grandpa." He also earned himself the nicknames, "The Pope of Prayer" and "The Pope of the Cross" for his spirituality,

Francis Newman said Pius IX was so popular because "his personal presence was of a kind that no one could withstand. . . the main cause of his popularity was the magic of his presence. . . Unlike most of his predecessors, Pius had a vibrant social life, taking frequent walks around Rome, granting an unprecedented number of audiences, hosting weekly parties in the Quirinal gardens, and speaking daily to crowds in the Piazza."[xxviii] He was the first pope to be photographed—not a rectory went without his picture. With his characteristically sharp sense of humor, he once quipped that he was the number one attraction for tourists in Rome. Before him, common folk didn't know what popes looked like, and they were often shrouded in mystery.[xxix]

Bl. Pius IX was a Marian pope, who described Mary as a Mediatrix of Salvation in his encyclical "Ubi Primum." In 1854, he promulgated the dogma of the Immaculate Conception, articulating a belief held for centuries by the Catholic faithful that the Mother of God was conceived in her mother's womb without original sin. His pontificate represented the height of missionary work to that time, and in 1862, he convened 300 bishops to the Vatican for the canonization of twenty-six Japanese martyrs. His 1864 Syllabus of Errors was a strong condemnation against liberalism, modernism, moral relativism, secularization, and separation of church and state.

The papal states were in danger of a takeover by Giuseppe Garibaldi who desired to march under the slogan Roma o Morte (Rome or Death). In a surprising expression of love for this anticlerical Italian revolutionary, the pope once remarked, "If you see Garibaldi, tell him that I know he curses me daily; but that I always bless him." And once, he so won over Garibaldi's troops imprisoned in his own jails that they wept and kissed his hands."[xxx]

Pius IX primary legacy is the First Vatican Council, which he convened in 1869, by far the largest Council in history. The Council formally deplored the pantheism, materialism, and atheism of the time, and declared the doctrine of "papal infallibility."[xxxi] When Antonelli, the money manager, warned the pope that infallibility would alienate many people, he rejoined, "I have the Blessed Virgin on my side."[xxxii]

This decree was promulgated on July 18, 1870, and not a moment too soon. The very next day saw the declaration of the Franco-Prussian War and the instant withdrawal of French troops from Rome, followed by the Italian occupation of the city, which brought the Council to a somewhat abrupt finish. The Vatican Council ended. Liberal Italy swallowed Rome and the remaining Papal States, leaving Vatican City the size of a small town. As the papacy's financial struggle deepened, Pio Nono said, "I may be infallible, but I am certainly bankrupt."[xxxiii]

THE WARNING

The idea of papal infallibility, however, was a reach no president, prime minister, or dictator could rival. His appeal for public worldwide support of the Holy See after he became what he called "the prisoner of the Vatican" resulted in the revival and spread to the whole Catholic Church of Peter's Pence, which is used today to enable the Pope "to respond to those who are suffering as a result of war, oppression, natural disaster, and disease."[xxxiv] Pope Pius IX was beatified by Pope John Paul II on September 3, 2000.

WORDS ABOUT THE WARNING:

"Since the whole world is against God and His Church, it is evident that He has reserved the victory over His enemies to Himself. This will be more obvious when it is considered that the root of all our present evils is to be found in the fact that those with talents and vigor crave earthly pleasures, and not only desert God but repudiate Him altogether. Thus it appears they cannot be brought back in any other way except through an act that cannot be ascribed to any secondary agency, and thus all will be forced to look to the supernatural. . . There will come a great wonder, which will fill the world with astonishment. This wonder will be preceded by the triumph of revolution. The church will suffer exceedingly. Her servants and her chieftain will be mocked, scourged, and martyred."[xxxv]

~Bl. Pope Pius IX

SAINT FAUSTINA KOWALSKA
POLAND (1905–1938)
Nun, Mystic, and Apostle of Divine Mercy

Saint Faustina Kowalska is one of the greatest mystics of the Church. She was the third of ten children born into a poor, Catholic, peasant family in Głogowiec, Poland. Her childhood was distinguished by hard work, obedience, acts of devotion, a love of prayer, and a tremendous sensitivity to human misery. In her famous work, the *Diary of Saint Maria Faustina Kowalska: Divine Mercy in My Soul,* she wrote: *"From the age of seven, I experienced the definite call of God, the grace of a vocation to the religious life. It was in the seventh year of my life that, for the first time, I heard God's voice in my soul; that is, an invitation to a more perfect life."*

After three years of schooling—all the education she would ever receive, she told her parents of her desire to enter a convent, but they prevented it. At sixteen, she worked as a housekeeper to help them and to support herself. Then the following happened when she was nineteen: *"Once I was at a dance with one of my sisters, and while everybody was having a good time, my soul was experiencing internal torments. As I began to dance, I suddenly saw Jesus at my side, Jesus racked with pain, stripped of his clothing, covered with wounds, Who spoke these words to*

229

me, *"How long shall I suffer and how long will you keep deceiving Me?"* *At that moment, the charming music stopped, and any company vanished from my sight; there remained Jesus and I. I took a seat by my dear sister, pretending to have a headache to hide what had taken place in my soul. After a while, I slipped out unnoticed, leaving my sister and all my companions behind, and made my way to the Cathedral of Saint Stanislaus Kostka. It was almost twilight; there were only a few people in the cathedral. Paying no attention to what was happening around me, I fell prostrate before the Blessed Sacrament and begged the Lord to be good enough to allow me to understand what I should do next. Then I heard these words, "Go at once to Warsaw. You will enter a convent there." I rose from prayer, came home and took care of things that needed to be settled. As best I could, I confided to my sister what took place within my soul. I told her to say goodbye to our parents, and thus, in one dress, with no other belongings, I arrived in Warsaw"* (Diary, #9-10).

In Warsaw, she knocked on numerous convent doors, but none opened for her. Finally, in August of 1925, she was accepted by the Congregation of the Sisters of Our Lady of Mercy and entered the order shortly thereafter: *"It seemed to me that I had stepped into the life of Paradise. A single prayer was bursting forth from my heart, one of thanksgiving"* (Diary, #17).

In her years in the convent, she worked as a cook, gardener and porter, and helped prostitutes on the streets to leave their profession and begin life anew. Sr. Faustina possessed a heart filled with the mercy for souls, a mercy she would soon be called to propagate. Her rigorous lifestyle and exhausting fasting on behalf of others left her weak, and she underwent great spiritual, moral, and physical sufferings in religious life. She sacrificed her life for sinners.

As her prayer life deepened, Sr. Faustina's soul was filled with extraordinary gifts: revelations, visions, hidden stigmata, participation in the Passion, bilocation, reading souls, prophecy, mystical engagement and marriage to the Lord. In spite of being so richly endowed with graces, she knew that they do not constitute sanctity. She wrote in her *Diary*: *Neither graces, nor revelations, nor raptures, nor gifts granted to a soul make it perfect, but rather the intimate union of the soul with God. These gifts are merely ornaments of the soul, but constitute neither its essence nor its perfection. My sanctity and perfection consist in the close union of my will with the will of God* (Diary #1107).

On February 22, 1931, after returning from prayer, she received her most intense vision and one that would forever change her life and the world. Jesus appeared to her wearing a dazzling white robe. One hand was raised in blessing and the other was touching His garment at the breast. Two large rays of light, one red and the other pale white, emanated from His heart.

Father Michael Sopoćko, St. Faustina's spiritual director and the person chosen by the Lord to propagate His message of Divine Mercy, was inspired by Sr. Faustina's holiness but didn't know if he quite believed in her visions. Doubts assailed him when Jesus persisted in His request that a Divine Mercy image be painted of His image in her vision, and a new Feast of Divine Mercy be celebrated on the Sunday following Easter, accompanied by extraordinary promises: *"On that day . . . The soul that will go to Confession and receive Holy Communion shall obtain complete forgiveness of sins and punishment."* (*Diary*, 699)

Fr. Sopoćko would later say: *"Led more by curiosity of what the picture would look like, rather than belief in the authenticity of Sister Faustina's visions, I decided to arrange the painting of the picture. . . Sister Faustina complained that the picture was not as beautiful as she saw it, but the Lord Jesus comforted her and said it was enough as it was, and He added: 'I am giving people a vessel with which they are to come to Me for graces. That vessel is this image with the inscription: Jesus, I trust in You.'"* In time, Fr. Sopoćko believed in Sr. Faustina's mystical experiences, especially when her prophecies concerning him were fulfilled: *"She foretold in detail difficulties and even persecutions that I was to encounter because of spreading the devotion of Divine Mercy and trying to establish the Feast of this name on Low Sunday. It was easier to bear that knowing that from the beginning, it was the will of God."*[xxxvi]

On April 19, 1935, Good Friday, Jesus told Sr. Faustina that He wished for His image to be publicly honored, and Fr. Sopoćko delivered the very first sermon on the Divine Mercy one week later. That same year, Jesus taught Sr. Faustina the Chaplet of Divine Mercy, a special prayer using rosary beads: *"Oh, what great graces I will grant to souls who say this Chaplet. Write down these words, My daughter. Speak to the world about My mercy; let all mankind recognize my unfathomable mercy. It is a sign for the end times; after it will come the day of justice. While there is still time, let them have recourse to the fount of my mercy; let them profit from the blood and water which gushed forth for them."* (*Diary*, #848)

In July of 1937, the first holy cards with the Divine Mercy image and the inscription, *"Jesus, I Trust in You,"* were created, and Faustina provided instructions for praying the Novena of Divine Mercy, which the Lord also dictated to her.

During the final years of her life, Sr. Faustina's health deteriorated significantly: she developed tuberculosis, which attacked her lungs and gastrointestinal tract. As a result, she suffered through two periods of hospital treatment, each lasting a few months. Fr. Sopoćko wrote: *"On September 26, [1938], she foretold me also her own death, that she would die in ten days, and she did die on October 5."* Physically ravaged, but spiritually united with God, Sr. Faustina passed away at age thirty-three, surrounded by the odor of sanctity. On April 30, 2000, St. Pope John Paul II canonized Sr. Faustina Kowalska, calling her *"The great apostle of Divine Mercy in our time."* The ceremony took place on the Sunday after Easter, the Sunday that was instituted by the Pope, at the request of Jesus Christ, as the Feast of Divine Mercy for the entire Church.[xxxvii]

WORDS ABOUT THE WARNING:

St. Faustina Kowalska experienced an illumination of her conscience and describes the moment in her *Diary*:

"Once I was summoned to the judgment [seat] of God. I stood alone before the Lord. Jesus appeared such as we know Him during His Passion. After a moment, His wounds disappeared, except for five: those in His hands, His feet, and His side. Suddenly, I saw the complete condition of my soul as God sees it. I could clearly see all that is displeasing to God. I did not know that even the smallest transgressions will have to be accounted for. What a moment! Who can describe it? To stand before the Thrice-Holy God!"[xxxviii]

~St. Faustina Kowalska

Message from Jesus Christ to St. Faustina Kowalska regarding the universal Illumination of Conscience:

"Write this: before I come as the Just Judge, I come as the King of Mercy. Before the day of justice arrives, this sign in the sky will be given to mankind. All light in the heavens will be extinguished, and there will be great darkness over the whole earth. Then the sign of the Cross will be seen in the sky, and from the holes where the hands and the feet of the

Savior were nailed will come forth a brilliant light, which will illuminate the Earth for a period of time. This will take place shortly before the last day. "xxxix

~*Diary* entry, August 2, 1934

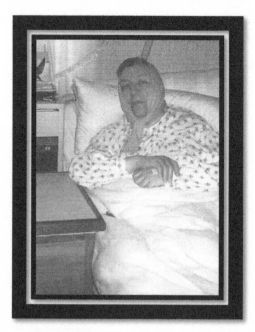

APPARITIONS OF OUR LORD AND OUR LADY AT HEEDE, GERMANY

(1937–1940, 1945)

GRETE GANSEFORTH
Mystic and Stigmatist
(1924?–1996)

On the evening of November 1, 1937, four girls, Anna Schulte, sisters Maria and Grete Ganseforth, and Susanna Bruns, ages twelve to fourteen, reported that the Blessed Virgin Mary had appeared to them as they walked past the church cemetery on their way to celebrate All Saints Day. The news was received in their small German village of Heede with skepticism and amusement, until the girls, previously occupied with worldly pleasures and amusements, switched to long and fervent prayer. On November 7, 4,000-5,000 villagers surrounded the girls during their apparition, and several priests claimed to witness Our Lady, as well. The next day, a crowd of over 7,000 gathered at the site.

Margaret (Grete), Susana, Ana y María en 1938

Our Lady hovered about one meter off the ground, with a small, light blue cloud under her feet. Appearing about eighteen years old, she was stunningly beautiful, with light blue eyes and wearing a decorated golden crown and a long white dress. On her left hand sat Baby Jesus with a golden globe topped by a cross in his right hand.

It was the eve of World War II. Hitler ruled Germany and forbade participation in this "superstitious nonsense." In 1939, the Gestapo seized the children and took them to the lunatic asylum of Göttingen. There, they were examined by psychiatric experts for four weeks and found perfectly healthy and normal. The children were released, but forbidden to go near the place of the apparitions, as were pilgrims, so Our Lady began appearing to the children elsewhere.

Our Lady asked to be invoked under the titles "Queen of the Universe" and "Queen of the Souls of Purgatory." She gave over 100 messages, primarily urgent appeals—sometimes through tears, for conversion, penance, and prayer. Five years after the last apparition on November 3, 1940, Grete began to see Our Lord and her guardian angel and although she did not see Our Lady, she heard her voice on numerous occasions from a brilliant light. On orders from her spiritual director, she kept a diary of her mystical events. Our Lord told Grete that He had singled her out to become His spouse by becoming a victim soul for the conversion of obstinate sinners. When she agreed, Our Lord gave her the wounds of the stigmata, and she shared in the Passion of Christ until she passed away in 1996. Today, her grave is visited by pilgrims, several of whom have claimed significant favors through the seer's intercession.[xl]

After years of investigation, the Bishop of Osnabrück, Helmut Hermann Wittler, declared the following on June 3, 1959, in a circular letter to the clergy of the diocese:

"The apparitions are undeniable proof of the seriousness and authenticity of these manifestations. . . In the apparitions and messages of Heede, we find nothing contrary to the Faith. Indeed, their similarity to the approved apparitions of Fatima, Lourdes, and La Salette give good indications of their authenticity."[xli]

Approbation of the apparitions has been graciously ratified with the installation of each successive bishop of Osnabrück, without a formal judgment being made. On August 22, 1977, a new chapel, "Mary Queen of the Universe," was consecrated on the grounds of the cemetery where Mary first appeared. Thirty-one years earlier, a statue of the same name had been placed in the cemetery by order of Bishop Hermann Wilhelm Berning, as directed by Our Lady through the visionaries. In 2000, Bishop Franz Josef Bode, elevated the church and chapel of Heede to the rank of Diocesan Shrines. The message containing the Mini-Judgment was given to Grete Ganseforth in 1945. It was published in Italian in 1949 in a booklet by Don Alfonso Cenni that received the Nihil Obstat and the Imprimatur.[xlii]

WORDS ABOUT THE WARNING:

Message from Jesus to Grete Ganseforth in 1945:

Humanity has not listened to My Holy Mother, who appeared at Fatima to urge mankind to do penance. Now I, Myself, have come to warn the world in this last hour: the times are serious! May people finally do penance for their sins; may they turn away with all their heart from evil and pray, pray much, in order to calm the indignation of God. May they often recite the Holy Rosary, in particular: this prayer is powerful with God. Less entertainments and amusements!

I am very near. The Earth will tremble and will suffer. It will be terrible, a Mini-Judgment. But do not fear. I am with you. You will rejoice and thank Me. Those who await Me will have My help, My grace, and My love. For those who are not in a state of grace, it will be frightening. The angels of justice are now scattered across the world. I will make Myself known to mankind. Every soul will recognize Me as their God. I am coming! I am at the door. The Earth will shake and moan.

My love has planned this action before the creation of the world. People do not listen to My calls: they close their ears; they resist grace and reject My mercy, My love, My merits. The world is worse than before the deluge. It agonizes in a quagmire of sin. Hatred and greed have infiltrated human hearts. All this is the work of Satan. The world lies in dense darkness. This generation deserves to be wiped out, but I wish to show it My mercy. The cup of God's anger is already spilling over onto the nations. The angel of peace will not delay in coming down to Earth. I want to heal and save. Through the wounds that bleed now, mercy will win and justice triumph.

But My faithful do not sleep, like the disciples in the Garden of Olives; rather, they constantly draw for themselves and others from the treasure of My merits and abundance. Prodigious things are being prepared. That which is coming will be terrible, like never before since the beginning of the world. I, Myself, am coming, and I will manifest My will.

All who have suffered in these last times are My martyrs, and they are preparing my harvest for the Church. They have taken part in My Via Dolorosa. That which is about to occur will greatly surpass everything that has happened before. The Mother of God and the angels will take part in it. Hell believes its victory is assured, but I will snatch it from its hand. Many curse me, and I must therefore allow them to fall into a world of misfortune; for many will be saved by this means. Blessed are those who suffer everything in reparation for those who offend me.

I will come with My peace. I will build My Kingdom with a small number of elect. This Kingdom will come suddenly, sooner than men think. . . I will make My light shine: a light which for some, will be a blessing, and for others, darkness. Mankind will recognize My love and My power.

My beloved children, the hour is near. Pray unceasingly, and you will not be confused. I am gathering My elect. They will come together from every part of the world, and they will glorify Me. I am coming! Blessed are those who are prepared. Blessed are those who await Me.[xliii]

ELIZABETH KINDELMANN
(1913–1985)
Wife, Mother, Mystic, and
Founder of The Flame of Love Movement

Elizabeth Szántò was a Hungarian mystic born in Budapest in 1913, who lived a life of poverty and hardship. She was the eldest child and the only one alongside her six twin-pairs of siblings to survive into adulthood. At age five, her father died, and at ten, Elizabeth was sent to Willisau, Switzerland to live with a well-to-do family. She returned to Budapest temporarily at age eleven to be with and care for her mom who was seriously ill and confined to bed. A month later, Elizabeth was scheduled to board a train from Austria at 10:00 a.m. in order to return to the Swiss family who decided to adopt her. She was alone and mistakenly arrived at the station at 10 p.m. A young couple took her back to Budapest where she spent the remainder of her life until she died in 1985.

Living as an orphan on the verge of starvation, Elizabeth worked hard to survive. Twice, she tried to enter religious congregations but was rejected. A turning point came in August, 1929, when she was accepted into the parish choir and there met Karoly Kindlemann, a chimney-sweeper instructor. They married on May 25, 1930, when she was sixteen and he was thirty. Together, they had six children, and after sixteen years of marriage, her husband died.

For many years to follow, Elizabeth struggled to care for herself and her family. In 1948, the Communist Nationalization of Hungary was a harsh master, and she was fired from her first job for having a statue of the Blessed Mother in her home. Always a diligent worker, Elizabeth never had good fortune in her long string of short-lived jobs, as she struggled to feed her family. Eventually, all of her children married, and in time, moved back in with her, bringing their children with them.

Elizabeth's profound prayer life led her to become a lay Carmelite, and in 1958 at age forty-five, she entered a three-year-period of spiritual darkness. Around that time, she also began to have intimate conversations with the Lord through inner locutions, followed by conversations with the Virgin Mary and her guardian angel. On July 13, 1960, Elizabeth started a diary at the Lord's request. Two years into this process, she wrote:

"Prior to receiving messages from Jesus and the Virgin Mary, I received the following inspiration: 'You must be selfless, for we will entrust you with a great mission, and you will be up to the task. However, this is only possible if you remain totally selfless, renouncing yourself. That mission can be bestowed upon you only if you also want it out of your free will."

Elizabeth's answer was "Yes," and through her, Jesus and Mary began a Church movement under a new name given to that immense and eternal love that Mary has for all her children: "The Flame of Love."

Through what became *The Spiritual Diary*, Jesus and Mary taught Elizabeth, and they continue to instruct the faithful in the divine art of suffering for the salvation of souls. Tasks are assigned for each day of the week, which involve prayer, fasting, and night vigils, with beautiful promises attached to them, laced with special graces for priests and the souls in purgatory. In their messages, Jesus and Mary say that The Flame of Love of the Immaculate Heart of Mary is the greatest grace given to mankind since the Incarnation. And in the not-so-distant future, her flame will engulf the entire world.

Cardinal Péter Erdő of Esztergom-Budapest, Primate of Hungary, established a commission to study *The Spiritual Diary* and the various recognitions that local bishops around the world had given to The Flame of Love movement, as a private association of the faithful. In 2009, the cardinal not only gave the Imprimatur to *The Spiritual Diary*, but recognized Elizabeth's mystical locutions and writings as authentic, a "gift to the Church." In addition, he gave his episcopal approval of the Flame of Love movement, which has formally operated within the Church for over twenty years. Currently, the movement is seeking further approbation as a Public Association of the Faithful. On June 19, 2013, Pope Francis gave it his Apostolic Blessing.

From the Diary of Elizabeth Kindelmann, titled *The Flame of Love of the Immaculate Heart of Mary: The Spiritual Diary* (Canadian) and the abridged version, titled *The Flame of Love* (United States)—

Diary entry of January 15, 1963:
"I saw the Lord's penetrating glance. My bodily eyes cannot stand that glance. I shut my eyes tightly. His glance is like a flash of lightening, which lights up everything. I saw all my sins. I cried for hours with greater sorrow than ever before. Jesus said, *'Let our glances meld together so they form one glance.'* My sinful eyes will be one with His divine eyes. He wants this for everyone. He said, *'Whoever walks with me will be joined with me in one glance.'*"

[On August 15, 1980] "The Lord said, *'The Church and the whole world are in danger. You cannot change this situation. Only the Holy Trinity, through the unified intercession of the Blessed Virgin, the angels, the saints, and the souls in purgatory, can help you.'*

"On March 27 [1963], the Lord said that the Spirit of Pentecost will flood the Earth with His power, and a great miracle will gain the attention of all humanity. This will be the effect of grace of the Flame of Love.

Due to lack of faith, Earth is entering into darkness, but Earth will experience a great jolt of faith. People will believe and will create a new world. By the Flame of Love, confidence and faith will take root. The face of the Earth will be renewed because *'something like this has not happened since the Word became Flesh.'* Earth, although flooded with sufferings, will be renewed by Our Lady's intercession.

The Lord asked me to take the messages to the bishop. Since the bishop was confirming nearby, I went to ask for an appointment. He told me to come to his home. I spoke with him for an hour and gave him the messages."

[On July 24, 1963], "Our Lady spoke, *'Do not abandon the battle. Through my Flame of Love, a new era of grace, never before known on Earth, will begin.'"*

"On August 1 (1963), [Our Lord] said, *'When the effect of grace of my Mother's Flame of Love pours out into all hearts, she will be venerated as never before. All will join in one gigantic prayer of petition. Give my messages to those in authority, and tell them not to impede My Mother who wants to pour out the Flame of Love.'"*

"On March 12, 1964, Jesus said in a thundering voice, *'Before the difficult times are upon you, prepare yourselves for the vocation I have called you to by renewed tenacity and a firm decision. You must not be lazy, uninterested, and indifferent because the great storm is brewing just ahead. Its gusts will carry away indifferent souls consumed by laziness. Only those souls with a genuine vocation will survive. The great danger that will soon erupt will begin when I will raise My hand. Give My words of warning to all the priestly souls. Let My words that warn you in advance shake them up.* [xliv]

Our Lady said, *'Earth is experiencing the calm before the storm, like a volcano about to explode. Earth is now in this terrible situation. The crater of hatred is boiling. I, the beautiful Ray of Dawn, will blind Satan. No dying soul should be condemned. My Flame of Love will now be lit. It will be a terrible storm, a hurricane that will want to destroy faith. In that dark night, heaven and Earth will be illuminated by the Flame of Love that I offer to souls.'*

Our Lady spoke, *'My Flame of Love is burning. It is so great that I cannot keep it any longer within me. It leaps out to you with explosive power. When it pours out, my love will destroy the satanic hatred that contaminates the world. The greatest number of souls will be set free. Nothing like this has existed before. This is my greatest miracle that I will do for all. . . No need for this miracle to be authenticated. I will authenticate the miracle in each soul. All will recognize the outpouring of the Flame of Love.* 'xlv

[Our Lady said:] 'The moment is near when my Flame of Love will ignite. At that moment, Satan will be blinded. [...] Everyone receiving this Flame will feel it because it will ignite and reach the whole world, not only in nations consecrated to me, but all around the Earth. It will spread to even the most inaccessible places because there is no place inaccessible to Satan. 'xlvi

'Once Satan is blinded,' Our Lord also promised, *'the decrees of Vatican Council II will be fulfilled in an extraordinary way.'* [Message from Jesus on October 25, 1964. The council had begun two years earlier.]xlvii *Let priests and their people gather in spiritual oneness. This outpouring will reach even the souls of the non-baptized.* '*'*xlviii

APPARITIONS OF OUR LADY AT GARABANDAL, SPAIN

(1961–1965)

Visionaries: CONCHITA GONZALEZ, MARI LOLI MAZON, MARI CRUZ GONZALEZ, AND JACINTA GONZALEZ

On the evening of June 18, 1961, four young girls, eleven and twelve years old, were playing together at the southern border of a small Spanish village of some eighty humble dwellings, called Garabandal. The hamlet was poor, Catholic, and untouched by modern conveniences, even telephones. Conchita, Mari Loli, Mari Cruz, and Jacinta went on a mischievous adventure to steal apples from their schoolteacher's tree, when they heard a loud boom, like a peal of thunder, but not a cloud was in the sky. "What a big fault we have committed!" Conchita," lamented. "Now that we have taken the apples that do not belong to us, the devil is happy and our poor guardian angel is sad."[xlix] A few minutes later, a dazzling angel appeared in front of them. He said nothing, and after a few short minutes, vanished. The angel would appear to the four girls eight more times in the succeeding days, without saying a word. Then finally, on the first of July, he spoke: *"I came to announce the visit of the Blessed Virgin Mary of Carmel. She will appear tomorrow, Sunday."*

The girls were overjoyed. "Let her come soon!" they told him.[1] News spread quickly, and the next day, many villagers and curiosity seekers from nearby villages, including priests, went to the spot where the girls said the angel appeared. On July 2, the Virgin Mary appeared to them with the Child Jesus and two angels—one of which was the angel they had seen, whom they now recognized as St. Michael. The girls spoke openly and familiarly with Our Lady as she smiled at them. Thus began a beautiful mother-daughter relationship of apparitions that would continue approximately 2000 times over the next four years, sometimes several times in a single day.

The visitations drew thousands of witnesses in huge crowds and featured mystical phenomena, much of it filmed or photographed. These interactions between Our Lady and the children became known as the ecstasies—when the children would fall to their knees and look upward, heavy as boulders and impervious to light and pain. They also included ecstatic walks, when the girls moved, for example, walking backward quickly through rough terrain with their heads and eyes tilted heavenward; and the returning of rosaries and medals to their proper owners—when the girls, still looking up, handed objects blessed by Our Lady to their rightful owners in a crowd, not knowing whose they were.

The Virgin Mary's first message to the world on October 18, 1961 was a call to a radical conversion of heart. In the words of the four visionaries: *"Many sacrifices must be made. Much penance must be done. We must pay many visits to the Blessed Sacrament. But first of all, we must be very good. Already the Cup is filling, and if we do not change, we shall be punished."* In a second message given for the world eight months later on June 19, 1962, Jacinta reported: *". . . the world is worse and must change much, but has not changed at all. What a pity that it does not change."* In a third message of June 23, 1962, Our Lady said, in the words of Mari Loli and Jacinta, now thirteen:

"The Virgin has told us: the world continues the same . . . that it does not change at all. Few will see God. They are so few that it causes the Virgin much sorrow. What a pity that it does not change. The Virgin told us that the chastisement is coming, seeing that the world is not changing. The Cup is filling up. How sad the Virgin was, although she didn't let us see it because she loves us so much and she suffers alone. She is so good! Be good, everyone, so that

the Virgin will be happy. She told us that we who are good should pray for those who are bad. Let us pray to God for the world, for those who do not know Him. Be good. . . be very good to everyone. "[li]

On June 18, 1965, Our Lady gave her last public message to Conchita at Garabandal. It was transmitted live on Spanish television. A video of Conchita in ecstasy along with events preceding the apparition can now be viewed on YouTube, in a video called "Garabandal Film 08—Second Message June 18th, 1965."[lii] Our Lady's words were of sadness and warning:

"Since my message of October 18, [1961] has not been complied with and has not been made known to the world, I tell you that this is the last one. Before, the Cup was filling, now it is overflowing. Many cardinals, many bishops, and many priests are on the road to perdition, and they are taking many souls with them. Less and less importance is being given to the Eucharist. You should turn the wrath of God away from yourselves by your efforts. If you ask for forgiveness with sincerity of heart, He will forgive you. I, your Mother, through the intercession of the Archangel Michael, want to tell you to amend your lives. The last warnings are upon you. I love you very much and do not want your condemnation. Pray to Us with sincerity, and we will grant your requests. You must make more sacrifices. Reflect on the Passion of Jesus."

The second message caused particular controversy over the words "many cardinals, many bishops and many priests are on the road to perdition." Conchita was asked many times to verify this information and responded many times that Mary stressed the importance of the priesthood, focusing attention on priests above others.[liii]

Besides these messages, the visionaries forecast a "Warning," a "Miracle," and a "Chastisement." Within a year of the Warning, a great miracle will take place for a quarter of an hour and will leave a permanent sign in Garabandal, which can be seen and photographed, but not touched. Conchita will announce the coming Miracle to the world, eight days in advance. The sick who come to Garabandal on that day will be cured, unbelievers will be converted. "The sign that will remain," says Conchita, "will be able to be seen, photographed, and televised but it will not be able to be touched. It will appear clearly that it is something not of this world, but of God."

The very last apparition was a private one to Conchita on November 13, 1965. *"Tell me, Conchita,"* said Our Lady with maternal care, *"tell me about my children. They are all under my mantle. I love you so much, and I desire your salvation."* Reminding Conchita of the importance of prayer, she said: *"Why don't you visit my Son more often in the Blessed Sacrament? Why are you lead by laziness, and why don't you go and visit Him? He is waiting for you day and night. . ."*

Toward the end of their conversation, Conchita exclaimed, "Oh, how happy I am when I see you. Why don't you take me with you right now?"

Our Lady answered, *"Remember what I told you on your saint's day. When you go before God, you must show Him your hands full of good works, done by you for your brothers and for the glory of God; now your hands are empty."*

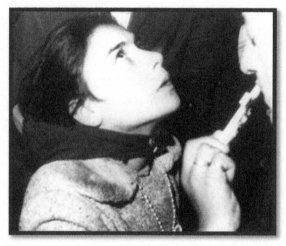

The day after this last apparition, an author of the events in Garabandal, Albrecht Weber, had a long conversation with Conchita, who asked him, "Can you imagine how somebody could kill children in the womb without thereby killing the mother?"

Albrecht answered, "No! What gave you that idea, Conchita?"

"Well, the Blessed Mother spoke about this, and she let me know that this will happen with the overflowing of the Cup." Conchita said this, trembling and disturbed, without being able to visualize what it really meant or how the killing could be effected. She would learn soon enough.[liv]

Where are the visionaries now? Conchita González moved to New York City where she met her husband and had four children. She was widowed on October 31, 2013.[lv]

Mari Loli Mazón moved to Brockton, Massachusetts, where she married, had four children—the fourth died young, and would live for the next twenty-seven years until her death in New Hampshire in 2009. Jacinta González became Jacinta Moynihan and is living in Oxnard,

California, with her husband and daughter. Mari Cruz González lives in Aviles, Spain and is married with four children.

The situation of the current ecclesiastical judgment of the apparitions at Garabandal is "Non-constat de supernaturalitate," which means "The supernatural origin has not been established," and it is open to new evaluations.[lvi] In an "Official Note" of July 8, 1965, Bishop Eugenio Beitia of Santander—the diocese containing Garabandal, wrote:

"We point out, however, that we have not found anything deserving of ecclesiastical censorship or condemnation either in the doctrine or in the spiritual recommendations that have been publicized as having been addressed to the faithful, for these contain an exhortation to prayer and sacrifice, to Eucharistic devotion, to veneration of Our Lady in traditional praiseworthy ways, and to holy fear of God offended by our sins. They simply repeat the common doctrine of the Church in these matters."[lvii]

An important number of contemporary saints have believed in the apparitions of Garabandal, such as St. Teresa of Calcutta,[lviii] St. Pope Paul VI,[lix] St. Josemaría Escrivá de Balaguer,[lx] and St. Padre Pio,[lxi] among others. St. Padre Pio encouraged people to go to Garabandal; when asked about its authenticity, he once answered curtly, "How many times must she appear there to be believed?"[lxii]

St. Pope John Paul II was also apparently a supporter of Our Lady's apparitions at Garabandal. When a copy of the 1993 version of the book by Albrecht Weber, *Garabandal Der Zeigefinger Gottes* (*Garabandal: The Finger of God*), was presented to Pope John Paul II, he later asked his secretary, Fr. (now Archbishop) Stanislaus Dziwisz, to write to the author. In a subsequent printing of the book in 2000, a portion of the Pope's message is reprinted on page 19:

"May God reward you for everything. Especially for the deep love with which you are making the events connected with Garabandal more widely known. May the message of the Mother of God find an entrance into hearts before it is too late. As an expression of joy and gratitude, the Holy Father gives you his apostolic blessing."

WORDS ABOUT THE WARNING:

Since the last apparition of Our Lady of Carmel at Garabandal, three of the seers, Conchita, Mari Loli, and Jacinta, have occasionally granted interviews. When they speak of the Warning, it often happens that new or supportive information, or a different perspective is revealed. To give a more complete picture of what they learned from the Blessed Mother regarding the event, below are chronological excerpts from various interviews.

Conchita on September 13, 14 and October 22, 1965:
"If I did not know about the other chastisement to come, I would say there is no greater chastisement than the Warning. Everybody will be afraid, but Catholics will bear it with more resignation than others. It will last for only a short time. The Warning comes directly from God. It will be visible in every part of the world, no matter where we live. It will be like an interior realization of our sins. Believers as well as unbelievers, wherever they are at the time, will see and feel it. Oh! Yes, the Warning will be very formidable! A thousand times worse than earthquakes. It will be like fire; it will not burn our flesh, but we will feel it corporeally and interiorly. All nations and every person on Earth will feel it. No one shall escape it. And unbelievers will feel the fear of God.

We could suffer it in the daytime, as well as the night, whether we are in bed or not. If we die during that time, it will be of fright. . . If I could only tell you how the Virgin described it to me! But the chastisement, that will be worse. . .

We will understand that the Warning comes to us because of our sins. I am tired of announcing it and having no one pay any attention to it.

We cannot imagine how much we offend God. The Blessed Mother told me that people know very well there is a heaven and a hell. But can't we see that we think about it only through fear and not for love of God? On account of our sins, we have only ourselves to blame for the Warning. And we must suffer it for Jesus, for the offenses committed against God."[lxiii]

Conchita in 1968:

Q: What about the many people who do not know Christ; how will they understand the Warning?

A: For those who do not know Christ, they will believe it is a Warning from God.

Conchita in 1973:

Q: How long will it last, a half hour, an hour?

A: I really don't know. I think that five minutes would be an adequate time.

Conchita to Dr. J. Dominguez in May, 1973:

A: The most important thing about that day is that everyone in the whole world will see a sign, a grace, or a punishment within themselves. They will find themselves all alone in the world, no matter where they are at that time, alone with their consciences right before God. . . Sometimes there are people who cannot see their own evil, for as it is said, they close the eyes of the soul not wanting to see inside. . . It is to open our soul to God and to bring repentance to us.

We will all feel the Warning differently because it will depend on our conscience. It will be very personal. Therefore, we will all react differently to it because your sins are different from mine.

Q: Will the Warning cause physical harm?

A: No, unless it is something that results from the shock, as, for example, a heart attack.

Mari Loli on July 27, 1975:

Q: It is said that you have mentioned that at the time of the Warning, everything will stop—even planes in the air. Is this true?

A: Yes.

Q: Can you tell us anything else about the Warning?

A: All I can say is that it is very near, and that it is very important that we get ready for it, as it will be a terrible event. It will make us realize all the sins we have committed.[lxiv]

Jacinta in February, 1977:

"The Warning is something that is just seen in the air, everywhere in the world, and immediately is transmitted into the interior of our souls. It will last for a very little time, but it will seem a very long time because of its effects within us. It will be good for our souls, in order to see in

249

ourselves our conscience—the good that we have failed to do, and the bad we have done. Then we will feel a great love toward our heavenly parents and ask forgiveness for all our offenses. The Warning is for us to draw closer to Him and to increase our faith. Therefore, one should prepare for that day, but not await it with fear. God does not send things for the sake of fear, but rather with justice and love. He does it for the good of all His children so they might enjoy eternal happiness and not be lost."

Conchita in 1977:

Q. You once said to Fr. Marcelino Andreu, "When you see the Warning, you will know we have opened up the end times." Can you explain what you meant by this?

A. The Virgin told us that the Warning and Miracle will be the last warnings or public spectacles that God will give us. This is why I believe that after them we will be near the end times.

Q. Do you have any words of advice for people in order that they might prepare for this event?

A. We must always be prepared with our souls in peace and not tie ourselves down so much to this world. Instead, we must think very often that we are here to go to heaven and to be saints.

Mari Loli in 1977:

Q. Do you have any words of advice for people in order that they might prepare for this event?

A. To do much penance, make sacrifices, visit the Blessed Sacrament every day that we are able to, and to pray the Holy Rosary daily.[lxv]

Mari Loli to Fr. Francis Benac, SJ, September 29, 1978:

"It will be an interior personal experience. It will look as if the world had come to a standstill, however, no one will be aware of that as they will be totally absorbed in their own experience. . . often when we do something wrong, we just ask with our lips for the Lord to forgive us, but now, He will help us sense that deep sorrow."

Conchita to Fr. Francis Benac, SJ, September 29, 1978:

"Privately, I have said that it is something like two stars clashing, making much noise and producing bright light, but causing no material damage to people, yet being very frightening. But, please, Father, it is just a mere comparison."

Conchita to Albrecht Weber, the author of Garabandal—Der Zeigefinger Gottes, *in 1965:*

A: When communism comes again, everything [the Warning] will happen.

Q: What do you mean by "comes again'"?

A: Yes, when it newly comes again.

Q: Does that mean that communism will go away before that?

A: I don't know. The Blessed Virgin simply said, "When communism comes again."[lxvi]

Mari Loli on October 19, 1982:

Q. Do you remember what the Blessed Mother said about the communist tribulation that is to precede the Warning?

A. It will look like the communists have taken over the whole world and it will be very hard to practice the religion, for priests to say Mass, or for people to open the doors of the churches.

Q. Is that what you meant when you said that it will seem as though the Church had disappeared?

A. Yes.

Q. It will be because of the persecution and not because the people would stop practicing their religion?

A. Yes, but I guess a lot of people will stop. Whoever practices it will have to go into hiding.

Q. You said that it would be very difficult for priests to say Mass. Was this something that the Blessed Mother told you or was it something that you thought yourself because of the communist tribulation?

A. From what I remember, it was something she said.

Q. And the Virgin said that it would seem as though the Church had disappeared?

A. Yes.

Jacinta on April 16, 1983:

A. The Virgin said that the Warning would come when conditions were at their worst. It wouldn't be just the persecution, either, because many people will no longer be practicing their religion.

Q. When the Warning comes, it will be seen and felt by everyone on Earth. Does this include little children who have not yet reached the age of reason?

A. Yes. That's why we felt sorry for them because it was such a terrifying experience.

Q. Can you tell us anything about what the world will be like when the Warning comes?

A. Bad. . .

Q. Do you remember when the Virgin told you that the Churches would unite?

A. The way she said it was all humanity would be within one Church, the Catholic Church. She also said it was very important to pray for this intention.[lxvii]

Conchita to a friend who said she was very much afraid of the Warning:
"Yes, but after the Warning, you will love God much more."

FATHER STEFANO GOBBI
ITALY (1930–2011)
Priest, Mystic, and Founder of
The Marian Movement of Priests

Father Stefano Gobbi was born in Dongo, Italy, north of Milan. As a layman, he managed an insurance agency, and then following a call to the priesthood, he went on to receive a doctorate in sacred theology from the Pontifical Lateran University in Rome. In 1964, was ordained at the age of 34.

In 1972, eight years into his priesthood, Fr. Gobbi traveled on pilgrimage to Fatima, Portugal. As he was praying at the shrine of Our Lady for certain priests who had renounced their vocations and were attempting to form themselves into associations in rebellion against the Catholic Church, he heard Our Lady's voice urge him to gather other priests who would be willing to consecrate themselves to the Immaculate Heart of Mary[lxviii] and be strongly united with the Pope and the Church. This was the first of hundreds of inner locutions that Fr. Gobbi would receive over the course of his life.

Guided by these messages from heaven, Fr. Gobbi founded the Marian Movement of Priests (MMP).[lxix] In the introduction of the de facto handbook of the MMP: *To the Priests, Our Lady's Beloved Sons*, it says of the movement:

It is a work of love which the Immaculate Heart of Mary is stirring up in the Church today to help all her children to live, with trust and filial hope, the painful moments of the purification. In these times of grave danger, the Mother of God and of the Church is taking action without hesitation or uncertainty to assist first and foremost the priests, who are the sons of her maternal predilection. Quite naturally, this work makes use of certain instruments; and in a particular way, Don Stefano Gobbi has been chosen. Why? In one passage of the book, the following explanation is given: "I have chosen you because you are the least apt instrument; thus no one will say that this is your work. The Marian Movement of Priests must be my work alone. Through your weakness, I will manifest my strength; through your nothingness, I will manifest my power" (message of July 16, 1973). . . *Through this movement, I am calling all my children to consecrate themselves to my Heart,*[lxx] *and to spread everywhere cenacles of prayer.*[lxxi]

Fr. Gobbi worked tirelessly to fulfill the mission Our Lady entrusted to him and a flurry of vocations and conversions followed him. By March of 1973, about forty priests had joined the Marian Movement of Priests, and by the end of 1985, Fr. Gobbi had boarded over 350 air flights and taken numerous journeys by car and train, visiting five continents several times over.[lxxii] Today the movement cites membership of over 400 Catholic cardinals and bishops, more than 100,000 Catholic priests, and millions of lay Catholics around the world, with cenacles of prayer and fraternal sharing among priests and lay faithful in every part of the world.

Fr. Gobbi's locutions from July 1973 to December 1997, printed in the book, *To the Priests, Our Lady's Beloved Sons*, received the Imprimatur of the Church.[lxxiii] The CDF took a cautious tone regarding Fr. Gobbi's messages, the seminal force of his fruitful apostolate, and asked the Marian Movement of Priests to change the title of his book from *Our Lady Speaks to Her Beloved Sons* to *To the Priests, Our Lady's Beloved Sons*. At the same time, the Church allowed that the book place the messages in the mouth of Our Lady.[lxxiv]

In November of 1993, the MMP in the United States, based in St. Francis, Maine, received an official papal blessing from Pope John Paul II, who maintained a close relationship with Fr. Gobbi and celebrated Mass with him in his private Vatican chapel annually for years.

Fr. Gobbi's last locution on December 31, 1997, to the Marian Movement of priests, contained a mother's tender gratitude toward her son:

I have now been guiding you for twenty-five years, with the words which I have spoken to the heart of this, my little son, whom I have chosen as an instrument for the realization of my maternal plan. During these years, I myself have carried him several times to every part of the world, and he has allowed himself to be led with docility, small and fearful but totally abandoned to me, like a little baby in the arms of his mother.

WORDS ABOUT THE WARNING:

According to Fr. Stefano Gobbi, Our Lady gave five messages concerning a coming Illumination of Conscience:

Message of May 22, 1988, Feast of Pentecost:
"With His divine love, He will open the doors of hearts and illuminate all consciences. Every person will see himself in the burning fire of divine truth. It will be like a judgment in miniature, and then Jesus Christ will bring His glorious reign in the world."

Message of October 2, 1992, Feast of the Holy Guardian Angels:
"What will come to pass is something so very great that it will exceed anything that has taken place since the beginning of the world. It will be like a judgment in miniature, and each one will see his own life and all he has done, in the very light of God.

To the first angel there befalls the task of making this announcement to all: "Give to God glory and obedience; praise Him, because the moment has come when He will judge the world. Go down on your knees before Him Who has made heaven and Earth, the sea and the springs of water."

Message of May 22, 1994, Feast of Pentecost:

"A new fire will come down from heaven and will purify all humanity, which has again become pagan. It will be like a judgment in miniature, and each one will see himself in the light of the very truth of God."

Message of June 4, 1995, Feast of Pentecost:

"Tongues of fire will come down upon you all, my poor children, so ensnared and seduced by Satan and by all the evil spirits who, during these years, have attained their greatest triumph. And thus, you will be illuminated by this divine light, and you will see your own selves in the mirror of the truth and the holiness of God. It will be like a judgment in miniature, which will open the door of your heart to receive the great gift of divine mercy.

And then the Holy Spirit will work the new miracle of universal transformation in the heart and the life of all: sinners will be converted; the weak will find support; the sick will receive healing; those far away will return to the house of the Father; those separated and divided will attain full unity.

In this way, the miracle of the Second Pentecost will take place. It will come with the triumph of my Immaculate Heart in the world. Only then will you see how the tongues of fire of the Spirit of Love will renew the whole world, which will become completely transformed by the greatest manifestation of divine mercy.

And so, I invite you to spend this day in the cenacle, gathered together in prayer with me, Mother of Mercy, in the hope and trembling expectation of the second Pentecost, now close at hand."[lxxv]

Message of May 26, 1996, the Feast of Pentecost:

"With an extraordinary cenacle of prayer and fraternity, you celebrate today the solemnity of Pentecost. You recall the prodigious event of the descent of the Holy Spirit, under the form of tongues of fire, upon the cenacle of Jerusalem, where the Apostles were gathered in prayer, with me, your heavenly Mother.

You, too, gathered today in prayer, in the spiritual cenacle of my Immaculate Heart, prepare yourselves to receive the prodigious gift of the Second Pentecost. The Second Pentecost will come to bring this humanity, which has again become pagan and which is living under the powerful influence of the evil one, back to its full communion of life with its Lord who has created, redeemed, and saved it.

Miraculous and spiritual tongues of fire will purify the hearts and the souls of all, who will see themselves in the light of God and will be pierced by the keen sword of His divine truth.

The second Pentecost will come to lead all the Church to the summit of her greatest splendor. The Spirit of Wisdom will lead her to perfect fidelity to the Gospel; the Spirit of Counsel will assist her and comfort her in all her tribulations; the Spirit of Fortitude will bring her to a daily and heroic witness to Jesus. Above all, the Holy Spirit will communicate to the Church the precious gift of her full unity and of her greatest holiness. Only then will Jesus bring into her His reign of glory.

The Second Pentecost will descend into hearts to transform them and make them sensitive and open to love, humble and merciful, free of all egoism and of all wickedness. And thus it will be that the Spirit of the Lord will transform the hearts of stone into hearts of flesh."[lxxvi]

MATTHEW KELLY
AUSTRALIA, UNITED STATES (1973–)
Husband, Father, Speaker, Writer, and Founder of the Dynamic Catholic Institute

Matthew Kelly was born in Sydney, Australia, in 1973. He is the fourth child of eight boys. His parents took them to church on Sunday, said grace before meals, and had a wonderful way of throwing out comments, like "God has been good to our family," which had a lasting impact on him as a child. Nevertheless, he doubted his faith for a time in his teens and once told his father that he didn't believe God anymore. Matthew says his father didn't get upset or fight back, but calmly gave the perfect answer: "God still believes in you."

One day, a physician friend of the family encouraged Matthew to look deeper into his faith and spend ten minutes each day, sitting in a church, maybe even praying. Matthew took up the challenge. Then one at a time, the family friend invited Matthew to add more spiritual practices: Bible reading, Daily Mass, the Rosary, and visits to a rest home, all of which led to a vibrant faith.

On April 7, 1993, when he was nineteen, Matthew knelt next to his bed to say his evening prayers, then climbed under the covers and reached for his Walkman to listen to music through his headphones. Oddly, he sensed a strong external presence and internal feeling urging him not to, but he proceeded to anyway. After only two or three seconds listening to music, the feeling was unmistakable, so he took off his headphones, knelt by his beside again, and said, "I am listening." At that moment, God the Father began speaking to him through inner locutions. The Father then asked that the messages He was giving be shared with the world, and so Matthew published them in a book with the simple title, *Words from God.*

With a family deeply steeped in business and an entrepreneurial spirit, dinner each night at the Kelly's was like an MBA class discussion. Everyone possessed an opinion, and Matthew had to assert himself to be heard. Unsurprisingly, he went to college business school, and because of his interest in the intersections between faith, ethics, and business, he began giving talks on the subject. As his speaking schedule intensified, Matthew took a semester off, planning to travel and speak (do the "God stuff"), then return to business school. He never went back.

Speaking led to writing, which boomeranged into a life of tireless, selfless, and continual service to the Catholic Church. Matthew has taken his deep, Australian voice, which booms on command, to fifty countries, and he continues to add to his many books, now published in over twenty-five languages. He is the founder of Floyd consulting and the Matthew Kelly Foundation, a charitable organization. With his zeal to share "the genius of Catholicism" with the world, he started a non-profit, The Dynamic Catholic Institute,[lxxvii] whose mission is to re-energize the Catholic Church in North America. Matthew married Meggie in 2009, and when he isn't on the road or at the office, he can be found at his home in Cincinnati, Ohio, doing his favorite job: playing with his five kids.

WORDS ABOUT THE WARNING:

The following excerpts are from Matthew Kelly's published book, *Words from God*, pages 70-72.[88]

Message to Matthew Kelly from God the Father on June 5, 1993:

---

[88] As with all the cited material in this book, this message is sourced here using a common and accepted literary practice known as "fair use".

"The Mini-Judgment is a reality. People no longer realize that they offend Me. Out of My infinite mercy, I will provide a Mini-Judgment. It will be painful, very painful, but short. You will see your sins; you will see how much you offend Me, every day.

I know that you think this sounds like a very good thing, but unfortunately even this won't bring the whole world into My love. Some people will turn even further away from Me; they will be proud and stubborn. Satan is working hard against Me.

Poor souls, all of you, robbed of the knowledge of My love. Be ready for this judgment of Mine. Judgment is the best word you humans have to describe it, but it will be more like this: you will see your own personal darkness contrasted against the pure light of My love.

Those who repent will be given an unquenchable thirst for this light. Their love for Me then will be so strong that, united with Mary's Immaculate Heart and the Sacred Heart of Jesus, the head of Satan shall be crushed, and he will be detained in hell forever. All those who love Me will join to help form the heel that crushes Satan.

Then, as you all die naturally, your thirst for this light will be quenched. You shall see Me, your God. You shall live in My love; you will be in heaven.

Now do you see how important these times are? Don't wait for this Mini-Judgment. You must start to look at yourselves more closely so that you can see your faults and repent. You are fortunate to have the faith needed to read, believe, and accept this message. You must not go away indifferent to it. You must examine yourself more every day and pray in reparation.

All of you, be like the blind man. Each day you should cry, "Lord, open My eyes," and My Son will open your eyes so that you can see your wretchedness and repent.

Pray now more than ever, and remember the world's standards are a false indication of My justice. I am your God, and while I am perfectly merciful to those who repent, I am perfectly just to those who do not.

Many people think that I, your God, won't mind. "It's only little," they say. But it's not a matter of minding. I want people to love Me. Love respects little things, as well as the big things; and in most cases, these little things are not so little.

Do not judge your actions or others' actions. You are unable to judge. You are incapable of judging because you cannot read a man's heart.

You must love Me with your whole heart, with your whole mind, with your whole soul, and with your whole strength.

Today is the day. Do your best to renounce yourself and let Christ reign in your lives. You will never be ready for the Mini-Judgment, but some will be more prepared than others. You must aim to be one of those and bring as many others as you can to be prepared, or as prepared as possible.

Above all, do not fear. I don't tell you all this to become scared. No, simply try to become better people each day. More than this I could not ask. I am your God. I am perfectly just and perfectly merciful. You are sons and daughters of Mine. Does not a father look after his children? I send this message to spare you from any pain I can; but the pain that you experience by seeing the darkness of your soul is an act of love on My behalf. Do you not see that this will return many, many souls to a fuller love of Me? This will save many souls from the fires of hell.

This is the most important of all My messages: I am the Lord, your God. You are My sons and daughters, whom I love very much, and My greatest delight is in being with you; and I want to be with you for eternity. Anything I do is done out of love for you, My children. Trust in Me, your Heavenly Father."[lxxviii]

JANIE GARZA
UNITED STATES (1955–)
Wife, Mother, Mystic, and Stigmatist

Mrs. Janie Garza is a visionary and locutionist with the visible stigmata, the wounds of Christ, on her body. She is the author of *Heaven's Messages for the Family: How to Become the Family God Wants You to Be* and *Heaven's Messages for the Family, Vol II: Messages from St. Joseph and the Archangels*. On May, 31, 2006, her bishop gave his full approbation for her to continue to speak and promulgate the messages from heaven that she has received. Mrs. Garza lives in Austin, Texas, with her husband, Marcelino, four sons, and a growing number of grandchildren.

Janie grew up in Austin, under the sharp tongue and hands of her abusive mother—the sole provider for her nine children—and her incessantly drunk stepfather. It was during Janie's one year at Catholic school (before her mother removed her without explanation) that Janie learned from the nuns of Jesus's presence in the Blessed Sacrament. As a child, she attended daily Mass and often sat in front of the Tabernacle, waiting for Jesus to come out. She had fallen in love.

Janie promised herself, when she was young, that she would never cause another to suffer. After getting married, while never abusive, she donned the pants of her family and took charge of all decision-making, many times considering divorce, if things didn't go her way. God had a plan to teach her, and other families through her, how to embrace her vocation as wife and mother in a more loving way, and on February 15, 1989, Our Lady appeared to Janie. This began a new trajectory in her life of regular visitations and messages from Mary, then Jesus, St. Joseph, St. Philomena and other saints, and the three archangels. To this day, Our Lady does not let Mrs. Garza learn of or read any messages from heaven received by other visionaries or locutionists, thus what she experiences stands on its own merit.[lxxix]

One day, Jesus and Mary asked that Mrs. Garza offer herself as a victim soul for the suffering of the Church, the unborn, and the conversion of families. Mrs. Garza and her husband then knelt before the Blessed Sacrament, where he expressed, *"Lord, I give You my wife to do with as you will. I know You will take care of her."* Subsequently, Janie has suffered from various ailments and has been given the stigmata and lives the Passion in her own body, particularly on Good Friday.[lxxx]

WORDS ABOUT THE WARNING:

The following excerpts are from Janie Garza's books, *Heaven's Messages for the Family: How to Become the Family God Wants You to Be* and *Heaven's Messages for the Family, Volume II: Messages from St. Joseph and the Archangels.*

Message of May 13, 1994:

St. Joseph: I, St. Joseph, bring God's blessings to you and to your family.

Janie: Thank you, beloved St. Joseph. Praised be the Eternal Father for His goodness forever and ever. Amen.

St. Joseph: My little one, I, St. Joseph, know that you have been struggling with the seriousness of the messages that you have received from Most Holy Mary and St. Michael. I am here to help you to understand these messages. You see, my little one, the people of God have ignored His warnings. The world does not understand the darkness that surrounds them. Many people continue to live in sin, and forget that the day is coming when they will be allowed to see the state of their souls. What a terrible time this will be for many, many souls.

Many will die, for they will not be able to withstand knowing the truth about the condition of their souls.

Janie: St. Joseph, could you explain why many people will die when they see their souls? I don't understand this, please help me to understand.

St. Joseph: My little one, the soul is where all truth lies, and no one can see or know your soul except the Eternal One. He alone knows all souls, and He alone will judge all souls. No one knows the truth except the Holy Trinity. If people knew the truth, they would choose not to sin, for the truth would enlighten their hearts to know how much sin separates them from the truth. The Truth is the Eternal Father. You cannot live in sin and say you know the truth, for you cannot have two masters. You must choose to live in darkness or to live in the light. For those who believe that they live in the light but continue to break every Commandment given by God, to these souls, I, St. Joseph, say that these souls will not be able to see the state of their souls and live.

Janie: This is hard for me to know. Are you saying that people who do not live God's Commandments will die when they see their souls?

St. Joseph: Yes, my little one, that's how it will be for many unless they repent and decide for conversion. There is still time for repentance, but time is growing shorter with each day that goes by.

Janie: What must I tell the people?

St. Joseph: Share with them that the Eternal One is calling them to return to Him and to accept His love and mercy, to amend their lives and to live the messages of prayer, fasting and conversion. All who repent will receive special graces to enter into the Sacred Heart of Jesus and the Immaculate Heart of Mary. To all who repent, God will shower His mercy on them. No one will be turned away, for God loves all His children.[lxxxi]

Message of September 9, 1995:

Jesus: Our humble servant, the illumination that will take place will be for a short period. During this time My Father will allow all of humanity to see the state of their souls as My Father sees their souls. This will be a time of great grace when many souls will repent and return to My Father. Those souls that die will die from great shock to see the state of the darkness which exists in their souls.

Janie: Beloved Savior, will the illumination scare people?

Jesus: The fear that will inflame their hearts is the holy fear of the immense power of My Father, especially for those many souls that have continued to deny the existence of My Father. These will be the souls that will experience tremendous fear.

Janie: Will all people convert?

Jesus: Many will convert, but many will not.

Janie: Oh, Jesus, will this happen very soon?

Jesus: Our humble servant, this will happen within a short period. Do not be distracted with dates, but prepare every day with strong prayer. Many who worry about these times will not live to see these things take place. This is why Holy Scripture warns everybody not to be concerned about tomorrow, for tomorrow is promised to no one. The present day has enough trials and crosses. Know that when We speak about such things to come; this is for the people to convert and abandon their evil ways. Every day is an opportunity for souls to convert. People should not wait for such things to come to convert, but they should convert now, before it's too late! The very fact that such judgments will come is because people refuse to convert and continue to live in darkness.[lxxxii]

Message of March 19, 1996:

Janie: Oh, we are so blessed to have you as Protector of the Family. Praised be God forever and ever.

St. Joseph: My little one, God's love for humanity is immense. He appeals to the world every second of the day to turn away from their sins. He gives them His love and mercy to help souls to convert. God will continue to appeal to His children to return back to His love and mercy. The time is coming when God will allow all His children to look deep into their souls and see their sins as God sees their sinful hearts. God will send an illumination throughout the world. This will be a time of great grace and conversion to many souls. Shortly after this great illumination of souls, God will send a great miracle for the world to see. After this great sign, the world will know peace. There will be great joy for all the faithful people of God. His children will be happy. There will be love in families everywhere. People will benefit from their labor, and they will build their homes and live to enjoy them. They will see their children's children, and all will live long lives.

Janie: Beloved St. Joseph, what should we do to prepare for this?

St. Joseph: Pray, my little one, pray. Remain faithful to all that the Holy Spirit directs you to do. Act in everything that Most Holy Mary is calling you to. Be a strong messenger of living her messages of peace, prayer, Holy Mass, fasting, conversion and reading Holy

Scripture. Do this as a family. Do not reject God's Most Holy Name so that He will not reject you. Decide to be a holy family, to pray together, to love, and to forgive one another. This is a time of decision for all of God's children. Live as God's people, leading good, simple and just lives. Open your hearts to God's love and mercy. Every family must consecrate themselves to the Sacred Heart of Jesus, to the Immaculate Heart of Mary,[lxxxiii] and to my intercession and protection, that We may lead you closer to God. We will prepare you for the things to come. Live as children of the Lord, and you will live through all these troubled times.

Janie: Please help us, beloved St. Joseph, we need your help.

St. Joseph: My little one, be prepared by living all that I, St. Joseph, have shared with you on a daily basis, living each day as if it was your last day. This is God's Holy Will for His children. Do not fear anything, but abandon yourself to the Holy Spirit who will help you to do the Holy Will of God.

Janie: Thank you for this, most humble St. Joseph.

St. Joseph: I give you my blessing. Live in God's peace.[lxxxiv]

SERVANT OF GOD, MARIA ESPERANZA
(1928–2004)
Wife, Mother, Mystic, Stigmatist, and Visionary of the Marian Apparitions at Betania, Venezuela
(1976–1990)

Maria Esperanza, born in Venezuela in 1928, had her first mystical experience when she was only five. As she was saying goodbye to her mother, who was leaving on a trip, Maria saw St. Therese of Lisieux emerge from the waters of the Orinoco River and toss a red rose toward her. Maria caught it and handed to her amazed mother. The rose had a uniquely beautiful velvety texture, and no roses could be found anywhere near.

Maria was a sickly child who suffered through more than one life-threatening illness. Once, at age twelve, she developed such an acute case of pneumonia that her doctor didn't think she would live more than three more days. Deeply faithful, Maria asked, "Mother of mine, would it be that you want me to come to you?" Then closing her eyes, she waited for an answer. When Maria opened them, the Blessed Virgin was smiling in front of her. Maria continued to live, fed through injections, and soon prayed for Christ to take her so she would no longer be a burden to her family. This time, Christ appeared, addressing her as *"My white rose."*

Remembering this moment years later, Maria commented, *"It's like radar the way He penetrates you with His eyes! It was so beautiful, beautiful eyes. . . His face was so gentle!"* But instead of granting her death, Jesus came with Mary to heal her. They explained to their "white rose" that life is a long series of trials, and that the bridge to heaven is constructed through struggles, purgation, and humility—especially humility. *"My daughter,"* Our Lady told her, *"when you begin your pilgrimage, you will have many sufferings. They are the pain of this Mother. Help me. Help me to save this world, which is going astray."*[lxxxv]

During her teenage years, Maria received several mystical graces, including the ability to read into hearts, and she often had the premonition of knowing when guests would arrive or when family or friends were ill. People at the receiving end of her prayers were often healed or received a word from her of the medical remedy they needed.

Maria desired to become a nun and entered a convent in 1954. However, on October 3 of that year, Saint Therese of the Child Jesus again appeared to her, throwing a red rose. This time, when Maria reached to catch it, something pinched her right palm, and blood began to seep from her hand. It was the beginning of her stigmata. *"This is not your vocation,"* St. Therese instructed her. *"Yours is to be a wife and mother."* Four days later, Our Lady told her to receive daily Communion, along with fasting, prayer, and penance, and that she would be a spiritual mother of souls. *"Also, you shall be the mother of seven children: six roses and a bud."* Maria would give birth to six girls and a boy.

After leaving the convent, Jesus told Maria to go to Rome where she would receive the blessing of Pope Pius XII. There, in front of the Church of the Sacred Heart of Jesus not one month later, on November 1, she met her husband to be, Geo Bianchini Gianni. After a courtship of two years, Maria went to speak to Msgr. Giulio Rossi, the parish priest of Saint Peter's Basilica in Vatican City, the papal enclave and one of the largest churches in the world. She asked him for special permission to marry in the Basilica's Chapel of the Choir of the Immaculate Conception. Msgr. Rossi noticed an aura around Maria Esperanza's face, which compelled him to bring her request to Pope Pius XII. The pope, who already knew of Maria, gave his authorization, and her wedding to Geo was celebrated on December 8, 1956.

Pope Pius XII was not the only saint familiar with Maria Esperanza. St. Padre Pio, in his later years, told people he expected to be visited by an extraordinary woman. "There is a young woman who is going to come from South America," he said. "When I leave, she will be your consolation." The two finally met when Maria heard St. Pio's "call," while in prayer to travel to him. She was near Rome, at the time, far away from his monastery at San Giovanni Rotondo, but she made the trip, and as she stood amidst a throng of people waiting to see the aged priest, he called out, *"Esperanza!"* On September 23, 1968, St. Pio would speak to her in a vision: *"Esperanza, I have come to say good-bye. My time has come. It is your turn."* As this was happening, Geo watched with amazement as his wife's face transfigured into that of Padre Pio's. The next day, they saw in the newspaper that he had died.

When Padre Pio was alive, Maria shared with him a vision she'd had as a child of a special plot of land where she was told the Virgin Mary would appear. Maria had seen an old house, a waterfall, and a grotto. *"From 1957 until 1974, we searched for this land in all of Venezuela,"* said Geo, who had oil concerns and a construction business in Caracas. When visiting a farm for sale, the couple finally found the place she had seen, and this would become the pilgrimage site of Finca Betania, Venezuela, now considered the "Lourdes" of South America. "Betania," as it is often called, became a holy site of great and documented miracles, where not only Maria, but close to two thousand people would see the Virgin Mary.

When the apparitions first began on March 25, 1976, Our Lady introduced herself as *"Mary, Reconciler of Peoples and Nations."* Maria Esperanza would go on to receive countless messages from Our Lady, sometimes more than one per day. On November 21, 1987, Bishop Pio Bello Ricardo, a Doctor in Psychology conducted an extensively thorough investigation of the apparitions, followed by three years of further reflection and discernment. In conclusion, he issued a pastoral letter declaring that the Betania apparitions *"are authentic and of a supernatural character."* The last paragraph of his "Pastoral Instruction on the Apparitions of the Blessed Virgin in Finca, Betania" begins, *"Ending this Pastoral Instruction, I thank the Lord for He has given our*

Diocese and our Country the privilege of the visit of Our Blessed Virgin; for in this period of our ecclesiastical history marked with a new evangelization, she encourages us to a renewal and deepening in faith, and to a projection of that faith into an integral conversion, in prayer and apostolic commitment; because in this divided world, she has come as Reconciler Of Nations. *"lxxxvi*

As instructed by Our Lady, Maria Esperanza ministered to pilgrims in Betania and visited many places around the world, giving talks and spreading a message of reconciliation between people of diverse backgrounds, and between people and their God. Maria exuded peace, compassion, love, and great hope, as her name "Esperanza" signified, and lived what she preached: *"We must serve and not seek to be served, and we must serve constantly, without feeling tired when we are bothered."lxxxvii*

Maria Esperanza, one of the greatest mystics of our time, received multiple and inexplicable gifts from God, including the stigmata, healing, bilocation, the reading of hearts, and the prophesying of future events— many yet to come. The United States was a country dear to Maria, and she sometimes traveled there on a divine mission. She warned the U.S. not to go to war in Iraq, despite rampant support for the war,[lxxxviii] and in 1992, saw a vision of the attack on the World Trade center—smoke rising from the two buildings and their collapse. In the days following this disturbing prophecy, she prayed for protection for that area of New York. Maria foresaw the outbreak of the AIDS epidemic and predicted another disease, as well as a threat to the United States by two nations, one large and one smaller, whom she said will conspire to provoke North America. The world will undergo wars, societal problems, and natural disasters, and "[God's] justice will start in Venezuela,"[lxxxix] she said. But the world will also go through a cleansing that will reawaken humanity. In 2004, at age 77, Maria Esperanza died in a New Jersey hospital from a mysterious Parkinson-like illness, which made it difficult for her to speak. Upon her death, she was surrounded by her loving family and the strong scent of roses.[xc]

WORDS ABOUT THE WARNING:

A few years before the apparitions began, Maria Esperanza received the following message from the Virgin Mary:

"This is the difficult hour for all humanity, and it is necessary to avoid misunderstandings among brethren; the nations must be united. . . the love of my Jesus will be the door that will open hearts to give access to a beautiful era that must revive people to a glorious teaching of unity. Take advantage of time because the hour is arriving when my Son will appear before everyone as Judge and Savior. You must be in the necessary conditions to live with Him on that Great Day. Do not think that it is distant."[xci]

The fourth message of Betania that Maria Esperanza received from Mary, Reconciler of Peoples and Nations:

"Little children, I am your Mother, and I come to seek you so that you may prepare yourselves to be able to bring my message of reconciliation: There is coming the great moment of a Great Day of Light. The consciences of this beloved people must be violently shaken so that they may "put their house in order" and offer to Jesus the just reparation for the daily infidelities that are committed on the part of sinners. . . it is the hour of decision for mankind."[xcii]

LUZ DE MARÍA DE BONILLA
COSTA RICA, ARGENTINA (1962?–)
Wife, Mother, Mystic, and Stigmatist

Luz de María de Bonilla is a Catholic mystic, Third Order Augustinian, and prophet from Costa Rica, currently residing in Argentina. She grew up in a very religious home with great devotion to the Eucharist, and as a child, experienced heavenly visits from her guardian angel and the Blessed mother, whom she considered her companions and confidants. In 1990, she received a miraculous healing from an illness, coinciding with both a visitation from the Blessed Mother and a new and more public calling to share her mystical experiences. Soon she would fall into profound ecstasy not only in the presence of her family—her husband and eight children, but also of people close to her who began to gather to pray; and they, in turn, formed a prayer cenacle, which accompanies her to this day.

After years of abandoning herself to the will of God, Luz de María began to suffer the pain of the Cross, which she carries in her body and soul. This first happened, she shared, on Good Friday: *"Our Lord asked me if I wanted to participate in His sufferings. I answered affirmatively, and then after a day of continuous prayer, that night, Christ appeared to me on the Cross and shared His wounds. It was indescribable pain, although I know that however painful it may be, it is not the totality of the pain that Christ continues to suffer for humanity.* "[xciii]

Luz de María's wounds are invisible most of the time, although no less painful. On several occasions during the year, they become visible. Prior to each time that Christ shares a visible expression of His Passion with her, Luz de María falls into a profound ecstasy, followed by manifestations of suffering. Wounds in her hands, feet, side and head become visible, and on occasions, tears of blood fall from her eyes and fill the entire room with fragrant perfume. She remains in this state from one to several hours, and when it comes to an end, her wounds heal, her flesh is regenerated completely, and only the blood that was shed remains.

It was on March 19 of 1992, that the Blessed Mother began to speak regularly to Luz de María. Since then, she has mostly received two messages per week and on occasion, only one. The messages originally came as internal locutions, followed by visions of Mary, who came to describe Luz de María's mission. *"I had never seen so much beauty,"* Luz said of Mary's appearance. *"It's something you can never get used to. Each time is like the first."*

Several months later, Mary and Saint Michael the Archangel introduced her to Our Lord in a vision, and in time, Jesus and Mary would speak to her of coming events, such as the Warning. The messages went from being private to public, and by divine command, she must communicate them to the world. The messages speak God's love, mercy, and His justice in the form of a purification—a fruit of the disobedience of present-day man, who is transforming himself into his own scourge.

This mission has taken Luz de María to various countries, especially in Latin America, where she speaks for radio interviews and at conferences. Called to travel constantly, she defines herself now as a "citizen of the world," and her work has spawned cenacles of prayer and gospel living around the globe. Christ warned her of the persecution, injustice, and slander that she would face from those who would not only reject the messages, but tirelessly seek to destroy and discredit her ministry. Luz de María accepts this, knowing that as His instrument, she must walk the same path that Christ walked on Earth: *"Amen, amen, I say to you, no slave is greater than his master nor any messenger greater than the one who sent him"* (John 13:16).

In the seer's words, *"The Blessed Mother asks us to understand fully what it means to be Christians, which is not something limited to a prayer, nor to be understood only as a historical inheritance. We have to live*

273

fused to Christ and live and work in the Divine Will. She tells me not to pray empty, repetitive prayers without attentiveness, but to pray for a closer, more intimate union with Our Lady, and thus the prayer attains an infinite value. She also asks us to know Christ and to recognize Him. That is why He calls us to the study of Sacred Scripture, so that we do not say yes to what is not the Divine Will. I have been told in the messages that we cannot say that we have faith if we do not act with charity, with love, with respect, with understanding, with hope—that is to say, live with the awareness that we are creatures of God."

Many of the prophecies Luz de María has received have already been fulfilled, including the attack on the Twin Towers in New York, which was announced to her eight days in advance. In the messages, Jesus and Mary express their profound sadness over man's disobedience of the Divine law, which has led him to align with evil and act against God. They warn the world of coming tribulations: communism and its coming peak; war and the use of nuclear weapons; pollution, famine, and plagues; revolution, social unrest, and moral depravity; a schism in the Church; the fall of the world economy; the public appearance and world domination of the antichrist; the fulfillment of the Warning, the Miracle, and the chastisements; the fall of an asteroid, and the change of terrestrial geography, among other messages. All this is not to frighten, but to urge man to turn his gaze toward God. Not all of God's messages are calamities. There are also proclamations of the resurgence of true faith, the unity of the people of God, the Triumph of the Immaculate Heart of Mary, and the final Triumph of Christ, the King of the Universe, when there will no longer be divisions, and we will be one people under the One God.[xciv]

Father José María Fernandez Rojas has remained beside Luz de María as her confessor from the beginning of her locutions and visions, and two priests work with her permanently. The messages she receives are audio recorded by two people and then transcribed by a nun. One priest makes spelling corrections, then another gives the messages a final review before uploading them to the website, www.revelacionesmarianas.com, to be shared with the world. The messages have been gathered into a book entitled, *Thy Kingdom Come*, and on March 19, 2017, Juan Abelardo Mata Guevara, SDB, Titular Bishop of Estelí, Nicaragua, granted them the Imprimatur of the Church. His letter began:

Estelí, Nicaragua, Year of Our Lord, March 19 of 2017
Solemnity of the Patriarch Saint Joseph

The volumes that contain "PRIVATE REVELATION" from heaven, given to Luz de María from the year 2009 to the present time, have been given to me for the respective ecclesiastic approval. I have reviewed with faith and interest these volumes entitled, THY KINGDOM COME, *and have come to conclusion that they are a call to humanity to return to the path that leads to eternal life, and that these messages are an exhortation from heaven in these times in which man must be careful not to stray from the Divine Word.*[xcv] *(See endnote for the entire letter.)*

WORDS ABOUT THE WARNING:

Messages from Jesus and Mary to Luz de María de Bonilla (www.revelacionesmarianas.com/english.htm):

Message of February 16, 2010, from Jesus Christ:

My Mother has announced throughout the whole world and across time what is now on the horizon. I do not call you through fear, but through love. In the same way that I gave Myself for you, I will enter inside each person with My Mercy. You shall see your actions, even though you do not want to see them; you will feel the offenses, even though you do not want to feel them. It will be a Warning within each of you; you will be alone with Me. This is the love of the King Who doesn't want His own to be lost, and proceeds with His plan.

I have entrusted My Word to you. Announce it to your brothers and sisters without fear. Today, My people are heroes, courageous souls who give their lives for Me. My people know they struggle against the world; My people are imprisoned and must rise up. That is why I will not leave you alone, that is why I will come, and those who have not believed will be put to shame.

Message of August 29, 2010, from Jesus Christ:

My Cross is Victory, and it will shine in the firmament for seven days and nights. It will radiate light constantly. It will be a preliminary sign for which My people have waited; and for those who do not believe, there will be great confusion. Science will try to give an explanation for that which has no scientific explanation.

Message of July 16, 2011, from Jesus Christ:

Beloved, remain alert. A sign in the sky will be seen by all. My Cross will shine through My wounds and illuminate everything in an instant. The sun will manifest great signs. What is incomprehensible to man will be reflected in the sky so that those who do not believe will believe.

Message of October 21, 2011, from Jesus Christ:

The announcement of the Warning causes some to laugh. But this, children, is a truth, just as My Mother's words, stating the dictates of the Trinity, are true. When the Warning happens, those who made fun of this divine decree will feel consumed by their own sin. We have called them to be aware of the seriousness of the moment in which they live, but like those who made fun of Noah, they will groan. The Warning, cosmic and spiritual, does not wait, and it will be fulfilled. I invite my faithful priests to call their flocks to reflect upon, recognize, and carefully avoid sin, which drowns, enslaves, and leads to eternal death.

Message of March 3, 2013, from the Blessed Virgin Mary:

How close this generation is to the Warning! And how many of you do not even know what the Warning is! In these times, my faithful instruments and my prophet [Luz de María] are mocked by those who consider themselves scholars of spirituality, by those who reach millions of souls through means of mass communication. They are misleading them and hiding the truth because I am the One revealing the will of the Trinity, the will of the Trinity already expressed in all of my apparitions, starting from long ago.

The Warning is not a fantasy. Humanity must be purified so that it does not fall into the flames of hell. People will see themselves, and in that moment, they will ache for not having believed, but they will have already misled many of My children who will not be able to recuperate so easily, for the godless will deny the Warning and attribute it to new technologies.[xcvi]

Message of July 24, 2014, from the Blessed Virgin Mary:

My beloved, the Warning is necessary; you must grow in faith and knowledge. In that moment, a mirror of your life will reflect your omissions, acts of disobedience, works, and personal behaviors. Love will be both your pardoner and executioner. In the face of this, some will revolt and reject My Son, for in the Warning, none will see the good or the evil of others, but only what is uniquely their own. Some will straighten their walk, others will deny My Son, thus becoming great persecutors of My elect.[xcvii]

Message of November 22, 2014, from Jesus Christ:

My beloved people, the examination of your consciences will come soon. . . Whatever moves will stop moving, for silence will reign on Earth. You will hear only the lamentations of those repenting for the wrongs they committed, and I will come with My love to once again welcome My lost sheep. Even then, some of My children will deny that the Warning came from My Kingdom and will rebel against Me, uniting with evil.[xcviii]

Message of January 9, 2015, from the Blessed Virgin Mary:

You will be given the freedom to examine your conscience, as an act of Divine Mercy for the salvation of souls. Man will say that it is an act caused by science; human explanations will be heard without delay.

Message of March 26, 2016 from the Blessed Virgin Mary:

Beloved children, in an instant, two heavenly bodies will approach one another and collapse. This event will be seen in the sky by all; then each human creature, in his soul, conscience, and essence, will see all the evil he has committed and the good he has failed to do.

Message of September 17, 2018 from Jesus Christ:

Shadows will cease to be shadows, but instead become a most terrible darkness that will obscure the light until the vault of the sky is illuminated by two celestial bodies, which will collide with one another, lighting up the entire Earth. The day will be brighter and the night will be like the day. I speak of the Warning, the moment in which each person will be alone before his own conscience and his sins—a moment so overpowering that some will not survive experiencing their own wickedness. They will not have the aid of another human being, as everyone will not only be undergoing their own personal experience, but also one in which everything on Earth will be frozen in time.

Message of May 10, 2018 from Jesus Christ:

Man does not look with mistrust upon the devil, instead he gladly follows and obeys him, acting contrary to the will of God. During the

THE WARNING

Warning, man will live in solitude for seconds without God. "And there will be wailing and grinding of teeth (cf. Luke 13:28a)."

Message of August 12, 2019 from Jesus Christ:
My love remains open for anyone who desires to journey with me. Children, you need to be living witnesses of My love and My charity for your brothers and sisters.

This isn't the time of lamentation. That moment will come soon. This is the moment of decision in which every human being will be blessed with my mercy so that, one by one, they see the sins they have committed throughout their lives, confessed or unconfessed. Thus, they will see the good they have done and have failed to do, the bad they have done, their sins of omission, their entire trajectory of life.

Those who behave and act in My likeness toward their neighbor, and repent with all their strength, force, and feelings, and confess their sins with a firm purpose of amendment, those children of mine will experience the Warning like every human being will, but not with the intensity of those who stoop in the mire of sin through disobedience, ignoring My calls, those of My Mother, and My faithful Saint Michael the Archangel.

My people, I want you to be honest, and for this, you must learn from your falls so that you can rise, so that in the refuge of My mercy, permeated by My love and love for your neighbor, you are saved, like the repentant thief; it is therefore essential that My children ask for forgiveness and learn how to forgive.

Luz de María de Bonilla's Experience of an Illumination of Conscience

The seer, Luz de María de Bonilla, was given a unique experience of the Warning, in that she didn't undergo it in the light of her own sins, but as one might experience it if he or she were in mortal sin and unprepared. Here, adapted from her own words, is how Luz de María described the occurrence:

In a very special way, our Lord has given me to understand that a comet will come near the earth, all of humanity will see it, which will create panic and compel many people to go to confession, but not for repentance.

In the sky, there will appear a sign, "a cross." For several days, people with faith will feel the need to confess their sins, to repent; the remainder will say that it was brought about by men and will turn against the Catholic Church, saying that it is trickery to frighten humanity.

In the midst of this confusion, including an earthquake, will come the Warning, which Our Lord permitted me to experience in part, on Holy Wednesday of Lent, 2008. I will describe it as follows:

I felt anguish in my being and my heart started beating rapidly, as though something was coming closer to me, but I could not tell what it was. . . something frightful, something distressful, that I couldn't figure out, though I knew something was going to happen.

I was in this state for around twenty minutes. Then the anxiousness began to increase. I started to feel as though my soul was leaving me because, little by little, I felt a terrible loneliness not only filling my spiritual being, but my physical body, as well. Then the loneliness became dreadful. Anxiety had me walking to and fro because the loneliness grew with each moment. I was totally aware that God was not in my being; my soul was desolate, anguished. I walked about seeking consolation but could not find it; the loneliness, the emptiness increased until the point of my feeling I was going out of my mind. My soul was left without

God! Then, as in a movie, sins started to unfold in me, perhaps the gravest that men could commit: I felt, or I should say was experiencing, everything because I felt them as my own. I was living them.

I felt what goes through the mind, through the heart, in the interior of people in the moments of suffering before they take their own life; I experienced what a baby feels when it is being aborted; I experienced the abuses committed by human beings when they are outraged; I experienced drug addiction, prostitution. All sorts of sins started to pass, one by one, within my soul. It was a terrible wretchedness. I felt I could not leave the house because God had abandoned me; I was living "the total absence of God." It is a terrifying emptiness that nothing can fill. Here on earth, men sin and repent, but the burden of the offense that sin causes is not felt because we have the presence of God.

I ambled aimlessly, in the terrible desolation of God's abandonment, and then I remembered that my husband did have God, so I looked for him, found him in his bedroom and said, "Please, lay your hands on my head. I need you to pass God to me because he has abandoned me!"

My husband, afraid, did not know what to do and asked, "What's happening to you?"

I responded in desperation, "I don't have God. He is gone. Please pass Him to me." My moans were coming from deep within my being.

"What prayer should I say?"

"It doesn't matter. Just pass God to me!"

He prayed, but I still felt the emptiness. This was truly a devastating and bitter experience. I think I was tempted by the demon to leave my house, get into the car, and look for one of the priests; but somehow, I knew that leaving the house could be a fatal move. I threw myself on the floor with my arms extended in the form of the cross and begged God to return to me. At that moment, my soul spoke to me! I knew it was my soul. She said some words, and as I kept repeating them, the Holy Spirit began to fill me. I was infused with a sense of peace I had never before experienced, a peace that satisfied and permeated me. My chest was bursting. Then I sensed something physical remain: a presence that I still feel to this day and that surrounds my whole chest.

That is how the Warning is going to be [for those in serious sin]. That is why people living in sin will be out of their minds. The devil will be waiting, will incite them to take their life, will try to take them as its own spoils before the hour of mercy comes. For those who are not with God, the Warning will be an unbearable moment in which they could end up placing themselves in the hands of the devil, who with its demoniac legions, will encircle souls, accusing them of their sins and telling them that God will not forgive them.

For those who are lukewarm, it will be a moment of repentance, of grace, because when they understand their errors, they will ask forgiveness and will convert. For those who are in God's grace, they will be filled with the presence of the Holy Spirit.

After the Warning, those who do not believe will give it a scientific explanation so that humanity will continue in error, sin will increase [for those who reject God and His Warning], and there will be persecution.

From that day on, my life has not been the same. During the Warning, God will make us aware of sin. I will never forget that day. I cried in those moments I did not feel God. I couldn't even think because the absence of God surpasses everything. I only sensed emptiness and felt in my flesh the sins that came one by one.

At the time of writing this message and whenever I talk about it, I cry; I cry because even just the memory of it hurts so much, and I always ask Our Jesus not to let me feel it again because I think I would not be able to endure it one more time.

This is my personal experience of the Warning, the recording of my experience of the suffering with Jesus. He has told me that that is what many souls will feel during the Warning, and it is only a drop of what he lived in Gethsemane for our sins.[xcix]

FR. MICHEL RODRIGUE[89]

Priest, Mystic, Exorcist, and Founder and Superior General of The Apostolic Fraternity of Saint Benedict Joseph Labre
(Founded in 2012)

Born into a faithful Catholic family of twenty-three children, Michel grew up poor. His family lived on a small piece of farmland, where hard work and bumpy trips to Sunday Mass with multiple children on horseback kept his family alive in body and spirit.

Like St. Padre Pio and other chosen souls, God the Father began speaking to Michel at the tender age of three. "When I was three years old," says Fr. Michel, "God began to speak to me, and we would have regular conversations. I remember sitting under a big tree behind our home on our family farm and asking God, 'Who made this tree?'

---

[89] To read more about Fr. Michel Rodrigue, go to www.CountdowntotheKingdom.com. Click on "Why Fr. Michel Rodrigue? A Virtual Retreat." Note: Fr. Michel Rodrigue's messages are not condemned by the Church, which has not made an ecclesial investigation. He remains a priest in good standing, obedient to the Church, and his new Fraternity is officially recognized within the Catholic Church. Read more on the last page of the End Notes.

'I did,' God answered. And when He pronounced the word, 'I,' I was suddenly given a vast view of the Earth, the universe, and myself, and I understood that everything was made and held in existence by Him. I thought that everyone talked to God the Father. From age three to six, the Lord instructed me in the faith and gave me a thorough theological education. He also told me, when I was three, that I would be a priest."

God the Father gave Michel such a thorough education in theology that when he attended the Grand Seminary of Quebec after high school, he tested out of his classes with an A+. Michel subsequently studied psychology and areas of theology, such as mariology, pneumatology, the writings of the Church Fathers, graduating with a doctorate in theology.

After founding and managing a shelter for homeless youth, which offered them psychological and spiritual care, Michel Rodrigue was ordained a diocesan priest at the age of thirty. He served as a parish priest for five years in northern Ontario until his bishop discerned that his talents would be best utilized forming future clergy. Fr. Michel then became a Sulpician priest teaching theology at the Grand Seminary of Montreal.

On Christmas Eve, 2009, Fr. Michel's priesthood took an extraordinary turn. He was awakened in the night by the presence of St. Benedict Joseph Labre, who stood by his bedside, shaking his shoulder to get his attention. Fr. Michel was awakened and heard the voice of God the Father say, "Stand." So Fr. Michel stood up. "Go to the computer." So he obeyed. "Listen and write." That is when God began to dictate the entire constitution for a new religious order, faster than Fr. Michel could type. He had to tell God to slow down!

Then God suddenly whisked Fr. Michel into a mystical flight to the land in the Diocese of Amos, Quebec, where He wanted the monastery built, and showed him in detail the monastery's design. God the Father told Fr. Michel that he would be the founder of this monastery. He would start a new fraternity in the Church called Fraternité Apostolique Saint Benoît-Joseph Labre (The Apostolic Fraternity of St. Joseph Benedict Labre) in order to prepare priests for the future of the Catholic Church.[c] Fr. Michel initially responded with feelings of panic, as his obligations were already overwhelming, but quickly realized that saying no to the Father wasn't an option. Today much of the monastery is now built, exactly as God desired.

God has gifted Fr. Michel Rodrigue with extraordinary intellectual and spiritual gifts, such as healing, reading souls, a photographic memory (which lessened after illness), prophecy, locutions, and visions.

He has a naturally joyful disposition and a ready laugh, while at the same time, a great seriousness concerning the things of God.[ci]

WORDS ABOUT THE WARNING:

Message from God the Father to Fr. Michel Rodrigue in 2018, concerning the Warning:

I do not want death and damnation for any one of you. So much suffering, so much violence, so many sins now occur on the Earth that I created. I now hear the cries of all the babies and children who are murdered by the sin of my children who live under the dominion of Satan. YOU SHALL NOT KILL. (These words were so strong.)

Pray and be confident. I do not want you to be like the ones who have no faith and who will tremble during the manifestation of the Son of Man. On the contrary, pray and rejoice and receive the peace given by my Son, Jesus. What sorrow when I must respect free will and come to the point of giving a Warning that is also part of My mercy. Be ready and vigilant for the hour of My mercy. I bless you, My children.

The following are excerpts from talks given by Fr. Michel Rodrigue in the years 2018 and 2019 in Canada and the United States:

"Over the last five years, God the Father has revealed many things to me about the near future, all of which I have shared with my bishop. Some of these are events that have already occurred. Others are yet to come. The times are urgent. When the Father gave me the fraternity [The Apostolic Fraternity of Saint Benedict Joseph Labre, which God asked Fr. Michel to found], He asked me to build it quickly because it will be a refuge for many priests who will come there.

One of the future events that the Father showed me represents, for me, a Pentecost. Others call it the Warning. At the close of Pope John the XXIII's convocation of Vatican II, he prayed to the Holy Spirit for a new Pentecost—not for the Church, but for the world. Soon, the day that he prayed for will happen. I saw it.

Suddenly, the stars, the sun, and the moon will not shine. All will be black. In the heavens, a sign of Jesus will appear and light up the sky and the world. He will be on the Cross—not in His suffering, but in His glory. Behind Him in a pale light will appear the face of the Father, the True God. It will be something, I assure you.

From the wounds in Jesus's hands, feet, and side, bright shining rays of love and mercy will fall onto the entire Earth, and everything will stop. If you are in an airplane, it will stop. If you are riding in a car, don't worry—the car will stop. If you ask me, "How can that be?" I will say, "God is God. He is the Father Almighty, Creator of heaven and Earth. Do you think He cannot stop matter? Do you believe that your small airplane will outrun Him? No."

Everything will be fixed in time, and the flame of the Holy Spirit will enlighten every conscience on Earth. The rays from Jesus's wounds will pierce every heart, like tongues of fire, and we will see ourselves as if in a mirror before us. We will see our souls, how precious they are to the Father, and we will see the evil within ourselves.

The illumination will last about fifteen minutes, and in this merciful pre-judgment, all will see immediately where they would go if they were to die right then: heaven, purgatory, or hell. More than seeing, however, they will feel pain of their sins, all of them, even the ones they have confessed in the Sacrament of Reconciliation. But the ones they have confessed will be experienced differently.

Those who would go to purgatory will see and feel the pains of their sin and purification. They will recognize their faults and know what they must correct within themselves. For those who are very close to Jesus, they will see what they must change in order to live in complete union with Him.

For the ones who would go to hell, they will burn. Their bodies will not be destroyed, but they will feel exactly what hell is like because they are already there. The only thing missing was the feeling. They will experience the beatings of the devil, and many will not survive because of their great sin, I assure you. But it will be for them a blessing, because they will ask for pardon. It will be their salvation.

The Father wants me to proclaim that you do not have to fear. For the one who believes in God, this will be a loving day, a blessed day. You will see what you must correct to accomplish more of His will, to be more submissive to the grace He wishes to give you for your mission on Earth. It will be one of the greatest signs given to the world since the Resurrection of Jesus Christ. The Father told me that the twenty-first century is His century. After the Warning, no one left on Earth will be able to say that God does not exist.

Many do not understand the Gospel of Matthew, Chapter 24:

Immediately after the tribulation of those days, the sun will be darkened, and the moon will not give its light, and the stars will fall from the sky, and the powers of the heavens will be shaken. And then the sign of the Son of Man will appear in heaven, and all the tribes of the earth will mourn, and they will see the Son of Man coming upon the clouds of heaven with power and great glory. And he will send out his angels with a trumpet blast, and they will gather his elect from the four winds, from one end of the heavens to the other. (Matthew 24:29-31)

Mourning will come when people experience their failures and the pain of their sin. They will express their contrition openly, unaware of their surroundings, because they will be so absorbed in the experience, like in Fatima [when the sun started to dance in the sky and plunged downward toward an estimated 70,000 people, who fell on their knees and confessed their sins publicly, afraid to die.]

After the Illumination of Conscience, another unparalleled gift will be granted to humanity: a period of repentance lasting about six and a half weeks, when the devil will not have the power to act. This means that everyone will have their complete free will to make a decision for or against the Lord. The devil will not bind a person's will and fight against him or her. The Lord will calm everyone's passions and appease their desires. He will heal everyone from the distortion of their senses, so after this Pentecost, all will feel that their entire bodies are in harmony with Him.

The first two and a half weeks [after the Warning], in particular, will be extremely important because the devil will not return at that time, but people's habits will, and they will then be harder to convert. All who have received the desire for the Lord, the sense that they need His salvation, will be marked on their forehead with a luminous cross [invisible to the human eye] by their guardian angel.

God has not given us three ways to travel, only two. There is no grey area in between the path of evil and the path of the Lord. Those who will say, "I don't know. I cannot make a decision," will not be able to remain indifferent. As God says in the Book of Revelation (3:16), *"So, because you are lukewarm, neither hot nor cold, I will spit you out of my mouth."* People will have to make a decisive choice, and you will understand why, because after that, they will be left with the consequences of their decision. The time of mercy will end, and the time of justice will begin. Jesus said this to St. Faustina Kowalska.

The Father said to me, "Renew your consecration to the Holy Hearts of Jesus and Mary."[90] This is important. You know that you are already blessed because you are being made aware. Why do you think that God has chosen you to be here? [Father Michel was speaking to a group of faithful Catholics.] Because you have a mission. When you go out, when you return to your home, you will feel something on your shoulder. What is it? The burden of Jesus, which is the mission of the Lord. If He is making you aware now of what will happen, it is because people will come back from their mystical experience of meeting God, searching for help, not knowing what to do. Some will be afraid; others will be in shock.

You have been chosen for this time to help guide these people into the Catholic Church to receive the Good News of Jesus. You can be young, old. Do not worry if you have problems with your legs, your back. There are plenty of backs in heaven, and the Lord can renew you better than any physician. Some of you will provide brief catechetical instruction for those who know nothing of the essentials of the Catholic faith.

First and foremost, people will need to be reconciled to God, so you will bring them to a priest for Confession. I assure you, the priests who are not in a state of grace will have a hard time because there will be long lines for Confession—I saw the lines! They will need protection and help. Please prepare the priests some sandwiches! I assure you, if people don't halt the line, we will not be able to go to the bathroom! Remember the Cure D'Ars, St. John Vianney, who was in the confessional for fourteen hours, at times.

If people are not baptized, you will bring them for baptismal preparation, which will happen quickly because time will be short. We will baptize en masse, as the Apostles did, by sprinkling water on the crowds and making the pronouncement: "I baptize you in the name of the Father, the Son, and the Holy Spirit." I assure you—I saw this, too.

When the devil returns after about six and a half weeks, he will disseminate a message to the world through the media, cell phones, TV's, et cetera. The message is this: A collective illusion happened on this date. Our scientists have analyzed this and found that it occurred at the same

---

[90] For a powerfully effective Marian consecration, order the book, *Mary's Mantle Consecration: A Spiritual Retreat for Heaven's Help,* endorsed by Archbishop Salvatore Cordileone and Bishop Myron J. Cotta, and the accompanying *Mary's Mantle Consecration Prayer Journal.* See www.MarysMantleConsecration.com.

time a solar flare from the sun was released into the universe. It was so powerful that it affected the minds of the people on Earth, giving everyone a collective illusion.

The devil fools us even now through the new "priests" of the world: television journalists who want you to think what they think, so they present news that is their opinion. They twist the truth, and you are hypnotized, manipulated into believing them.

Others have spoken of these times, but I am accountable for sharing only what the Father revealed to me. I will have to answer to God when I die, so I wish to be faithful to Him."[cii]

NOTES TO THE READER

AMAZON REVIEWS

If you were graced by this book, would you kindly post a short review of *The Warning* on Amazon.com? Your support will make a difference in the lives of souls and our future.

To leave a short review, go to Amazon.com and type in *The Warning*. Click on the book and scroll down the page. Next to customer reviews, click on "Write a customer review." Thank you, in advance, for your kindness.

AFTER THE WARNING

If you are interested in learning more about what God has revealed about the Warning, the events that precede and follow, and how to prepare, see www.CountdowntotheKingdom.com.

BOOK TRAILER

If you would like to view or share the trailer for this book, go to www.queenofpeacemedia.com/the-warning.

Queen of Peace Media Joyfully Announces That
The Warning
Will Be Made into a Movie by

Belladream
Films

If you'd like to know more about this effort, go to:

www.THEWARNINGMOVIE.com

OTHER BOOKS
BY THE AUTHOR

Available through
QueenofPeaceMedia.com and Amazon.com in
Print, Ebook, and Audiobook formats

Libros disponible en español
www.queenofpeacemedia.com/libreria-catolica

EL AVISO
Testimonios y Profecías de la Iluminación de Conciencia

EL MANTO DE MARÍA
Una Consagración Mariana para Ayuda Celestial

EL MANTO DE MARÍA
Diario de Oración para la Consagración

TRANSFIGURADA
El Escape de las Drogas, de la Calle y de la Industria del
Aborto, de Patricia Sandoval

HOMBRES JUNTO A MARÍA
Así Vencieron Seis Hombres la Más Ardua Batalla
de Sus Vidas

OF MEN AND MARY

HOW SIX MEN WON THE GREATEST BATTLE OF THEIR LIVES

"Of Men and Mary is superb. The six life testimonies contained within it are miraculous, heroic, and truly inspiring."

—Fr. Gary Thomas
Pastor, exorcist, and subject of the book and movie, "The Rite."

(See www.queenofpeacemedia.com/of-men-and-mary
For the book trailer and to order)

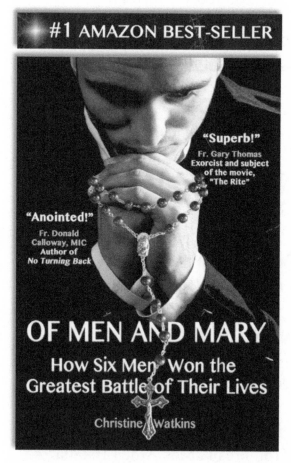

"Anointed!"
—Fr. Donald Calloway, MIC

Turn these pages, and you will find yourself surprisingly inspired by a murderer locked up in prison, a drug-using football player who dreamed of the pros, and a selfish, womanizing dare-devil who died and met God. You will root for a husband and father whose marriage was a battleground, a man searching desperately to belong, pulled by lust and illicit attractions, and an innocent lamb who lost, in a single moment, everyone he cared about most. And you will rejoice that their sins and their pasts were no obstacle for heaven.

FULL OF GRACE

MIRACULOUS STORIES OF HEALING AND CONVERSION THROUGH MARY'S INTERCESSION

"Christine Watkins's beautiful and touching collection of conversion stories are direct, honest, heart-rending, and miraculous."

—Wayne Weible
Author of *Medjugorje: The Message*

(See www.queenofpeacemedia.com/full-of-grace for the book trailer and to order)

In this riveting book, Christine Watkins tells her dramatic story of miraculous healing and conversion to Catholicism, along with the stories of five others: a homeless drug addict, an altar boy trapped by cocaine, a stripper, a lonely youth, and a modern-day hero.

Following each story is a message that Mary has given to the world. And for those eager to probe the deeper, reflective waters of discipleship—either alone or within a prayer group—a Scripture passage, prayerful reflection questions, and a spiritual exercise at the end of each chapter offer an opportunity to enliven our faith.

TRANSFIGURED

PATRICIA SANDOVAL'S ESCAPE FROM DRUGS, HOMELESSNESS, AND THE BACK DOORS OF PLANNED PARENTHOOD

Endorsed by
**Archbishop Salvatore Cordileone & Bishop Michael C. Barber, SJ,
And Fr. Donald Calloway, MIC**

**Disponible También en Español: TRANSFIGURADA
avalado por EMMANUEL
(See www.queenofpeacemedia.com/transfigured
for the book trailer, the companion DVD, and to order)**

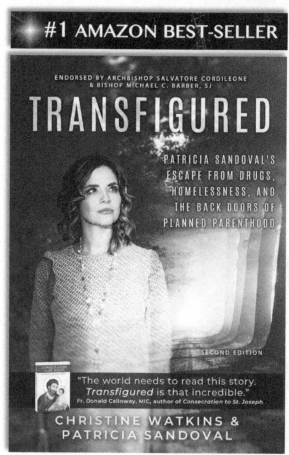

"Are you ready to read one of the most powerful conversion stories ever written? Seriously, are you? It's a bold and shocking claim, I admit. But the story you are about to have the pleasure of reading is so intense and brutally candid that I wouldn't be surprised if it brings you to tears multiple times and opens the door to an experience of mercy and healing. This story is made for the big screen, and I pray it makes it there someday. It's that incredible. . . What you are about to read is as raw, real, and riveting as a story can get. I couldn't put this book down!"

**—Fr. Donald
Calloway, MIC**
Author of
Consecration to St. Joseph and *No Turning Back*

MARY'S MANTLE CONSECRATION

A SPIRITUAL RETREAT FOR HEAVEN'S HELP

Disponible también en español—*El Manto de María:*
Una Consagración Mariana para Ayuda Celestial

Endorsed by **Archbishop Salvatore Cordileone** and
Bishop Myron J. Cotta

**(See www.MarysMantleConsecration.com
to see a video of amazing testimonies and to order)**

"I am grateful to Christine Watkins for making this disarmingly simple practice, which first grew in the fertile soil of Mexican piety, available to the English-speaking world."

—Archbishop Salvatore Cordileone

"Now more than ever, we need a miracle. Christine Watkins leads us through a 46-day self-guided retreat that focuses on daily praying of the Rosary, a Little fasting, and meditating on various virtues and the seven gifts of the Holy Spirit, leading to a transformation in our lives and in the people on the journey with us!"

—Fr. Sean O. Sheridan, TOR
Former President, Franciscan University of Steubenville

MARY'S MANTLE CONSECRATION

PRAYER JOURNAL
to accompany the consecration book

Disponible también en español—
El Manto de Maria: Diario de Oración para la Consagración

PREPARE FOR AN OUTPOURING
OF GRACE UPON YOUR LIFE

(See www.MarysMantleConsecration.com
to see a video of amazing testimonies and to order)

St. Pope John Paul II said that his consecration to Mary was "a decisive

turning point in my life." It can be the same for you.

This *Prayer Journal* with daily Scriptures, saint quotes, questions for reflection and space for journaling is a companion book to the popular *Mary's Mantle Consecration,* a self-guided retreat that has resulted in miracles in the lives and hearts of those who have applied themselves to it. This prayer journal will take you even deeper into your soul and into God's transforming grace.

WINNING THE BATTLE FOR YOUR SOUL

JESUS' TEACHINGS THROUGH MARINO RESTREPO, A ST. PAUL FOR OUR CENTURY

Endorsed by Archbishop-Emeritus, Ramón C. Argüelles
"This book is an authentic jewel of God!"
—**Internationally renowned author, María Vallejo-Nájera**

(See **The Warning: Testimonies and Prophecies of the Illumination of Conscience** to read Marino's testimony)

Marino Restrepo was a sinful man kidnapped for ransom by Colombian terrorists and dragged into the heart of the Amazon jungle. In the span of just one night, the Lord gave him an illumination of his conscience followed by an extraordinary infusion of divine knowledge. Today, Marino is hailed as one of the greatest evangelizers of our time.

In addition to giving talks around the world, Marino is the founder of the Church-approved apostolate, Pilgrims of Love.

This book contains some of the most extraordinary teachings that Jesus has given to the world through Marino Restrepo, teachings that will profoundly alter and inform the way you see your ancestry, your past, your purpose, and your future.

IN LOVE WITH TRUE LOVE

THE UNFORGETTABLE STORY OF SISTER NICOLINA

(See www.QueenofPeaceMedia.com and Amazon.com)

In this seemingly loveless world of ours, we might wonder if true love is attainable. Is it real, or is it perhaps a dancing illusion captured on Hollywood screens? And if this love dares to exist, does it satisfy as the poets say, or fade in our hearing like a passing whisper?

The souls are few who have discovered these answers, and one of them is Nicolina, a feisty, flirtatious girl who fell in love with the most romantic man in all of post-war Germany.

Little did they imagine the places where love would take them.

This enthralling real-life story is a glimpse into the grand secrets of true love—secrets that remain a conundrum to most, but are life, itself for a chosen few. Little-known chambers within the Heart of Love lie in hope to be discovered, and through this little book, may you, like Nicolina, enter their mystery and find life, too.

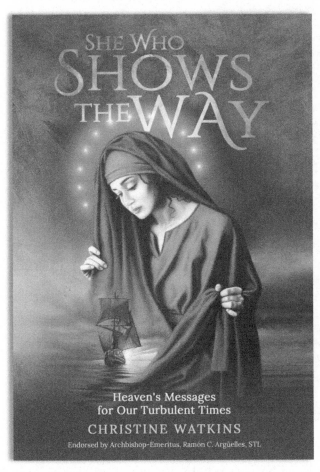

MARIE-JULIE JAHENNY

PROPHECIES AND PROTECTION
FOR THE END TIMES

(See **www.QueenofPeaceMedia.com. Soon on Amazon.com**)

Marie-Julie Jahenny (1850-1941) is one of the most extraordinary mystics in the history of the Church. This humble peasant from devout parents in Britanny, France, received numerous visitations from heaven and lived

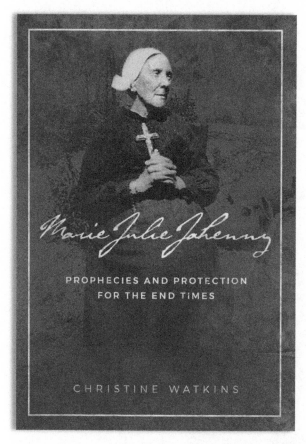

with multiple wounds of the stigmata for most of her long life. Jahenny's selfless spirit endures as a gift to the Church, for she received knowledge of what lies on the horizon of our current era.

Jahenny was supported by her local bishop, Msgr. Fournier of Nantes, who said of her, "I see nothing but good."

In addition to Jahenny's special mission from the Lord to spread the love of the Cross, she was called to prepare the world for the coming chastisements, which precede and prepare the world for the glorious renewal of Christendom in the promised era of peace.

Through Marie-Julie, the Lord has given help, remedies, and protection for the times we now live in, and those soon to come. As Christ said to her on several occasions, "I want My people to be warned."

PURPLE SCAPULAR

OF BLESSING AND PROTECTION
FOR THE END TIMES

Jesus and Mary have given this scapular to the world for our times!

Go to **www.queenofpeacemedia.com/product/purple-scapular-of-blessing-and-protection** to read about all of the incredible promises given to those who wear it in faith.

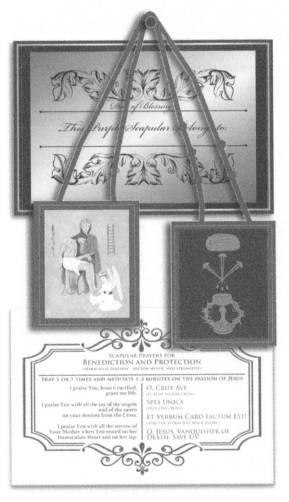

Our Lady's words to the mystic, stigmatist, and victim soul, Marie-Julie Jahenny: "My children, all souls, all people who possesses this scapular will see their family protected. Their home will also be protected, **foremost from fires**. . . for a long time my Son and I have had the desire to make known this scapular of benediction…

This first apparition of this scapular will be a new protection for the times of the chastisements, of the calamities, and the famines. All those who are clothed (with it) shall pass under the storms, the tempests, and the darkness. They will have light as if it were plain day. Such is the power of this unknown scapular. . ."

THE CROSS OF FORGIVENESS

FOR THE END TIMES

On July 20, 1882, Our Lord introduced **THE CROSS OF FORGIVENESS** to the world through the French mystic, Marie-Julie Jahenny. He indicated that He would like it made and worn by the faithful during the time of the chastisements. It is a cross signifying pardon, salvation, protection, and the calming of plagues.

Go to **www.queenofpeacemedia.com/product/cross-of-forgiveness** to read about all of the graces and protection given to those who wear it in faith.

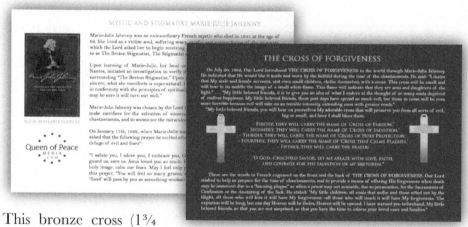

This bronze cross (1¾ inches tall and 1 inch wide) is a gift for our age and a future time when priests may not be readily available: "My little beloved friends, you will bear on yourselves My adorable cross that will preserve you from all sorts of evil, big or small, and later I shall bless them. . . My little children, all souls that suffer, and those sifted out by the blight, all those who will kiss it will have My forgiveness—all those who will touch it will have My forgiveness." The expiation will be long, but one day Heaven will be theirs, Heaven will be opened."

THE FLAME OF LOVE

THE SPIRITUAL DIARY
OF ELIZABETH KINDELMANN

(Go to www.QueenofPeaceMedia.com/flame-love-love-book-bundle) to receive the Flame of Love book bundle at cost!

Extraordinary graces of literally blinding Satan, and reaching heaven quickly are attached to the spiritual practices and promises in this spiritual classic. On August 2, 1962, Our Lady said these remarkable words to mystic and victim soul, Elizabeth Kindelmann:

"Since the Word became Flesh, I have never given such a great movement as the Flame of Love that comes to you now. Until now, there has been nothing that so blinds Satan."

THE FLAME OF LOVE

In this special talk, Christine Watkins introduces the Flame of Love of the Immaculate Heart of Mary.

This worldwide movement in the Catholic Church is making true disciples of Jesus Christ in our turbulent times and preparing souls for the Triumph of Our Lady's Heart and the New Pentecost. See www.ChristineWatkins.com. Email cwatkins@queenofpeacemedia.com.

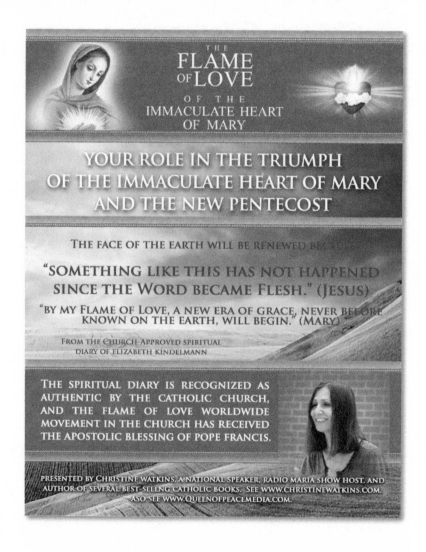

ABOUT THE AUTHOR

Christine Watkins is a popular Catholic author and keynote speaker. She was an anti-Catholic atheist about to die from her sins when she received a divine healing. Watkins brings to life stories of faith, including her own, and fascinating topics of Catholic spirituality. See www.ChristineWatkins.com.

Queen of Peace
MEDIA
.com

END NOTES

[i] Biblical writers and secular historians both record that Judas Iscariot paid a sum of thirty pieces of silver to betray Jesus, and they indicate that the money went to purchase a "potter's field," which was used for the burial of poor aliens (Matthew 27:3-10).

[ii] Hugh Ross, "Fulfilled Prophecy: Evidence for Reliability of the Bible," August 22, 2003, Reason to Believe, accessed July 12, 2019, https://www.reasons.org/explore/blogs/todays-new-reason-to-believe/read/tnrtb/2003/08/22/fulfilled-prophecy-evidence-for-the-reliability-of-the-bible.

[iii] Mark Mallett, "Prophecy Properly Understood," May 2, 2014, The Now World: Reflections on Our Times, accessed July 12, 2019, https://www.markmallett.com/blog/2014/05/02/prophecy-properly-understood. *Message of Fatima, Theological Commentary* by Pope Benedict XVI.

[iv] Centuries before Jesus was born, God told His people of their coming Messiah. The Old Testament was written between 1450 BC and 430 BC, and through it, the Lord shares in uncanny detail what will happen when He comes to Earth.

Genesis first mentions how the Messiah would be the offspring of the woman (Eve), and a descendant of Abraham and Judah. Deuteronomy says that He will be a prophet like Moses.

The Psalms reveal He will be the Son of God, sneered at and mocked, betrayed by a friend, accused by false witnesses and hated without a cause. They speak of how the Messiah will be crucified, pierced through His hands and feet, but his bones not broken; He will be given vinegar and gall to drink, and men will gamble for his clothing; He will be the "stone the builders rejected" who will become "the head cornerstone," who will ascend to heaven.

The prophet Isaiah speaks of how the Messiah will be born of a virgin, His first spiritual work will be in Galilee; He will make the blind see and the deaf hear, and he will be rejected, beaten, mocked, and spat upon, and silent in front of His accusers. He will be killed, crucified with criminals, buried with the rich, and as is also mentioned by the prophet Jeremiah, part of a new and everlasting covenant.

The prophet Daniel says He will come at a specific time; Micah announced He will be born in Bethlehem; Zechariah mentions that His disciples will forsake him, He will enter Jerusalem, riding on a donkey, and sold for thirty pieces of silver; and Malachy declares that the Messiah will enter the Temple with authority.

Taken from "Messianic Prophecies: The Bible's predictions about Jesus, written centuries before He was born, accessed July 13, 2019, http://www.clarifyingchristianity.com/m_prophecies.shtml

[v] Apostolado de Garabandal, "Conchita's Trip to Rome," https://www.apostoladodegarabandal.com/en/a-viagem-de-conchita-a-roma and home page: https://www.apostoladodegarabandal.com/en, accessed July 4, 2020.

[vi] YouTube: "Kisah Nyata Priest Has Near Death Experience and Almost Goes to Hell," accessed May 6, 2020, https://www.youtube.com/watch?v=o9pbvu3BGrQ

YouTube: "Father Steven Scheier's Judgment Experience," https://www.youtube.com/watch?v=9VFE8ToVatI, accessed July 23, 2019, aired April 15, 1997 on "Mother Angelica Live" on EWTN.

Personal interview by the author with Fr. Steve Sheier, August 20, 2012.

Joseph Pronechen, "Wake-Up Call Changes Priest," National Catholic Register, August 28-September 10, 2011, Volume 87, No. 18, pp. B1 and B4.

Rev. Stephen Scheier, "God's Merciful Judgment: Father Steve Scheier's Story," Signs and Wonders for Our Times, Summer 2002, Vol. 14, No. 2, pp. 50-55.

"God's Merciful Judgment: A Priest," a recording of a talk by Fr. Steven Scheier at the Arizona Mir Conference, 2009. Glorious Sounds Network, P.O. Box 37854, Phoenix, AZ 85069

[vii] The Book of Daniel serves as the major apocalyptic Book of the Old Testament, as Chapters 7-12 foretell the End Times. The prophecy of Daniel 12:1 speaks of a time of great "distress" unsurpassed in history, when Michael will arise. This period is called the Great Tribulation by Jesus in Matthew 24:21 and is further referenced in Revelation 7:14. The great nations of the world have risen against the Lord; but God will protect His people and His Kingdom shall prevail and last forever.

[viii] "See Drawing Heaven—Akiane Kramarik," https://www.youtube.com/watch?v=md4cMFVniZY, accessed July 23, 2019, "Did Akiane Kramarik and Colton Burpos See Yeshua (Jesus)?", accessed May 6, 2020, https://www.youtube.com/watch?v=NNx0kbNuqBg

[ix] Used with permission and excerpted from the book: Now I Walk on Death Row (Chosen Books: 20110, the true story of a high-powered lawyer with prestige, power, and unthinkable paychecks at his fingertips, who became a humble lay chaplain.

[x] Used with permission from Thomas Petrisko's The Miracle of the Illumination of All Consciences (St. Andrew's Productions: 2000), pp. 105-114.

[xi] For an updated timeline on the Church's official position on Medjugorje, see https://www.tektonministries.org/timeline-of-churchs-response-to-medjugorje-2/

[xii] See http://www.marinorestrepo.com/about-us.html

[xiii] James 3:1-12

[xiv] See the Catechism of the Catholic Church, #1446:
Christ instituted the sacrament of Penance for all sinful members of his Church: above all for those who, since Baptism, have fallen into grave sin, and have thus lost their baptismal grace and wounded ecclesial communion. It is to them that the sacrament of Penance offers a new possibility to convert and to recover the grace of justification. The Fathers of the Church present this sacrament as "the second plank [of salvation] after the shipwreck which is the loss of grace."

[xv] Exodus 34:6-7, Deuteronomy 5:8-10, Leviticus 26:39

[xvi] Revelation 12:7-12

[xvii] Where purgatory is found in the Bible:
"Then the master called the servant in. 'You wicked servant,' he said, 'I canceled all that debt of yours because you begged me to. Shouldn't you have had mercy on your fellow servant just as I had on you?' In anger his master handed him over to the jailers to be tortured, until he should pay back all he owed. "This is how my heavenly Father will treat each of you unless you forgive your brother or sister from your heart." (Matt.18:32-35)

"Settle matters quickly with your adversary who is taking you to court. Do it while you are still together on the way, or your adversary may hand you over to the judge, and the judge may hand you over to the officer, and you may be thrown into prison. Truly I tell you, you will not get out until you have paid the last penny." (Matt. 5:25)

"But each one should build with care. For no one can lay any foundation other than the one already laid, which is Jesus Christ. If anyone builds on this foundation using gold, silver, costly stones, wood, hay or straw, their work will be shown for what it is, because the Day will bring it to light. It will be revealed with fire, and the fire will test the quality of each person's work. If what has been built survives, the builder will receive a reward. If it is burned up, the builder will suffer loss but yet will be saved—even though ONLY as one ESCAPING THROUGH THE FLAMES." (1 Cor. 3:11-15)

Jesus teaches us, "Come to terms with your opponent or you will be handed over to the judge and thrown into prison. You will not get out until you have paid the last penny." (Matt. 5:26,18:34; Luke 12:58-59) The word "opponent" (antidiko) is likely a reference to the devil (see the same word for devil in 1 Peter 5:8) who is an accuser against man (c.f. Job 1.6-12; Zech. 3.1; Rev. 12.10), and God is the judge. If we have not adequately dealt with Satan and sin in this life, we will be held in a temporary state called a prison, and we won't get out until we have satisfied our entire debt to God. This "prison" is purgatory where we will not get out until the last penny is paid.

Jesus says, "Be perfect, even as your heavenly Father is perfect." We are only made perfect through purification, and in Catholic teaching, this purification, if not completed on earth, is continued in a transitional state we call purgatory. (Matt. 5:48)

Jesus says, "And anyone who says a word against the Son of man will be forgiven; but no one who speaks against the Holy Spirit will be forgiven either in this world or in the next." (Matt. 12:32) Jesus thus clearly provides that there is forgiveness after death. The phrase "in the next" (from the Greek "en to mellonti") generally refers to the afterlife (see, for example, Mark 10.30;

Luke 18.30; 20.34-35; Eph. 1.21 for similar language). Forgiveness is not necessary in heaven, and there is no forgiveness in hell. This proves that there is another state after death, and the Church for 2,000 years has called this state purgatory.

Luke 12:47-48—When the Master comes (at the end of time), some will receive light or heavy beatings but will live. This state is not heaven or hell, because in heaven there are no beatings, and in hell we will no longer live with the Master.

1 Cor. 15:29-30—Paul mentions people being baptized on behalf of the dead, in the context of atoning for their sins (people are baptized on the dead's behalf so the dead can be raised). These people cannot be in heaven because they are still with sin, but they also cannot be in hell because their sins can no longer be atoned for. They are in purgatory. These verses directly correspond to 2 Macc. 12:44-45 which also shows specific prayers for the dead, so that they may be forgiven of their sin.

Phil. 2:10—Every knee bends to Jesus, in heaven, on earth, and "under the earth" which is the realm of the righteous dead, or purgatory.

2 Tim. 1:16-18—Onesiphorus is dead but Paul asks for mercy on him "on that day." Paul's use of "that day" demonstrates its eschatological usage (see, for example, Rom. 2.5,16; 1 Cor. 1.8; 3.13; 5.5; 2 Cor. 1.14; Phil. 1.6,10; 2.16; 1 Thess. 5.2,4,5,8; 2 Thess. 2.2,3; 2 Tim. 4.8). Of course, there is no need for mercy in heaven, and there is no mercy given in hell. Where is Onesiphorus? He is in purgatory.

Heb. 12:14—without holiness no one will see the Lord. We need final sanctification to attain true holiness before God, and this process occurs during our lives and, if not completed during our lives, in the transitional state of purgatory.

[xviii] Romans 5:20

[xix] Psalm 90:4, 2 Peter 3:8–9

[xx] Matthew 16:26, Mark 8:36

[xxi] Evelyn Waugh, *Edmund Campion* (Ignatius Press; First edition, 2012).

[xxii] Francis Johnston, *Fatima: The Great Sign* (Rockford, Illinois: Tan Books and Publishers, 1980), pp. 54-66.

Gale Thomson, "Campion, Edmund," Encyclopedia.com, 2007, accessed July 27, 2019, https://www.encyclopedia.com/humanities/news-wires-white-papers-and-books/campion-edmund

"St. Edmund Campion, SJ (1540-1581)," IgnatianSpirituality.com: A Service of Loyola Press, accessed July 27, 2019, https://www.ignatianspirituality.com/ignatian-voices/16th-and-17th-century-ignatian-voices/st-edmund-campion-sj/

Todd Aglialoro, "Edmund Campion," Catholic Answers, September 1, 1994, accessed July 27, 2019, https://www.catholic.com/magazine/print-edition/edmund-campion

[xxiii]Evelyn Waugh, *Two Lives: Edmund Campion and Ronald Knox* (Continuum; 2005), p. 113. Note: A certain Catholic scholar has argued that St. Campion is speaking here of the final judgment and not the Illumination of Conscience. That could not be so because the final judgment is not simply a day of change in the world. It is the end of the world. Also, St. Edmund's audience, his persecutors, would already be familiar with the final judgment in Scripture, therefore St. Edmund would not be pronouncing anything new to them, as he seems to be doing in this quote.

[xxiv] Mark Regis, "Blessed Anna-Maria Taigi," Garabandal Journal, January-February 2004, pp. 6-8.

Albert Bessieres, SJ, translated from the French by Rev. Stephen Rigby, *Wife, Mother and Mystic* (Tan Books, 1970).

[xxv] Thomas W. Petrisko, *The Miracle of the Illumination of All Consciences* (St. Andrew's Productions, 2000; second printing 2002), p. 27.

[xxvi] Fr. Joseph Iannuzzi, *The Antichrist and the End Times* (Saint Andrew's Productions, 2019), p. 36.

[xxvii] Fr. Gaudentius Rossi, Missionary priest, *The Christian Trumpet: Impending General Calamities, The Universal Triumph of the Church, the Coming of Antichrist, The Last Judgment, and the End of the World* (Thomas Richardson and Sons; London, 1875) accessed July 27, 2019, https://archive.org/details/TheChristianTrumpetOr/page/n5/mode/2up?%2Fq=taigi

[xxviii] Alec R. Vidler, *The Church in an Age of Revolution* (Penguin Books, 1962), pp. 146, 153.

[xxix] Donald R. McClarey, "Pio Nono: First Pope to be Photographed," The American Catholic: Politics and Culture from a Catholic Perspective, September 30, 2013, accessed June 27, 2019, https://www.the-american-catholic.com/2013/09/30/pio-nono-first-pope-to-be-photographed/

[xxx] Holland, Joe, *Modern Catholic Social Teaching: The Popes confront the Industrial Age 1740-1958* (Paulist Press, 2003), p. 57.

[xxxi] Pope Pius IX introduced the doctrine of papal infallibility, which led to the First Vatican Council declaring the Roman pontiff infallible, his definitions "being irreformable of themselves, and not from the consent of the Church"; his infallibility was, however, restricted only to those occasions "when he speaks "ex cathedra," a Latin phrase which means "from the chair," meaning when he officially teaches in his capacity of the universal shepherd of the Church a doctrine on a matter of faith or morals and addresses it to the entire world.

[xxxii] Jason Berry, *Render Unto Rome: The Secret Life of Money in the Catholic Church* (Broadway Books, 2012), p. 48.

[xxxiii] Ibid.

[xxxiv] "Peter's Pence." Washington: United States Conference of Catholic Bishop, accessed July 27, 2019, http://www.usccb.org/catholic-giving/opportunities-for-giving/peters-pence/index.cfm

[xxxv] Rev. R. Gerald Culleton, *The Prophets and Our Times* (Tan Books and Publishers, 1941), p. 206, accessed July 29, 2019, http://ia800200.us.archive.org/2/items/TheProphetsAndOurTimes/TheProphetsAndOurTimes.pdf

[xxxvi] Rev. Michael Sopoćko, "My Memories of the Late Sister Faustina," January 27, 1948,

The Congregation of the Sisters of Our Lady of Mercy, accessed July 1, 2019, https://www.faustyna.pl/zmbm/en/blessed-fr-michal-sopocko/

xxxvii "Mary Faustina Kowalska, 1905-1938, Vatican News Services, accessed July 1, 2019, http://www.vatican.va/news_services/liturgy/saints/ns_lit_doc_20000430_faustina_en.html

xxxviii St. Faustina Kowalska, *Diary of Saint Maria Faustina Kowalska: Divine Mercy in My Soul, 3rd Edition* (Marian Press, 2005), #35.

xxxix Ibid., #83.

xl "Grete Ganseforth," Visions of Jesus Christ, accessed July 13, 2019, http://www.visionsofjesuschrist.com/weeping1790.html

xli John Carpenter, "Queen of the Universe, Heede, Germany, 1937-1945, August 12, 2016, accessed June 30, 2019, http://www.divinemysteries.info/queen-of-the-universe-heede-germany-1937-1945/

xlii D. Alfonso Cenni, *I SS. Cuori di Gesu e di Maria. La Salvezza del Mondo. Le Loro Apparizioni, Promesse e Richieste. Nihil Obstate Ex Parte Ordinis Il P. Generale D. Pier-Damiano Buffadini, February 24, 1949. Imprimatur Sublaci. Simon Laurentius O.S. B. Ep, tit. Abb. Ord. June 3, 1949. Accessed June 23, 2019,* https://gloria.tv/like/uaZeA21Rv8dW4nTWH4kAWfMQQ

xliii D. Alfonso Cenni, *I SS. Cuori di Gesu e di Maria. La Salvezza del Mondo. Le Loro Apparizioni, Promesse e Richieste. Nihil Obstat Ex Parte Ordinis Il P. Generale D. Pier-Damiano Buffadini, February 24, 1949. Imprimatur Sublaci. Simon Laurentius O.S.B. Ep, tit. Abb. Ord. June 3, 1949. Accessed June 23, 2019,* https://gloria.tv/like/uaZeA21Rv8dW4nTWH4kAWfMQQ

xliv Kindelmann, *The Flame of Love of the Immaculate Heart of Mary*, p. 205.

xlv Kindelmann, *The Flame of Love* (Children of the Father Foundation; 2015-2018), pp. 44-45.

xlvi Elizabeth Kindelmann, La Flamme d'Amour, p. 79. http://www.salvemaria.ca/en-pdf/flame10-book-p78-121-toblindsatank.pdf, accessed September 19, 2019. See also https://www.theflameoflove.org/spiritual_diary.html, accessed September 19, 2019.

xlvii Kindelmann, *The Flame of Love* (Children of the Father Foundation; 2015-2018), p. 87.

xlviii Ibid., p.110.

xlix Fr. Adof Faroni, SDB, *Garabandal—Conchita's Diary: A Tale of Innocence* translated from the Spanish, 101 Foundation, p. 7.

l Ibid., p. 30.

li "Four Messages of Our Lady Carmel of Garabandal, St. Michael's Garabandal Center for Our Lady of Carmel, Inc., accessed July 2, 2019, http://www.garabandal.org/News/Message_7.shtml

lii "Garabandal Film 08—Second Message June 18th, 1965." YouTube, accessed July 2, 2019, https://www.youtube.com/watch?v=uNmCB_j3Vhg

liii F. Sanchez-Ventura y Pascual, *The Apparitions of Garabandal* (San Miguel, 1966), p. 171.

liv Albrecht Weber, *Garabandal Der Zeigefinger Gottes [Garabandal: The Finger of God]* (Weto-Verlag Meersburg; Auflage), 2000.

lv "The Four Seers These Days," Apostolado de Garabandal: Lingue Portuguesa, accessed, July 2, 2019, https://www.apostoladodegarabandal.com/en/as-quatro-videntes-nos-dias-de-hoje/

lvi Colin B. Donovan, STL, "Garabandal," EWTN Expert Answers, accessed July 4, 2019, https://www.ewtn.com/expert/answers/garabandal.htm

lvii Michael O'Neill, "Exploring the Miraculous," December 7, 2015, Our Sunday Visitor, p. 224.

lviii St. Mother Teresa of Calcutta, the famous founder of the Missionaries of Charity wrote:

"It was in 1970 that I heard about the apparitions of San Sebastian de Garabandal for the first time . . . From the beginning, I felt that the 'events' were authentic . . ." (Letter of November 10, 1987 to Msgr. Del Val). During her frequent trips to the United States, notably to New York, Mother Teresa had the opportunity of meeting Conchita, who has lived on Long Island since 1972. This was the beginning of a strong human and spiritual friendship with Conchita and her family, which never faltered. Mother Teresa became the godmother of Conchita's third daughter, Anna Maria.

[lix] The November 7, 1968 bulletin of Peru's Legion Blanca under the imprimatur of Mgr. Alfonso Zapana Belliza, Bishop of Tacna, Peru, quotes the late Pope Paul VI as having said at a private audience these inspiring words: "Garabandal the most beautiful story of humanity since the birth of Jesus Christ! It is also the second sojourn of the most Holy Virgin on this earth, and we have no adequate words to express our gratitude."

Pope Paul VI had all the while shown a very special interest in the apparitions. At an audience given to Fr. Jose Escalda, SJ, the latter mentioned there were many opponents of the apparitions even amongst his own people. His Holiness promptly rejoined: "It doesn't matter; tell these gentlemen that it is the Pope who has said that it is most important and most urgent to make these messages known to the world."

The visionary, Conchita, had a private audience with Pope Paul VI, and His Holiness said to her, "Conchita, I bless you and with me, the whole Church blesses you." Accessed July 3, 2019, http://www.garabandal.org/church.shtml.

[lx] The link between St. Josemaría Escrivá de Balaguer and the Garabandal apparitions is not well known. In the summer of 1962, the saint spent a few days on holiday in Suances, Cantabria and visited Garabandal, accompanied by several young men who were members of Opus Dei. He spoke cheerfully and profoundly to the girls. News of this visit came out by chance, years later, when somebody showed the girls a prayer card asking for St. Josemaría Escrivá de Balaguer's intercession, printed during his canonization. It was then that the girls joyfully recounted the meeting. He would not have risked his reputation, if he did not believe in the apparitions, by telling others about his trip and conversation with the girls. This was also confirmed by Mother Nieves.

Video with Mother Neives (in Spanish) on You Tube, "Testimonio de la presencia de San Jose Maria Escriba de Balaguer en GARABANDAL," accessed July 3, 2019, https://www.gloria.tv/video/jPSe82pAqv8P2arkSMTbzqMe4

[lxi] St. Padre Pio wrote (typed) the following letter in Italian to the four Garabandal visionaries. At the time, they didn't know who Padre Pio was. A photograph of the letter can be found on this webpage accessed on July 3, 2019, Garabandal News, "The Original Letter of Padre Pio to the Seers of Garabandal" by Juan Hervás, November 2, 2108, https://garabandalnews.org/2018/11/02/the-letter-of-padre-pio-to-the-seers-of-garabandal/:

Dear girls,

At nine o'clock this morning the Blessed Virgin Mary told me about you, oh dear girls, about your visions and she told me to say to you:

"Oh blessed girls of San Sebastian de Garabandal, I promise that I will be with you until the end of the centuries, and you will be with me until the end of the world, and then united with me in the glory of paradise."

Together with this I am sending you a copy of the Holy Rosary of Fatima, which the Blessed Virgin has ordered me to send you. The Blessed Virgin dictated this rosary, and she wants it to be propagated for the salvation of sinners and the preservation of humanity from the terrible punishments, with which the good God is threatening.

I give you a recommendation: pray and make others pray, because the world is on the road to perdition.

They do not believe in you or in your conversations with the white Lady, but they will believe when it is too late.
March 3, 1962

In 1967, Conchita had been called to Rome by Cardinal Ottaviani, Prefect of the Holy Office, now called the Sacred Congregation for the Doctrine of the Faith. It was during this time that Conchita had a private audience with Pope Paul VI. Since Conchita had to wait a day before meeting with Cardinal Ottaviani, it was decided that she, accompanied by her mother and the other members of the party, would visit Padre Pio at San Giovanni Rotondo.

One of the prophesies of Our Lady regarding the Miracle was that the Holy Father would see it wherever he may be at that time and Padre Pio would see it too. After the death of Padre Pio, Conchita visited Lourdes at the request of Fr. Cennamo OFM, the Superior of the Capuchin Order, who was well known by Padre Pio. Conchita asked Father Cennamo, "How is it the Virgin told me Padre Pio was supposed to see the Miracle and he has died?"

He answered, "He saw the Miracle before he died. He told me so himself."

Another significant event concerns the veil which covered the face of Padre Pio after his death. Fr. Cennamo was told by Padre Pio before his death to give the veil to Conchita. On handing the veil to her, Fr. Cennamo told her that he did not believe in the apparitions of Garabandal until Padre Pio told him to give the veil to her.

"Padre Pio and Garabandal," Garabandal, www.garabandal.ie, accessed July 4, 2019, http://www.garabandal.ie/padre-pio-and-garabandal/

Conchita recounts: "I had the veil in front of me, as I was writing later that evening, when suddenly the whole room became filled with fragrance. The perfume so strong I started to cry."

Barry Hanratty, "Padre Pio at Garabandal: The Association between the Famed Stigmatist and the Events at Garabandal is Real," Garabandal: The Message of Our Lady of Mount Carmel, July/September 1997, pp. 10-13, accessed, July 3, 2019, https://www.garabandal.us/wp-content/uploads/2013/02/padre_pio.pdf

[lxii] Michael Brown, *The Final Hour* (Queenship Publications, 1997) p. 141.

[lxiii] Ramon Pérez, *Garabandal: The Village Speaks*, translated from the French by Matthews, Annette I. Curot, The Workers of Our Lady of Mount Carmel, 1981, pp. 50-51.

[lxiv] Ramon Pérez, *Garabandal: The Village Speaks*, translated from the French by Matthews, Annette I. Curot, The Workers of Our Lady of Mount Carmel, 1981, pp. 51-52.

[lxv] Garabandal International Magazine, October-December, 2014, accessed July 4, 2019, http://www.garabandal.org.uk/magazine.html

[lxvi] Barry Hanratty, "The Warning," Garabandal Journal, Vol. 3. No. 1, January-February, 2004, pp. 5-6.

[lxvii] Interview with Jacinta conducted by Barry Hanratty April 16,1983, St. Michael's Garabandal Center for Our Lady of Carmel, Inc., accessed July 4, 2019, http://www.garabandal.org/News/Interview_with_Jacinta.shtml

[lxviii] For a powerfully effective Marian consecration, order the book, *Mary's Mantle Consecration: A Spiritual Retreat for Heaven's Help,* endorsed by Archbishop Salvatore Cordileone and Bishop Myron J. Cotta, and the accompanying *Mary's Mantle Consecration Prayer Journal.* See www.MarysMantleConsecration.com.

[lxix] Colin B. Donovan, STL, "Marian Movement of Priests," EWTN Expert Answers, accessed July 4, 2019, https://www.ewtn.com/expert/answers/MMP.htm

[lxx] For a powerfully effective Marian consecration, order the book and journal: *Mary's Mantle Consecration: A Spiritual Retreat for Heaven's Help,* endorsed by Archbishop Salvatore Cordileone and Bishop Myron J. Cotta. See www.MarysMantleConsecration.com.

[lxxi] National Headquarters of the Marian Movement of Priests in the United States of

America, Our Lady Speaks to Her Beloved Priests, 10th Edition (Maine; 1988) p. xiv.

lxxii Ibid. p. xii.

lxxiii Cardinal Bernardino Echeverría Ruiz, OFM, Cardinal Ignatius Moussa Daoud, and Cardinal John Baptist Wu provided their Imprimatur for Gobbi's book.

lxxiv Church officials asked that the following words be put at the beginning of MMP's book, *To the Priests, Our Lady's Beloved Sons*: "The messages contained in this book must be understood not as words spoken directly by Our Lady, but received, in the form of interior locutions, by Don Stefano Gobbi."

lxxv Marian Movement of Priests, Fr. Stefano Gobbi, *To the Priests: Our Lady's Beloved Sons; 17th English Edition* (St. Francis, Maine: Marian Movement of Priests, 1996), p. 920.

lxxvi Marian Movement of Priests, Fr. Stefano Gobbi, *To the Priests: Our Lady's Beloved Sons; 1996 Supplement* (St. Francis, Maine: Marian Movement of Priests, 1996), pp. 973-974.

lxxvii www.dynamiccatholic.com

lxxviii Matthew Kelly, *Words from God* (Batemans Bay, Australia: Words from God, 1993), p. 70-72.

lxxix This information is corroborated by Fr. Neil Buchlein, Pastor of St. Mary Queen of Heaven, Madison, WV, and of St. Joseph the Worker, Whitesville, WV. To listen a radio interview with Janie Garza on "As the Spirit Leads," WTMR radio in Pennsylvania. go to: Our Blessed Mother's Children, "Janie Garza's Silver Anniversary of Messages from the Blessed Mother," accessed June 18, 2019, http://www.blessedmotherschildren.com/daily-ramblings/janie-garzas-silver-anniversary-of-messages-from-the-blessed-mother.

lxxx Fr. Joseph Amalfitano, Pastor Emeritus of Immaculate Conception Parish in Marcus Hook, Pennsylvania, and spiritual director of the National Centre for Padre Pio in Barto, PA, knows Janie Garza personally, and confirmed with the author that Janie suffers the Passion in her body, in particular, on Good Friday.

lxxxi Janie Garza, *Heaven's Messages for the Family, Vol. II: Messages from St. Joseph and the Archangels*, (St. Dominic Media, 1999) p. 45-46.

lxxxii Janie Garza, *Heaven's Messages for the Family: How to Become the Family God Wants You to Be* (Saint Dominic Media, 1998), p. 329.

lxxxiii For a powerfully effective Marian consecration, order the book, *Mary's Mantle Consecration: A Spiritual Retreat for Heaven's Help,* endorsed by Archbishop Salvatore Cordileone and Bishop Myron J. Cotta, and the accompanying *Mary's Mantle Consecration Prayer Journal.* See www.MarysMantleConsecration.com.

lxxxiv Garza, *Heaven's Messages*, pp. 201-202.

lxxxv "Maria Esperanza: Modern-Day Mystic and Messenger of Hope," Mystics of the Church, accessed July 4, 2019, http://www.mysticsofthechurch.com/2010/10/maria-esperanza-modern-day-mystic-and.html

lxxxvi Archbishop Pio Bello Ricardo, "Pastoral Instruction on the Apparitions of the Blessed Virgin in Finca, Betania," https://www.ewtn.com/catholicism/ library/pastoral-instruction-on-the-apparitions-of-the-blessed-virgin-in-finca-betania-3647, accessed July 4, 2019.

lxxxvii Sources: Michael Brown, *The Bridge to Heaven—Interviews with Maria Esperanza of Betania* (Betania Publications: 2003).

"Mrs. Maria Esperanza: Messenger of Reconcilation," Maria Esperanza, Servant of God, accessed July 4, 2019, http://mariaesperanza.org/mrs-maria-esperanza-messenger-of-reconciliation/

"Maria Esperanza: Modern-Day Mystic and Messenger of Hope," Mystics of the Church, accessed July 4, 2019, http://www.mysticsofthechurch.com/2010/10/maria-esperanza-modern-day-mystic-and.html

lxxxviii Michael Brown, "Esperanza's Recent Sun Prophecies Fulfilled? Great Seer's Health Also Improves," Spirit Daily, accessed July 14, 2019, https://www.spiritdaily.org/Prophecy-seers/Esperanza/esperanzairaqafter.htm

lxxxix Michael Brown, "Sit in Venezuela Accents Mystery of Why Certain Spots are Specifically Chosen," Spirit Daily, accessed July 4, 2019, https://www.spiritdaily.org/betaniaspot.htm

xc Michael Brown, "The Incredible Story of Maria Esperanza," Spirit Daily, accessed July 7, 2019, https://www.spiritdaily.org/Prophecy-seers/Esperanza/Esperanza_story.htm

xci *The Appeals of Our Lady: Apparitions and Marian Shrines in the World.* "Apparition of the Virgin Mary at Betania." http://www.therealpresence.org/eucharst/misc/BVM/91_BETANIA_96x96.pdf, accessed September 16, 2019.

xcii Signs and Wonders for Our Times, Volume 15-n.2, Featured Article from www.sign.org, p. 37.

xciii "Revelamos Quen Es la Vidente Luz de María," Foros de la Virgen María, accessed July 13, 2019, https://forosdelavirgen.org/118869/luz-de-maria-reportaje/

xciv Ibid.

xcv

Estelí, Nicaragua, Year of Our Lord, March 19 of 2017
Solemnity of the Patriarch Saint Joseph

The volumes that contain "PRIVATE REVELATION" from heaven, given to Luz de María from the year 2009 to the present time, have been given to me for the respective ecclesiastic approval. I have reviewed with faith and interest these volumes entitled, THY KINGDOM COME, and have come to conclusion that they are a call to humanity to return to the path that leads to eternal life, and that these messages are an exhortation from heaven in these times in which man must be careful not to stray from the Divine Word.

In each revelation given to Luz de María, Our Lord Jesus Christ and the Blessed Virgin Mary guide the steps, the work, and the actions of the people of God in these times in which humanity needs to return to the teachings contained in Holy Scripture.

The messages in these volumes are a treatise of spirituality, divine wisdom, and morality for those who welcome them with faith and humility, so I recommend them for you to read, meditate upon, and put into practice.

I DECLARE that I have not found any doctrinal error that attempts against the faith, morality and good habits, for which I grant these publications the IMPRIMATUR. Together with my blessing, I express my best wishes for the "Words of Heaven" contained here to resonate in every creature of good will. I ask the Virgin Mary, Mother of God and Our Mother, to intercede for us so that the will of God be fulfilled

". . . on Earth as it is in heaven (Mt, 6:10)."
IMPRIMATUR
Juan Abelardo Mata Guevara, SDB
Head Bishop of Estelí, Nicaragua

xcvi Bonilla, *Venga,* Imprimatur of Bishop Guevara, Message of March 3, 2013, from the Blessed Virgin Mary, p. 56, Revelaciones Marianas, https://www.revelacionesmarianas.com/libros/en/2013.pdf, accessed September 17, 2019.

xcvii Ibid., p. 175, https://www.revelacionesmarianas.com/libros/en/2014.pdf, accessed September 17, 2019.

xcviii Ibid.

xcix Luz de María de Bonilla, "The Great Warning of God to Humanity: Prophecies and Revelations Given to Luz de María de Bonilla," Revelaciones Marianas, accessed July 13, 2019, https://www.revelacionesmarianas.com/en/warning.html

[c] Talks by Fr. Rodrigue (2 CD sets) can be purchased through Peter Frank at missionangelshq@gmail.com. All proceeds go to supporting the construction of the new monasteries, which God the Father has told Fr. Rodrigue are important for the Church's future: Fraternité Apostolique Saint Benoît-Joseph Labre (Apostolic Fraternity of St. Benedict Joseph Labre). See www.Countdowntothekingdom.com

[ci] From the following live recorded talks of Fr. Michel Rodrigue: "The Merciful Father" in Dominique du Rosaire, Amos, Quebec on October 23, 2017; "The Times Are Urgent for the Church" in Barry's Bay on Thursday July 12, 13, 2018; "When the Holy Spirit Speaks to the Church" in Bancroft on Thursday, October 11, 2018; "The Holy Spirit Speaking to the Church" in North Brunswick, October 27, 2018, Canada. Talks on February 22-24, 2019, at Gospa House in North Hills, California, United States.
See www.Countdowntothekingdom.com

[cii] Ibid. For more of what God the Father has revealed about the time after the Illumination of Conscience, see www.Countdowntothekingdom.com. Talks by Fr. Rodrigue (2 CD sets) can be purchased through Peter Frank at missionangelshq@gmail.com. See footnote xciv.

More on Fr. Michel Rodrigue:

Fr. Michel is the Superior General of The Apostolic Fraternity of Saint Benedict Joseph Labre in Quebec, Canada, and a priest in good standing with the Church. There is a misconception on the Internet that two bishops have condemned Fr. Michel's messages. They have not condemned them but personally "disavowed" them, which is a statement of personal opinion to which they are entitled. One bishop wrote that he personally does not believe in the Warning, the Chastisements, the Three Days of Darkness, the Era of Peace, which have been prophesied by many mystics in the Church throughout the world and over time. In the Church-approved apparitions at Fatima, for example, Our Lady prophesied a period of peace. In the Church-approved apparitions in Akita, Japan, Our Lady prophesied a chastisement. In the Church-approved apparitions in Betania, Venezuela, Our Lady prophesied The Warning, etc. The Church is not now contradicting itself and saying that it disavows those realities mentioned by Our Lady, due to a bishop's letter regarding another messenger. Even a bishop, according to the Church, does not have to believe in the authentic words and approved apparitions of the Blessed Mother. In the case of Fr. Rodrigue's messages, an ecclesial investigation to make an official determination has not occurred.

An example of a proper ecclesial investigation of the mystical phenomena of locutions and apparitions, versus a bishop's personal opinion, is that of Bishop Pio Bello Ricardo of Betania, Venezuela, who at first was personally skeptical of the apparitions within his diocese. He did not believe in them and would not stand by them. This was his personal opinion; but he was open to learning more. Then after an extensive investigation of the apparitions, followed by three years of further reflection, scrutiny, and discernment, he gave the apparitions a positive Church pronouncement.

A more well-known case of a bishop's personal disapproval of an authentic supernatural occurrence, approved by the Church after a proper ecclesial investigation, is St. Faustina Kowalska's messages of Divine Mercy. Not everyone in Rome approved of the devotion. The head of the Holy Office, Cardinal Alfredo Ottaviani, petitioned Pope Pius XII to sign a condemnation of Saint Faustina's work and visions, but he was denied.

To clarify matters relating to Fr. Michel's history, status in the Church, and work in exorcism ministry, he has written a public letter, which can be read under the title, "Fr. Michel Rodrigue Breaks His Silence and Responds to Bishops and the Faithful," on the website: www.countdowntothekingdom.com. See https://www.countdowntothekingdom.com/fr-michel-rodrigue-breaks-his-silence-and-responds-to-bishops-and-the-faithful/.

Made in the USA
Las Vegas, NV
04 July 2021